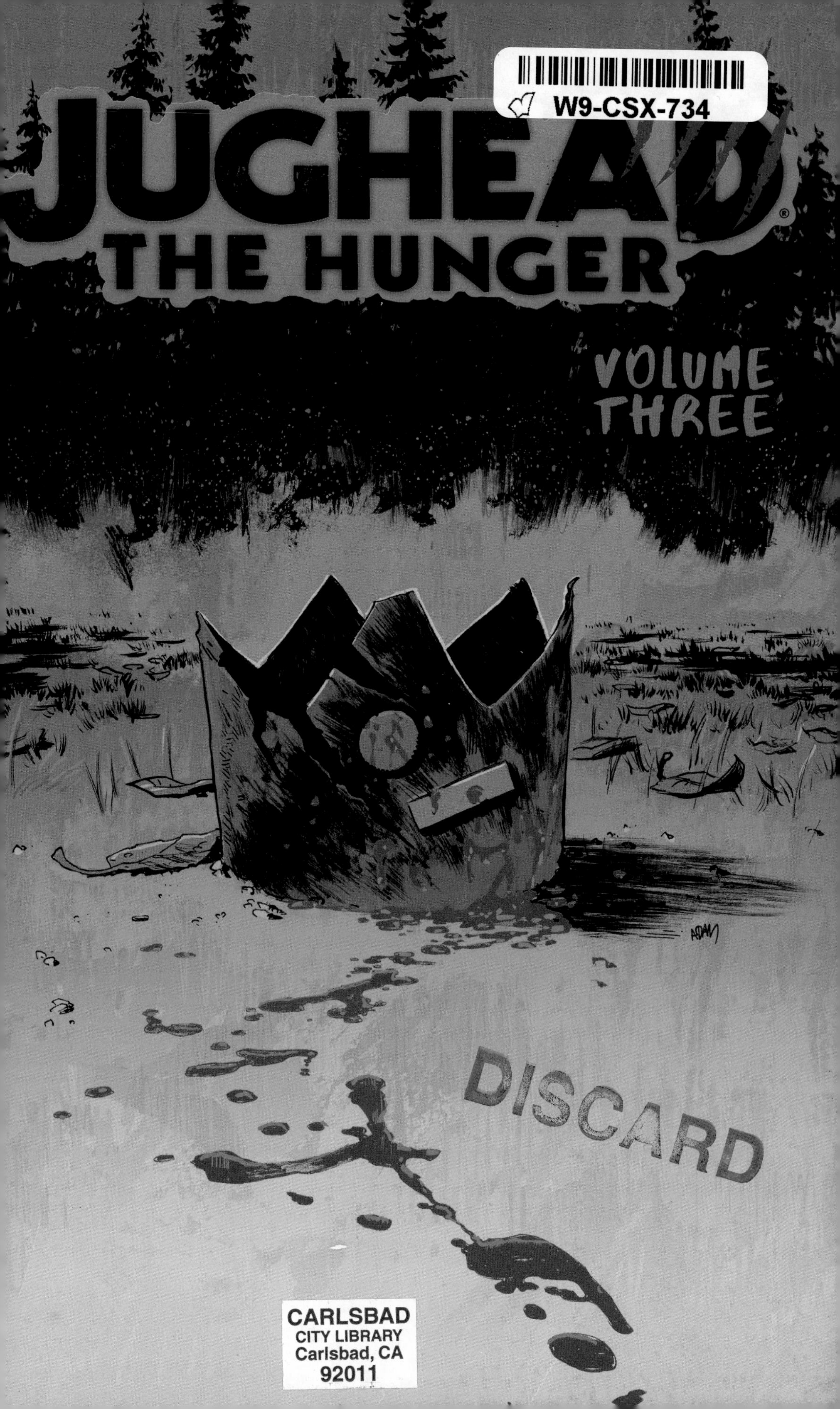
JUGHEAD®
THE HUNGER
VOLUME THREE
ADAM

JUGHEAD
THE HUNGER

SCRIPT:
Frank Tieri

ART:
Joe Eisma

COLORS:
Matt Herms

LETTERS:
Jack Morelli

EDITORS:
Alex Segura
Jamie Lee Rotante

ASSOCIATE EDITOR:
Stephen Oswald
ASSISTANT EDITOR:
Vincent Lovallo

GRAPHIC DESIGN:
Kari McLachlan

EDITOR-IN-CHIEF
Victor Gorelick

PUBLISHER
Jon Goldwater

PREVIOUSLY...

JUGHEAD JONES hails from a long line of werewolves, and his friend BETTY COOPER's ancestral history of werewolf hunters tracks just as far back! Betty's aunt, ELENA COOPER, was once in love with Jughead's uncle, JONAH JONES, which ended in heartbreak and pain for both families. Yet despite their familial differences, Betty stood up to her family, determined to help her friend escape the wrath of her huntress aunt. While Jughead did everything he could to escape with minimal damage to others, there was a more pressing issue at stake: where was his little sister, JELLYBEAN? Little did he know, Jellybean was captured by the pack of recently-turned werewolves, including VERONICA LODGE, REGGIE MANTLE, CHERYL BLOSSOM, MOOSE MASON and MR. WEATHERBEE.

Fortunately, Jughead and Betty, with help of ARCHIE ANDREWS, were able to fight off the pack and save Jellybean—though, werewolf blood runs in the family and she might not be so "safe" after all. In the process of running the werewolves out of RIVERDALE (those that weren't completely eviscerated), Reggie and Veronica were also framed as the RIVERDALE RIPPERS—much to the chagrin of Veronica's father, HIRAM LODGE, who is determined to do whatever it takes to clear his daughter's good name.

Betty, Archie and Jughead may have calmed things down for now—but what kind of messes have been left in the wake of Jughead's rampage? And what new ones are about to rise?

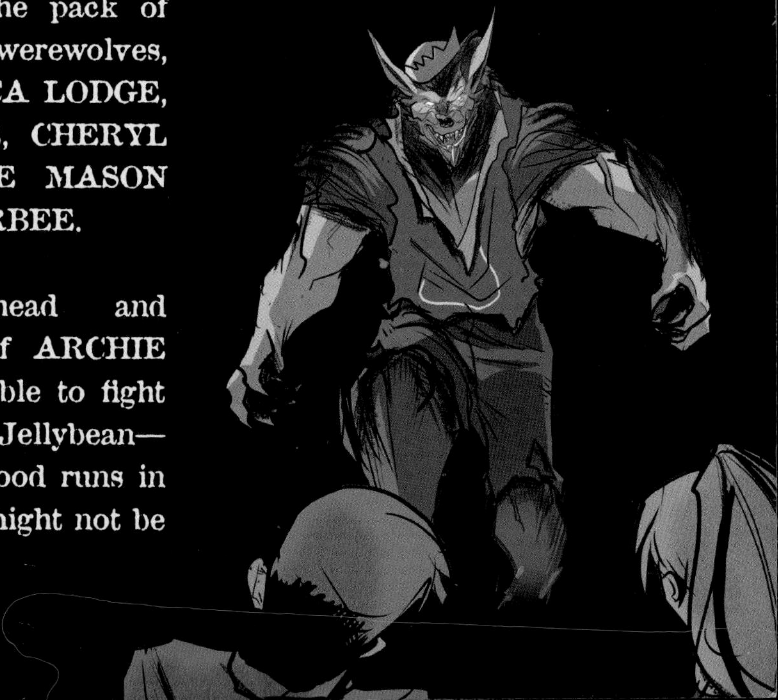

FRANKENMOOSE MEETS WOLFJUG: PART 1

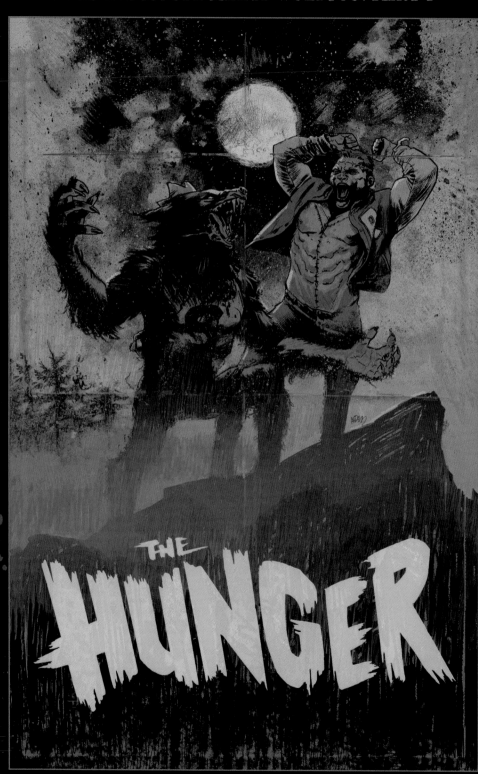

THE HUNGER

COVER ART Adam Gorham

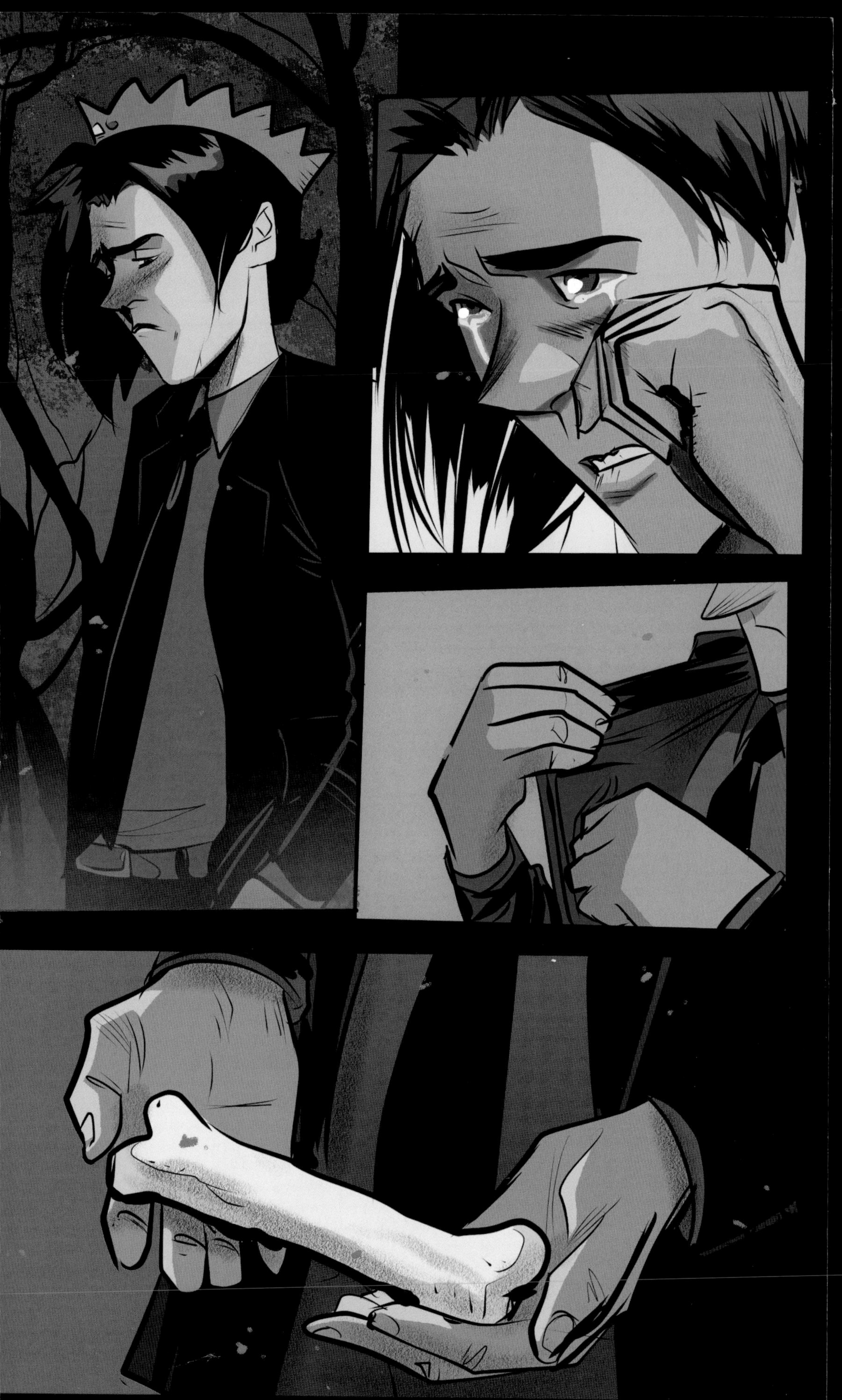

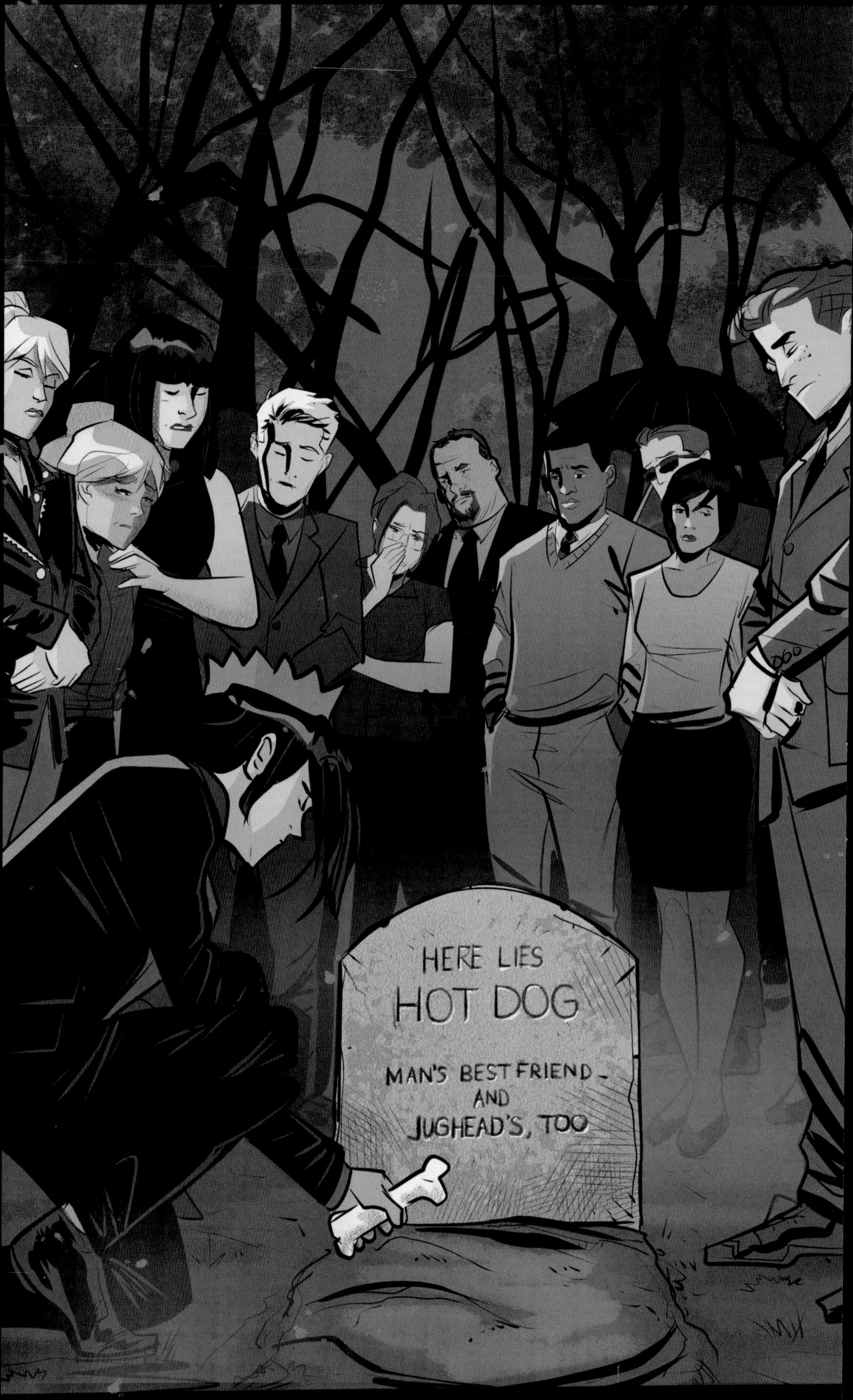
HERE LIES
HOT DOG
MAN'S BEST FRIEND -
AND
JUGHEAD'S, TOO

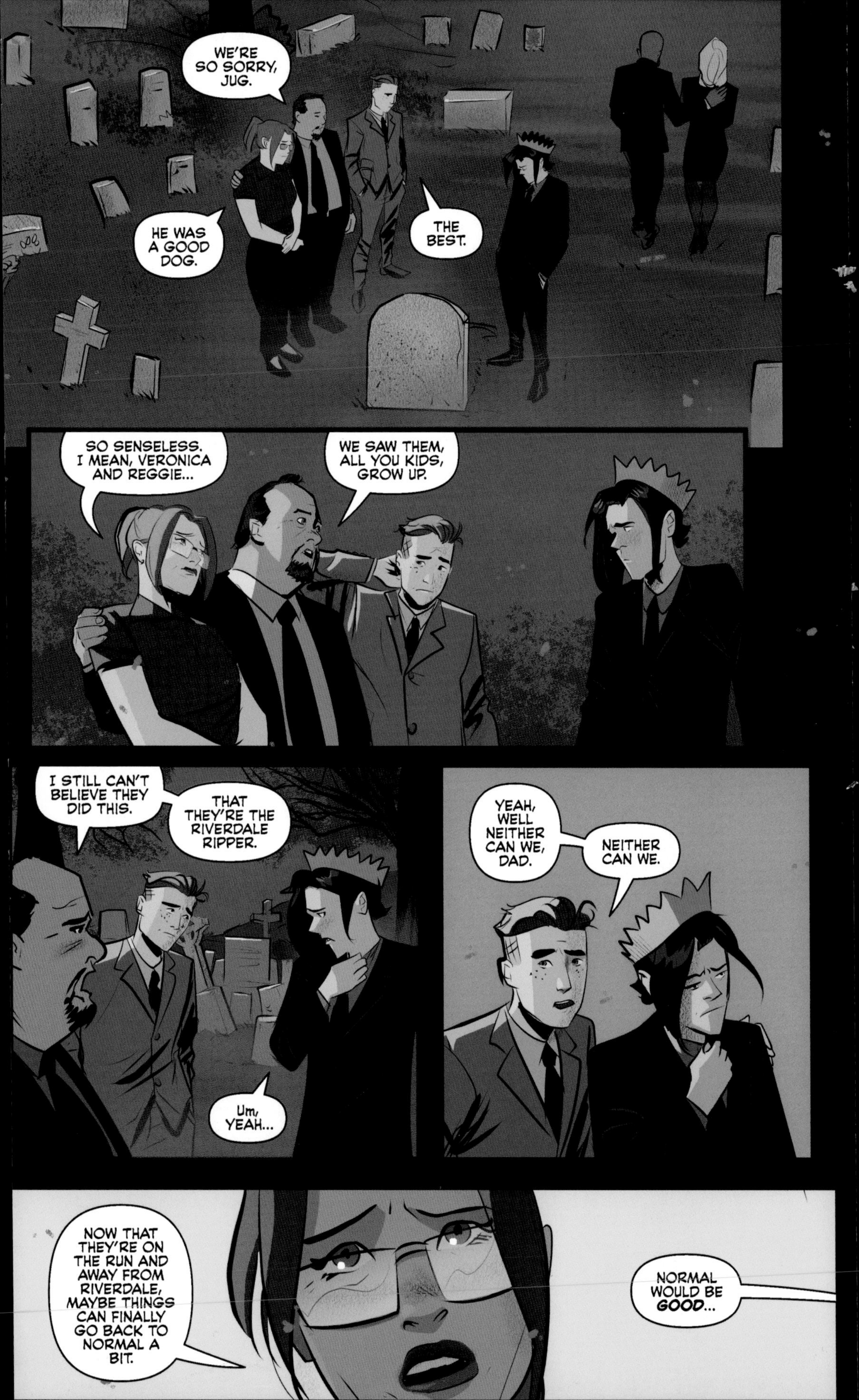
WE'RE SO SORRY, JUG.
HE WAS A GOOD DOG.
THE BEST.
SO SENSELESS. I MEAN, VERONICA AND REGGIE...
WE SAW THEM, ALL YOU KIDS, GROW UP.
I STILL CAN'T BELIEVE THEY DID THIS.
THAT THEY'RE THE RIVERDALE RIPPER.
Um, YEAH...
YEAH, WELL NEITHER CAN WE, DAD.
NEITHER CAN WE.
NOW THAT THEY'RE ON THE RUN AND AWAY FROM RIVERDALE, MAYBE THINGS CAN FINALLY GO BACK TO NORMAL A BIT.
NORMAL WOULD BE **GOOD**...

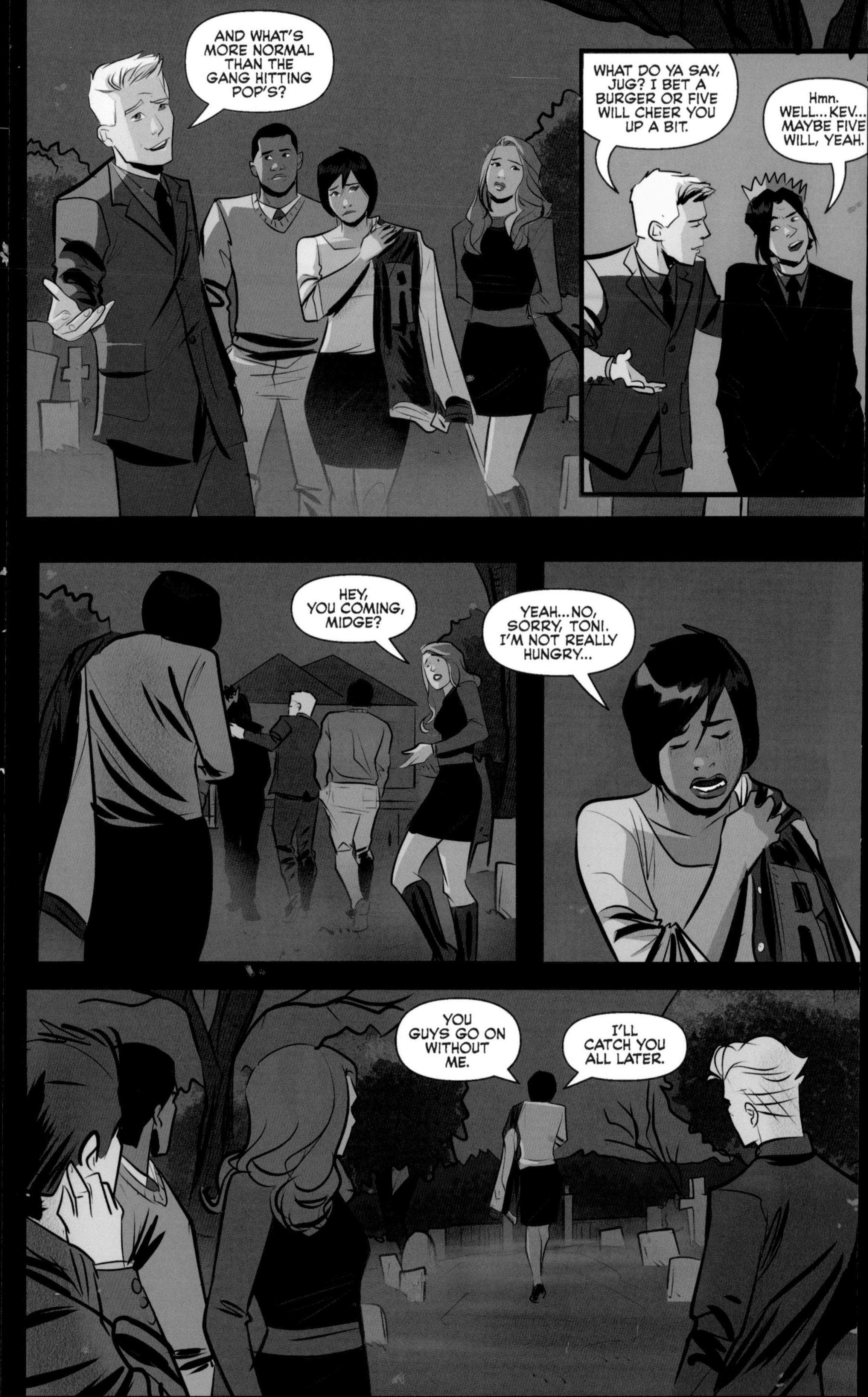
AND WHAT'S MORE NORMAL THAN THE GANG HITTING POP'S?
WHAT DO YA SAY, JUG? I BET A BURGER OR FIVE WILL CHEER YOU UP A BIT.
Hmn. WELL...KEV... MAYBE FIVE WILL, YEAH.
HEY, YOU COMING, MIDGE?
YEAH...NO, SORRY, TONI. I'M NOT REALLY HUNGRY...
YOU GUYS GO ON WITHOUT ME.
I'LL CATCH YOU ALL LATER.

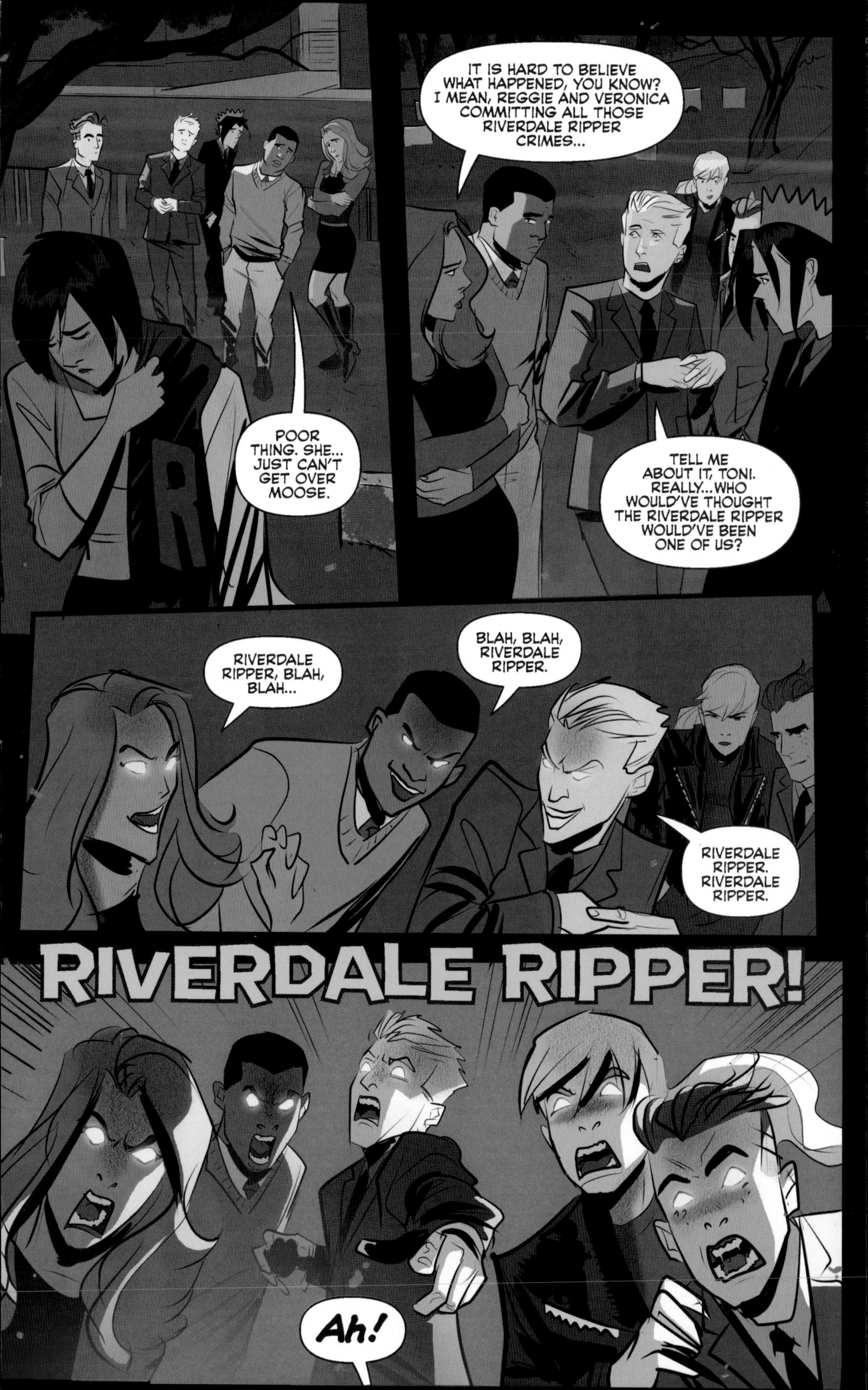
POOR THING. SHE... JUST CAN'T GET OVER MOOSE.
IT IS HARD TO BELIEVE WHAT HAPPENED, YOU KNOW? I MEAN, REGGIE AND VERONICA COMMITTING ALL THOSE RIVERDALE RIPPER CRIMES...
TELL ME ABOUT IT, TONI. REALLY...WHO WOULD'VE THOUGHT THE RIVERDALE RIPPER WOULD'VE BEEN ONE OF US?
RIVERDALE RIPPER, BLAH, BLAH...
BLAH, BLAH, RIVERDALE RIPPER.
RIVERDALE RIPPER. RIVERDALE RIPPER.
RIVERDALE RIPPER!
Ah!

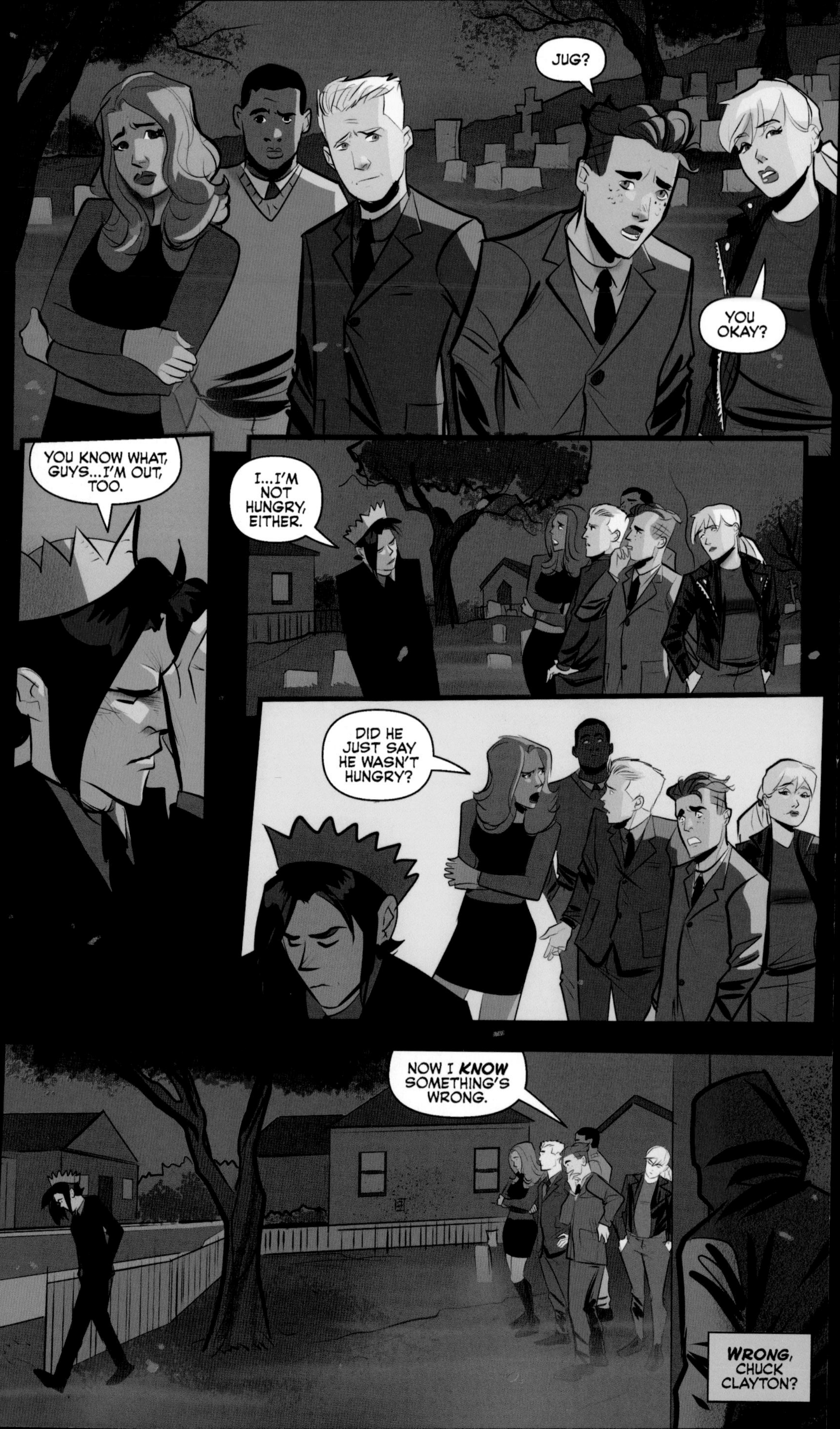
JUG?
YOU OKAY?
YOU KNOW WHAT, GUYS...I'M OUT, TOO.
I...I'M NOT HUNGRY, EITHER.
DID HE JUST SAY HE WASN'T HUNGRY?
NOW I KNOW SOMETHING'S WRONG.
WRONG, CHUCK CLAYTON?

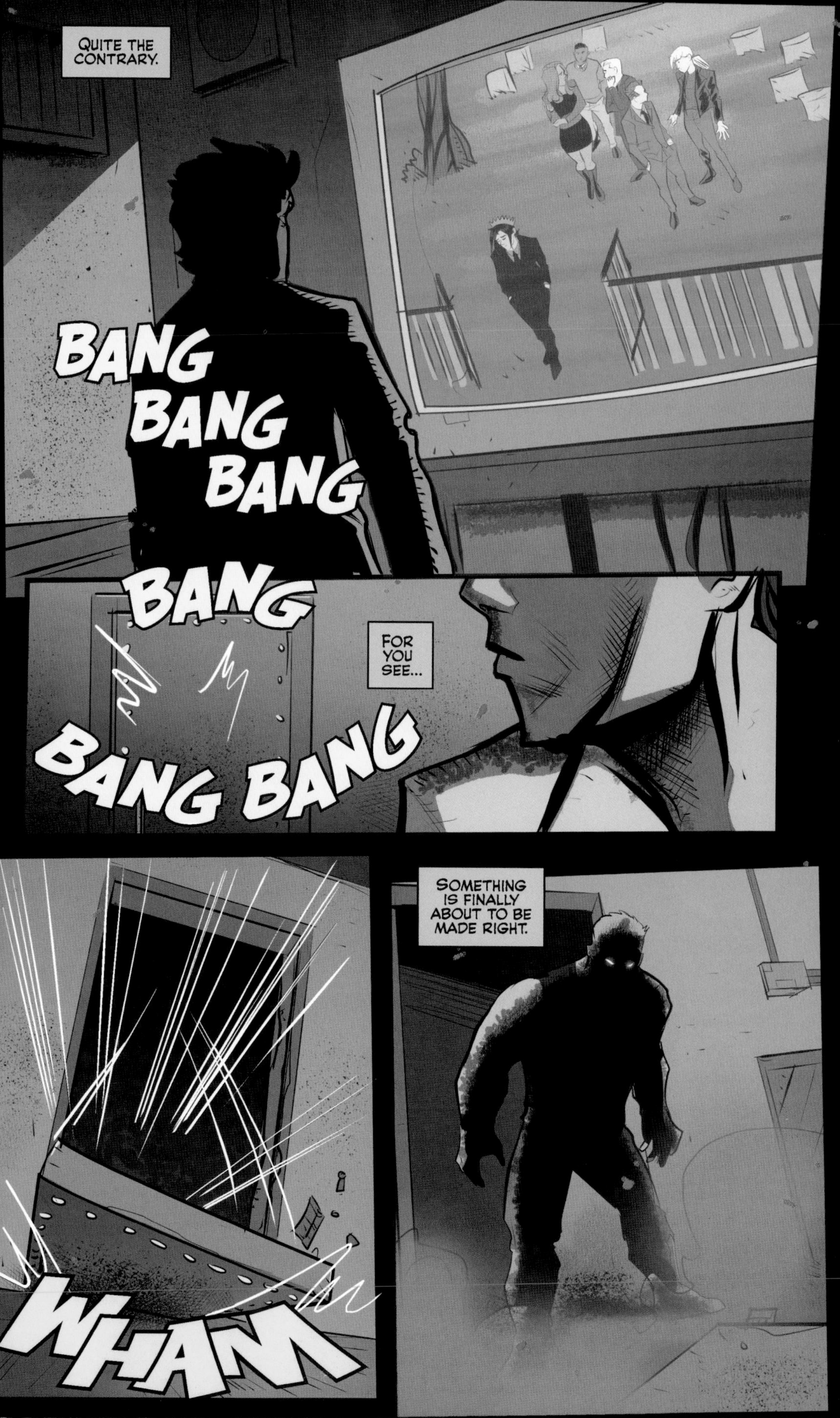
QUITE THE CONTRARY.
BANG
BANG
BANG
BANG
FOR YOU SEE...
BANG BANG
WHAM
SOMETHING IS FINALLY ABOUT TO BE MADE RIGHT.

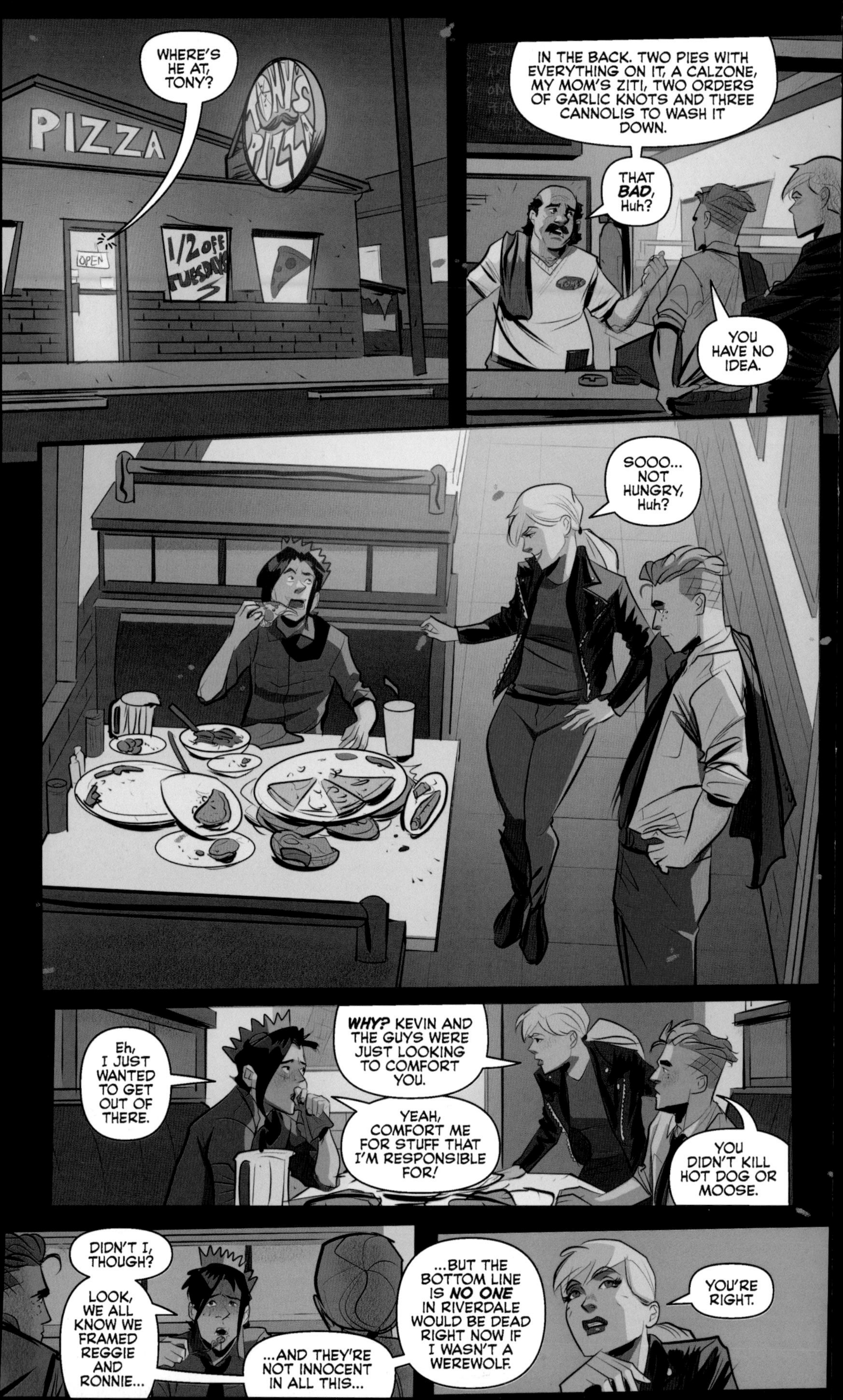

WHERE'S HE AT, TONY?
PIZZA
TONY'S PIZZA
OPEN
1/2 OFF TUESDAYS
IN THE BACK. TWO PIES WITH EVERYTHING ON IT, A CALZONE, MY MOM'S ZITI, TWO ORDERS OF GARLIC KNOTS AND THREE CANNOLIS TO WASH IT DOWN.
THAT **BAD**, Huh?
YOU HAVE NO IDEA.
SOOO... NOT HUNGRY, Huh?
Eh, I JUST WANTED TO GET OUT OF THERE.
WHY? KEVIN AND THE GUYS WERE JUST LOOKING TO COMFORT YOU.
YEAH, COMFORT ME FOR STUFF THAT I'M RESPONSIBLE FOR!
YOU DIDN'T KILL HOT DOG OR MOOSE.
DIDN'T I, THOUGH?
LOOK, WE ALL KNOW WE FRAMED REGGIE AND RONNIE...
...AND THEY'RE NOT INNOCENT IN ALL THIS...
...BUT THE BOTTOM LINE IS **NO ONE** IN RIVERDALE WOULD BE DEAD RIGHT NOW IF I WASN'T A WEREWOLF.
YOU'RE RIGHT.

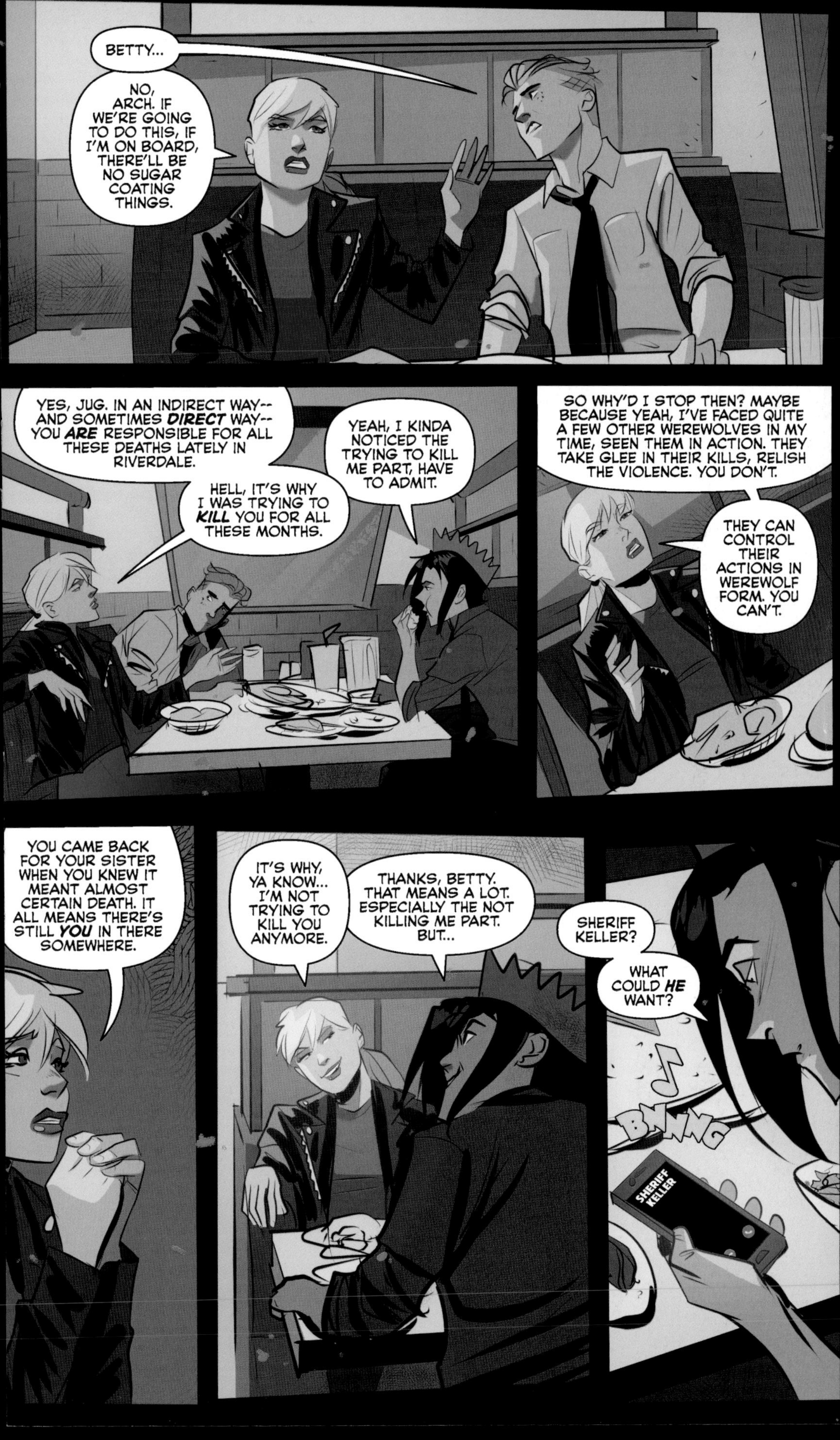
BETTY...
NO, ARCH. IF WE'RE GOING TO DO THIS, IF I'M ON BOARD, THERE'LL BE NO SUGAR COATING THINGS.
YES, JUG. IN AN INDIRECT WAY--AND SOMETIMES DIRECT WAY--YOU ARE RESPONSIBLE FOR ALL THESE DEATHS LATELY IN RIVERDALE.
HELL, IT'S WHY I WAS TRYING TO KILL YOU FOR ALL THESE MONTHS.
YEAH, I KINDA NOTICED THE TRYING TO KILL ME PART, HAVE TO ADMIT.
SO WHY'D I STOP THEN? MAYBE BECAUSE YEAH, I'VE FACED QUITE A FEW OTHER WEREWOLVES IN MY TIME, SEEN THEM IN ACTION. THEY TAKE GLEE IN THEIR KILLS, RELISH THE VIOLENCE. YOU DON'T.
THEY CAN CONTROL THEIR ACTIONS IN WEREWOLF FORM. YOU CAN'T.
YOU CAME BACK FOR YOUR SISTER WHEN YOU KNEW IT MEANT ALMOST CERTAIN DEATH. IT ALL MEANS THERE'S STILL YOU IN THERE SOMEWHERE.
IT'S WHY, YA KNOW... I'M NOT TRYING TO KILL YOU ANYMORE.
THANKS, BETTY. THAT MEANS A LOT. ESPECIALLY THE NOT KILLING ME PART. BUT...
BNNNG
SHERIFF KELLER
SHERIFF KELLER?
WHAT COULD HE WANT?

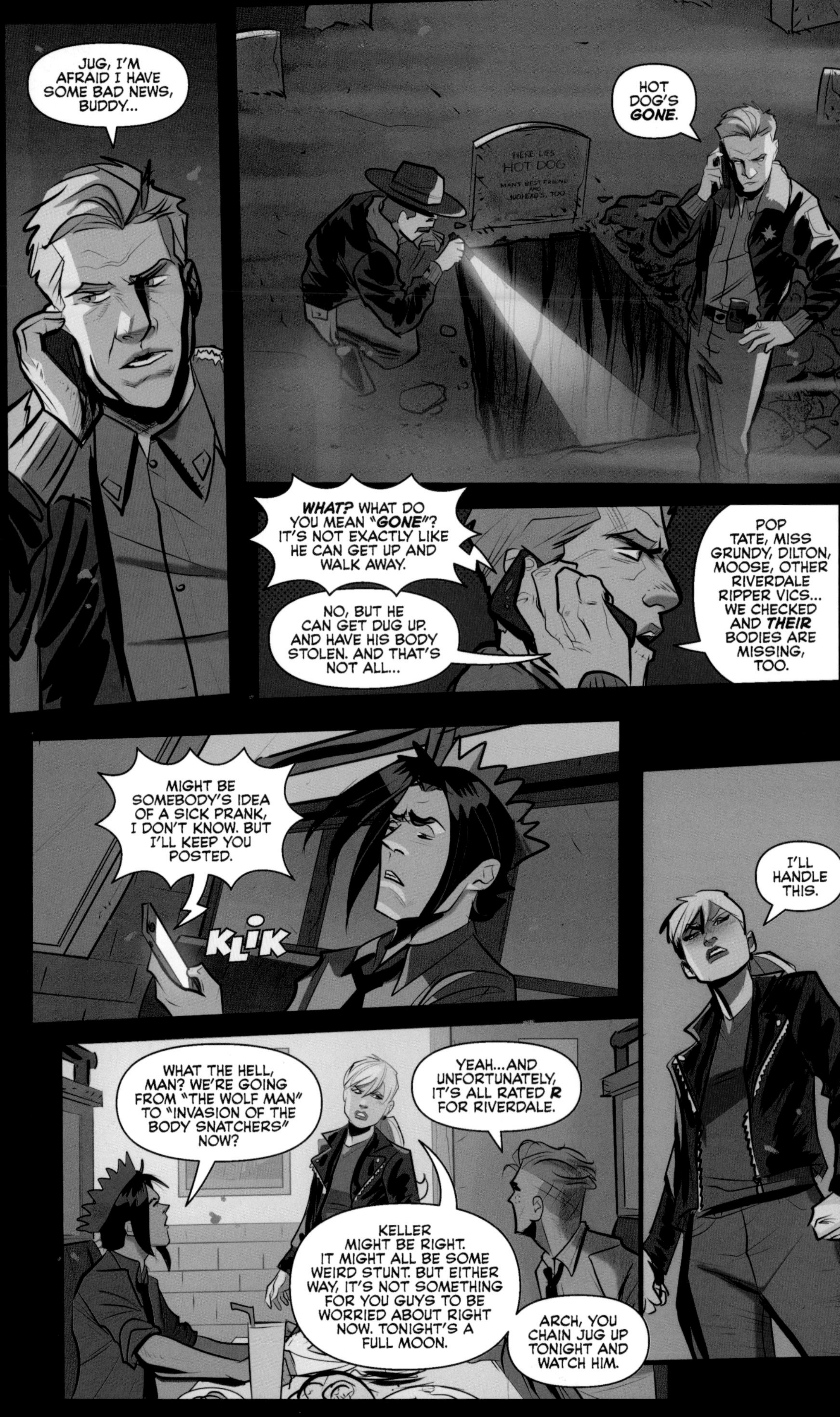
JUG, I'M AFRAID I HAVE SOME BAD NEWS, BUDDY...
HOT DOG'S **GONE**.
HERE LIES HOT DOG MAN'S BEST FRIEND AND JUGHEAD'S, TOO
WHAT? WHAT DO YOU MEAN "***GONE***"? IT'S NOT EXACTLY LIKE HE CAN GET UP AND WALK AWAY.
NO, BUT HE CAN GET DUG UP. AND HAVE HIS BODY STOLEN. AND THAT'S NOT ALL...
POP TATE, MISS GRUNDY, DILTON, MOOSE, OTHER RIVERDALE RIPPER VICS... WE CHECKED AND ***THEIR*** BODIES ARE MISSING, TOO.
MIGHT BE SOMEBODY'S IDEA OF A SICK PRANK, I DON'T KNOW. BUT I'LL KEEP YOU POSTED.
KLIK
I'LL HANDLE THIS.
WHAT THE HELL, MAN? WE'RE GOING FROM "THE WOLF MAN" TO "INVASION OF THE BODY SNATCHERS" NOW?
YEAH...AND UNFORTUNATELY, IT'S ALL RATED ***R*** FOR RIVERDALE.
KELLER MIGHT BE RIGHT. IT MIGHT ALL BE SOME WEIRD STUNT. BUT EITHER WAY, IT'S NOT SOMETHING FOR YOU GUYS TO BE WORRIED ABOUT RIGHT NOW. TONIGHT'S A FULL MOON.
ARCH, YOU CHAIN JUG UP TONIGHT AND WATCH HIM.

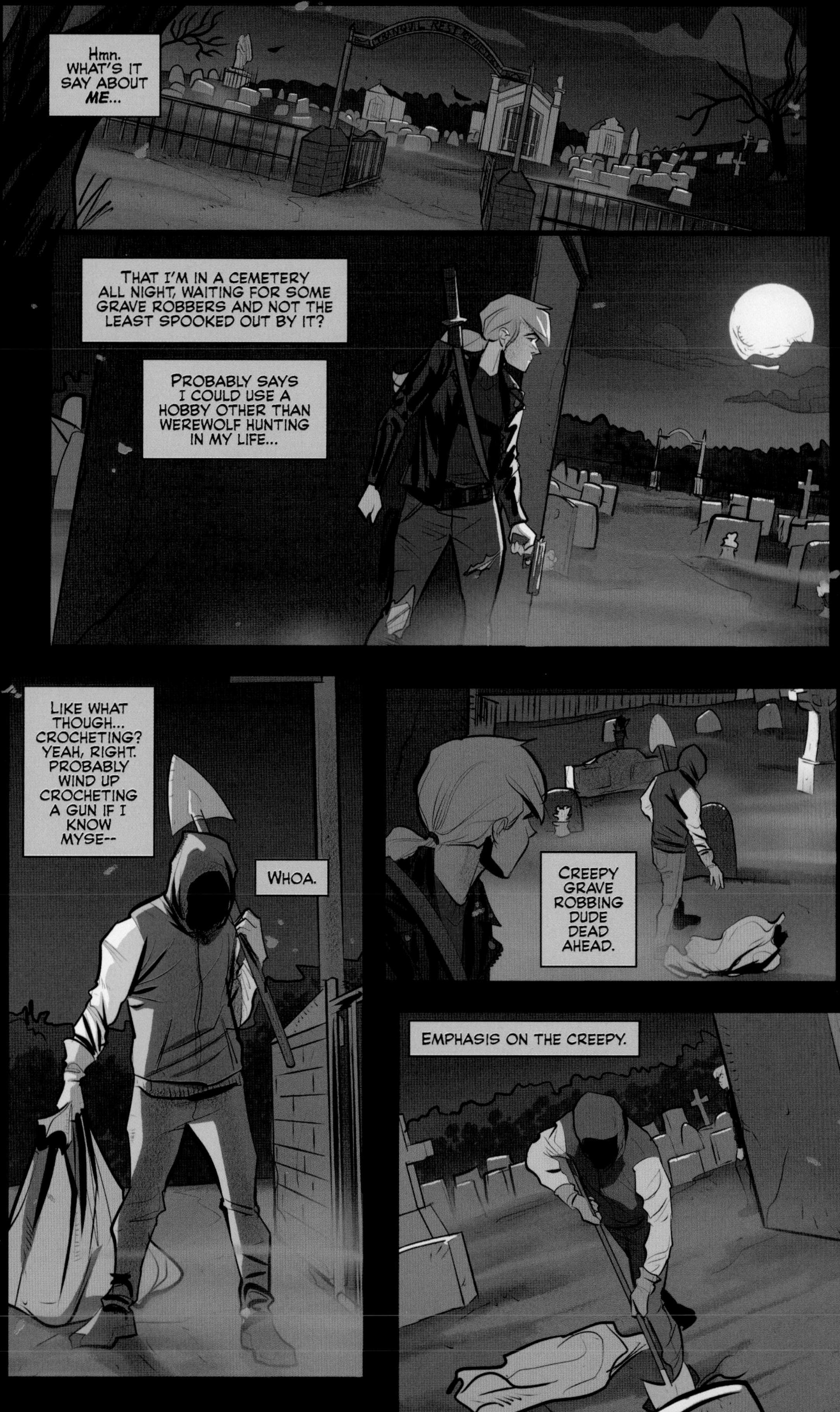

Hmn. WHAT'S IT SAY ABOUT *ME*...
THAT I'M IN A CEMETERY ALL NIGHT, WAITING FOR SOME GRAVE ROBBERS AND NOT THE LEAST SPOOKED OUT BY IT?
PROBABLY SAYS I COULD USE A HOBBY OTHER THAN WEREWOLF HUNTING IN MY LIFE...
LIKE WHAT THOUGH... CROCHETING? YEAH, RIGHT. PROBABLY WIND UP CROCHETING A GUN IF I KNOW MYSE--
WHOA.
CREEPY GRAVE ROBBING DUDE DEAD AHEAD.
EMPHASIS ON THE CREEPY.

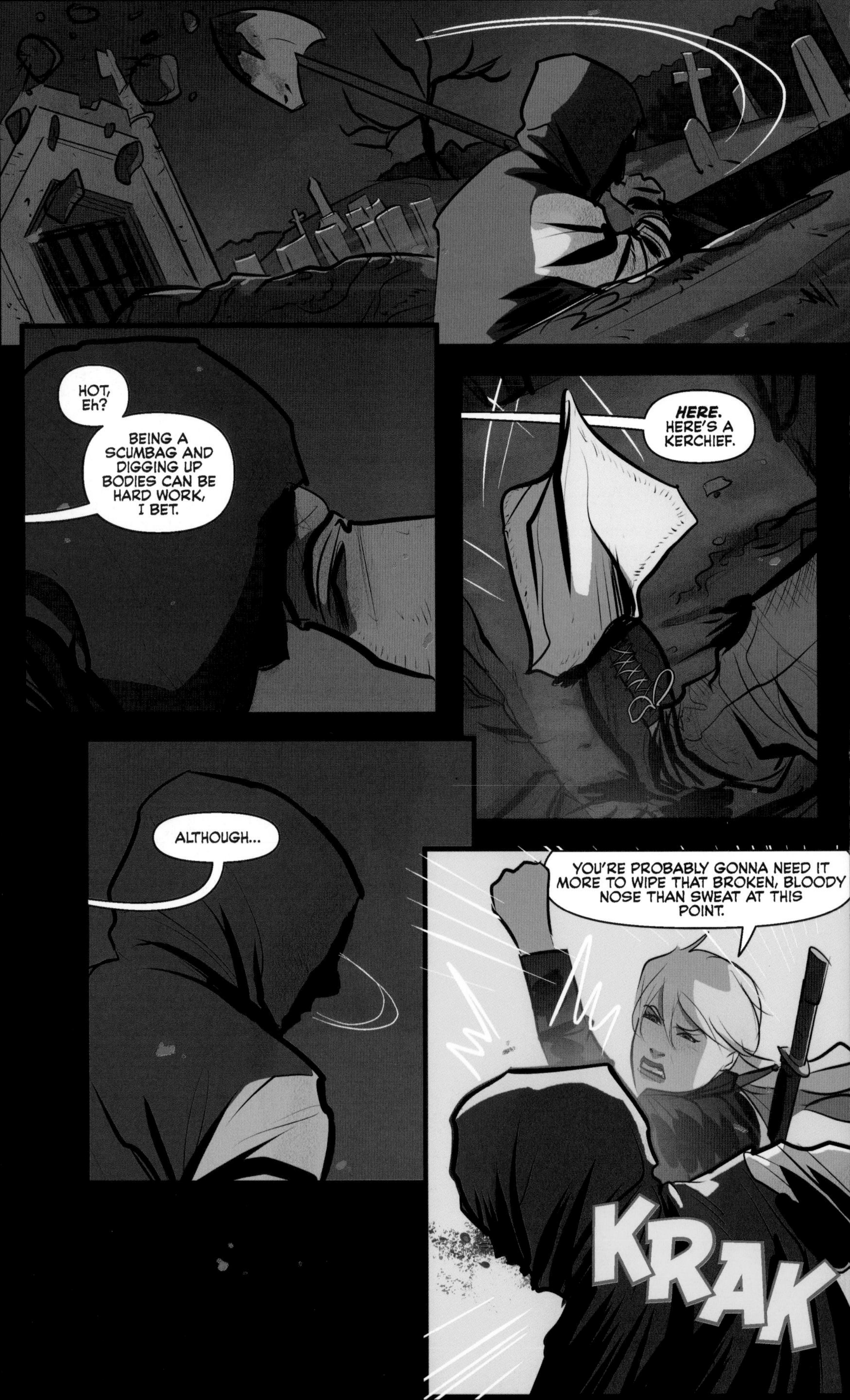
HOT, Eh?
BEING A SCUMBAG AND DIGGING UP BODIES CAN BE HARD WORK, I BET.
HERE. HERE'S A KERCHIEF.
ALTHOUGH...
YOU'RE PROBABLY GONNA NEED IT MORE TO WIPE THAT BROKEN, BLOODY NOSE THAN SWEAT AT THIS POINT.
KRAK

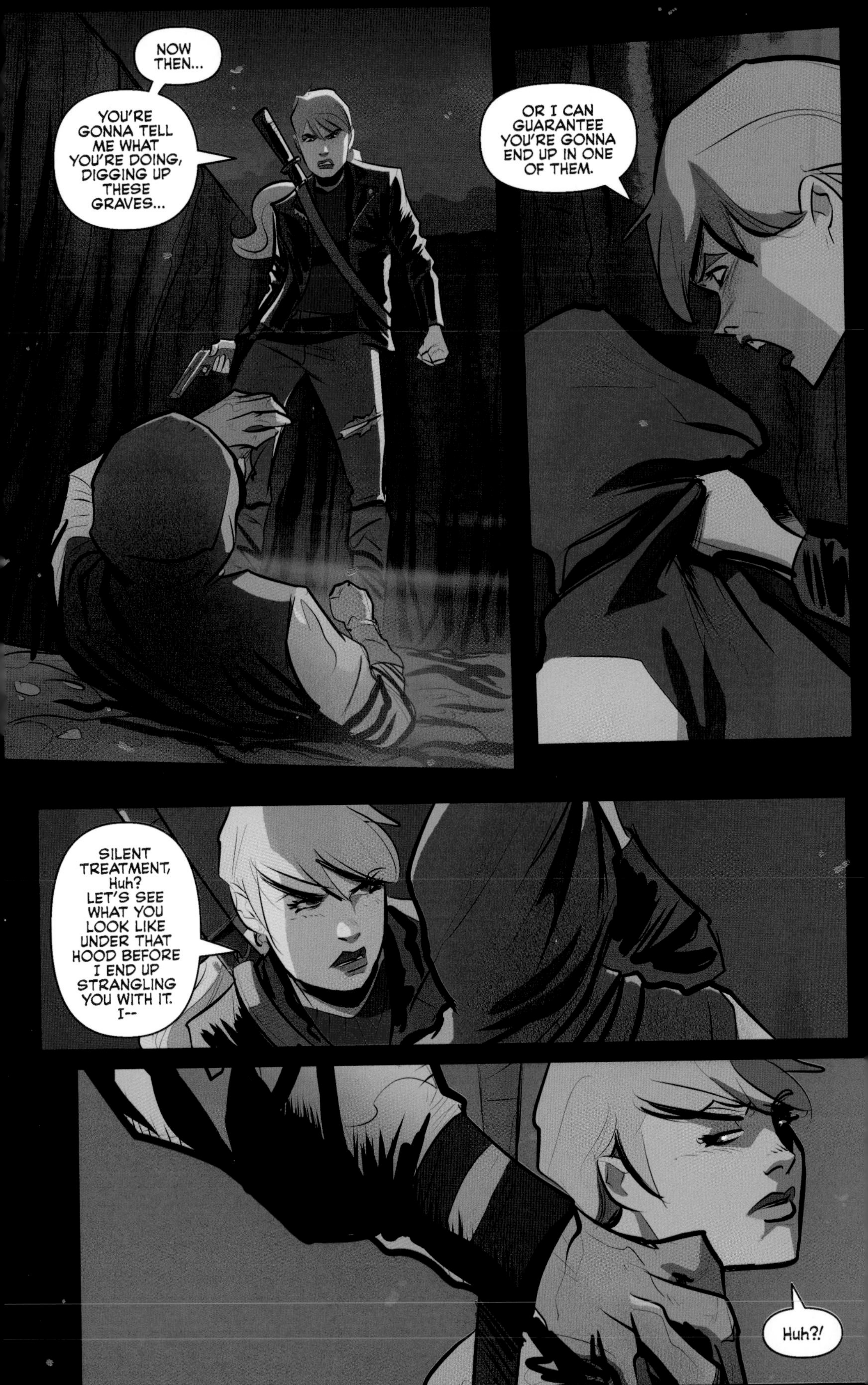
NOW THEN...
YOU'RE GONNA TELL ME WHAT YOU'RE DOING, DIGGING UP THESE GRAVES...
OR I CAN GUARANTEE YOU'RE GONNA END UP IN ONE OF THEM.
SILENT TREATMENT, Huh? LET'S SEE WHAT YOU LOOK LIKE UNDER THAT HOOD BEFORE I END UP STRANGLING YOU WITH IT. I--
Huh?!

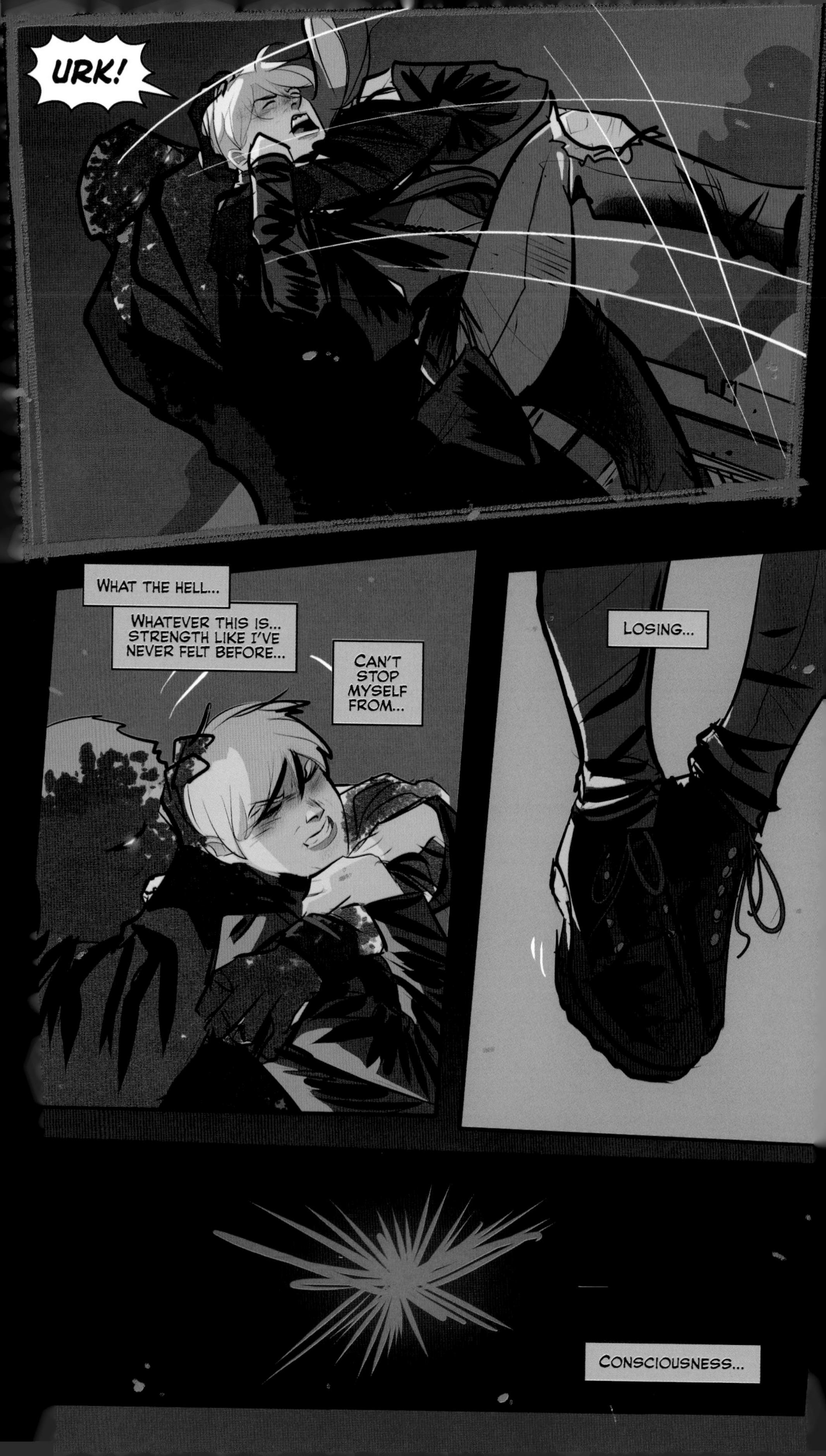
URK!
WHAT THE HELL...
WHATEVER THIS IS... STRENGTH LIKE I'VE NEVER FELT BEFORE...
CAN'T STOP MYSELF FROM...
LOSING...
CONSCIOUSNESS...

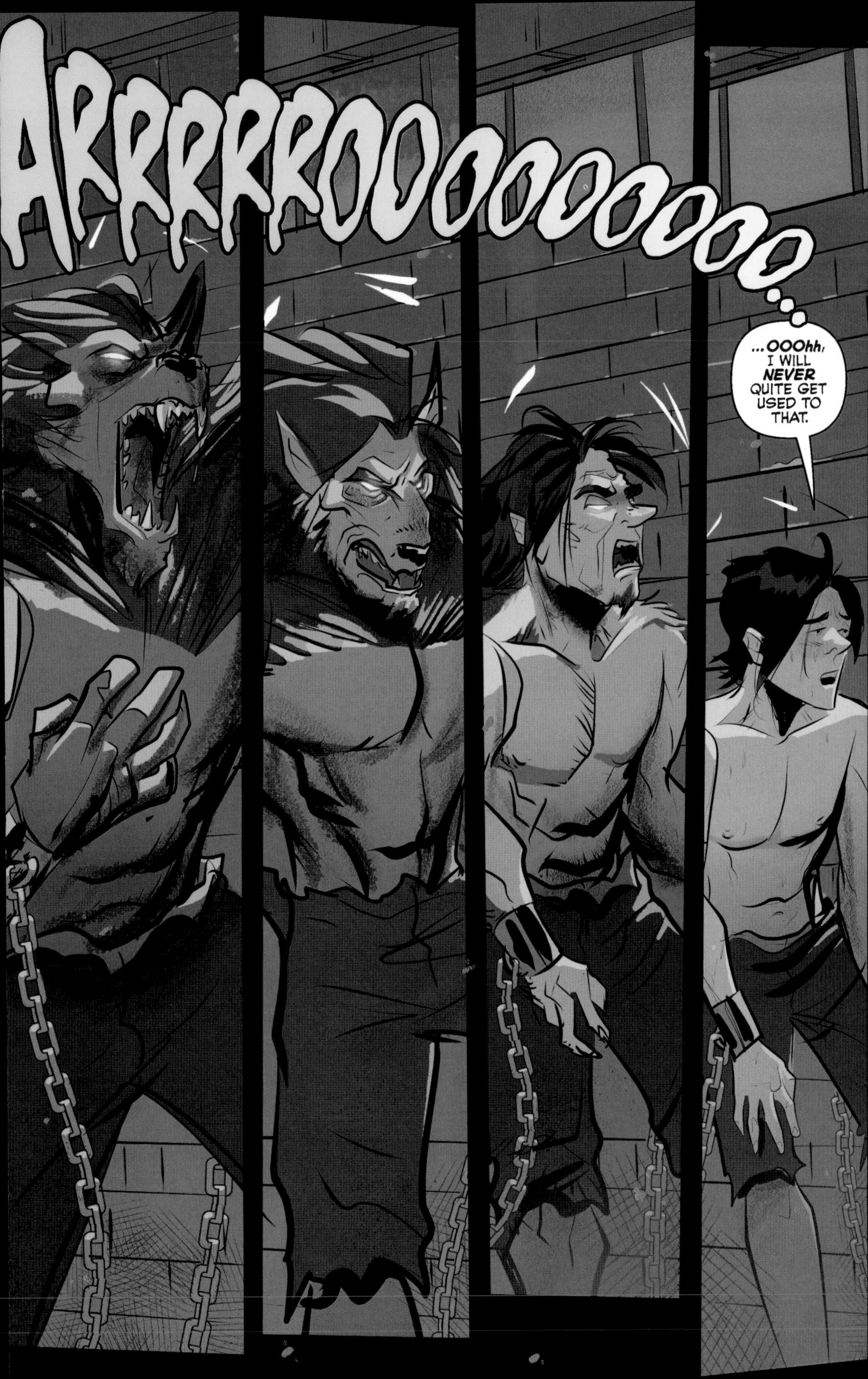
ARRRRROOOOOOOOOO...
...OOOhh, I WILL NEVER QUITE GET USED TO THAT.

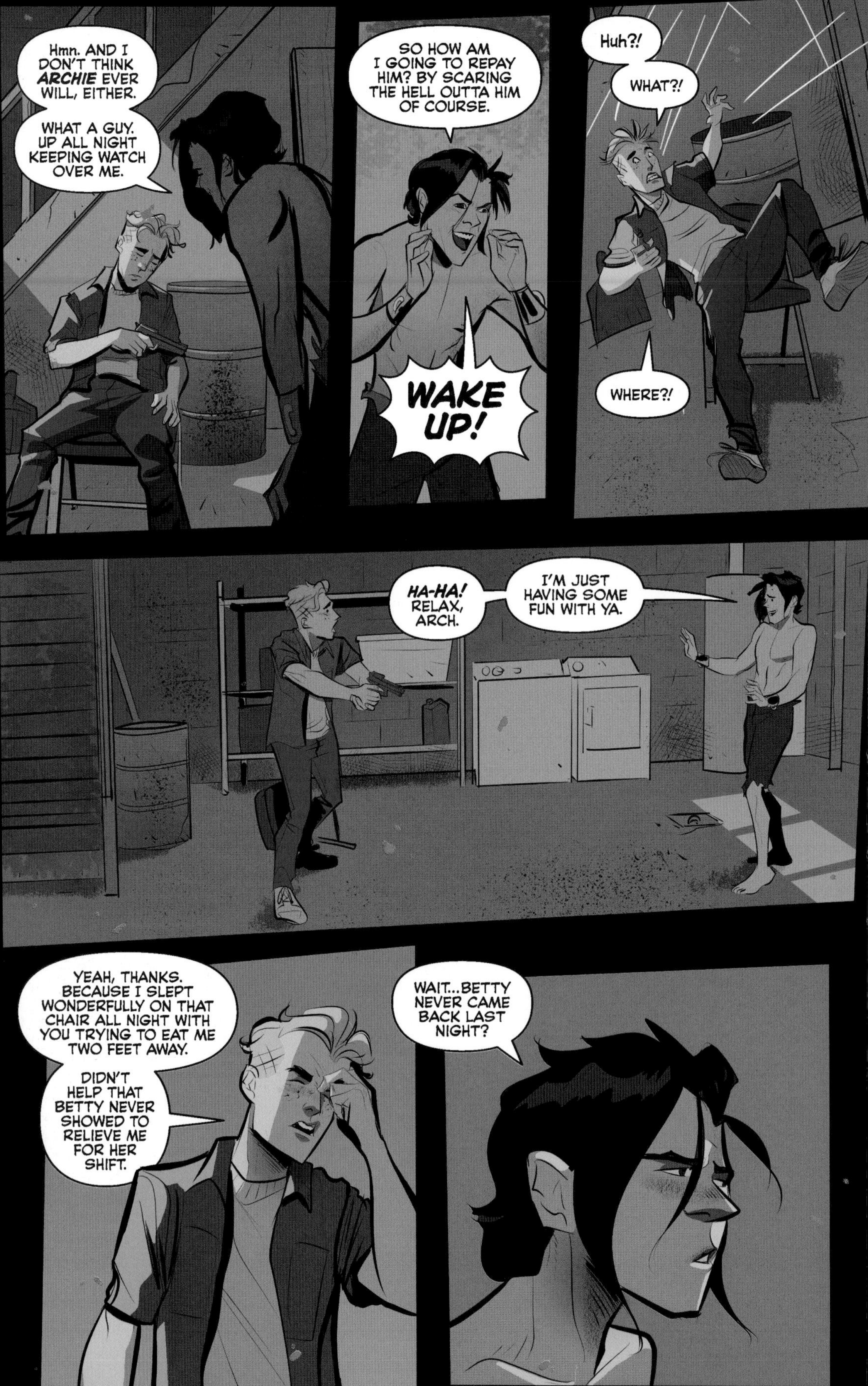
Hmn. AND I DON'T THINK ARCHIE EVER WILL, EITHER.
WHAT A GUY. UP ALL NIGHT KEEPING WATCH OVER ME.
SO HOW AM I GOING TO REPAY HIM? BY SCARING THE HELL OUTTA HIM OF COURSE.
WAKE UP!
Huh?!
WHAT?!
WHERE?!
HA-HA! RELAX, ARCH.
I'M JUST HAVING SOME FUN WITH YA.
YEAH, THANKS. BECAUSE I SLEPT WONDERFULLY ON THAT CHAIR ALL NIGHT WITH YOU TRYING TO EAT ME TWO FEET AWAY.
DIDN'T HELP THAT BETTY NEVER SHOWED TO RELIEVE ME FOR HER SHIFT.
WAIT...BETTY NEVER CAME BACK LAST NIGHT?

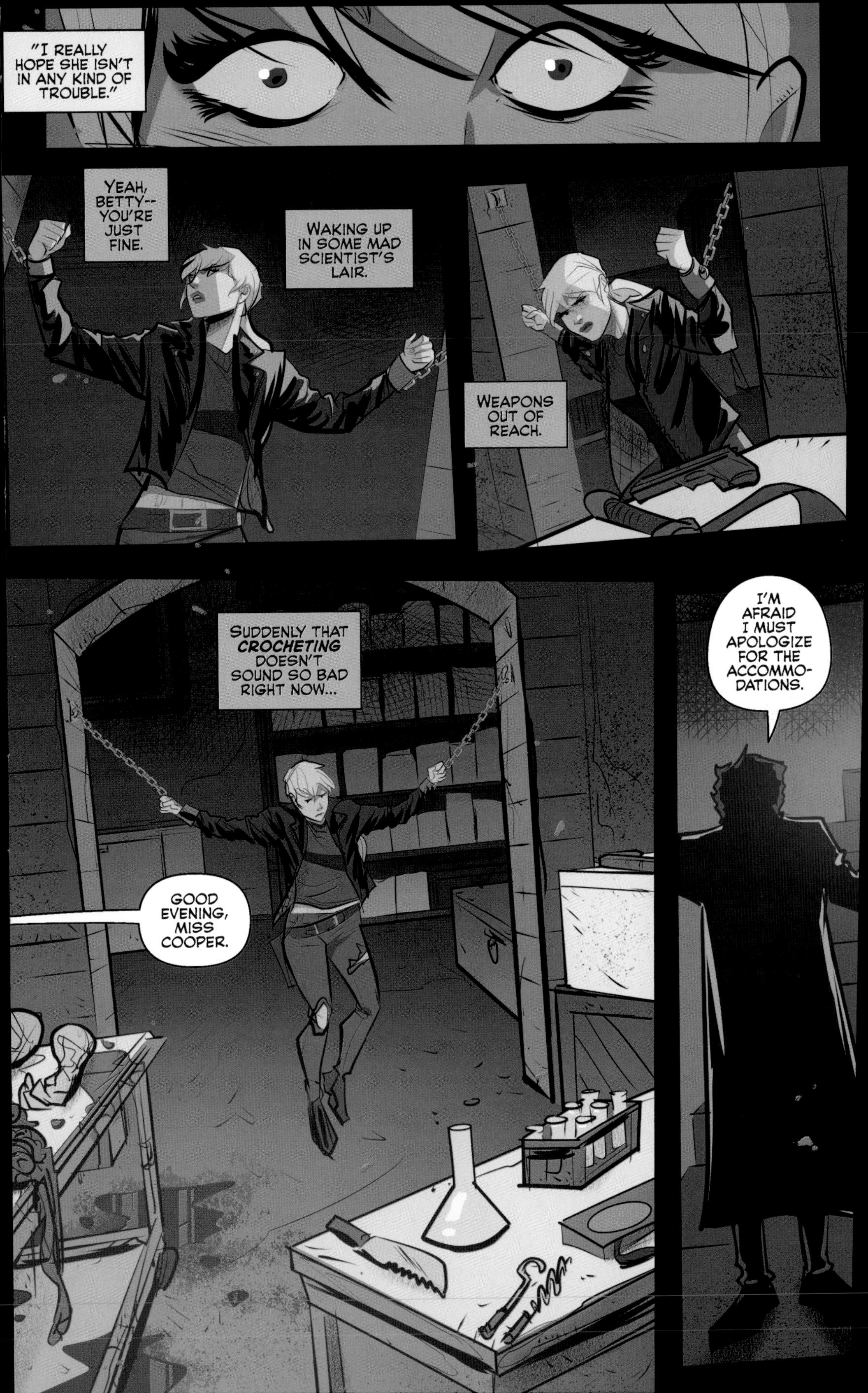
"I REALLY HOPE SHE ISN'T IN ANY KIND OF TROUBLE."
YEAH, BETTY-- YOU'RE JUST FINE.
WAKING UP IN SOME MAD SCIENTIST'S LAIR.
WEAPONS OUT OF REACH.
SUDDENLY THAT CROCHETING DOESN'T SOUND SO BAD RIGHT NOW...
GOOD EVENING, MISS COOPER.
I'M AFRAID I MUST APOLOGIZE FOR THE ACCOMMO-DATIONS.

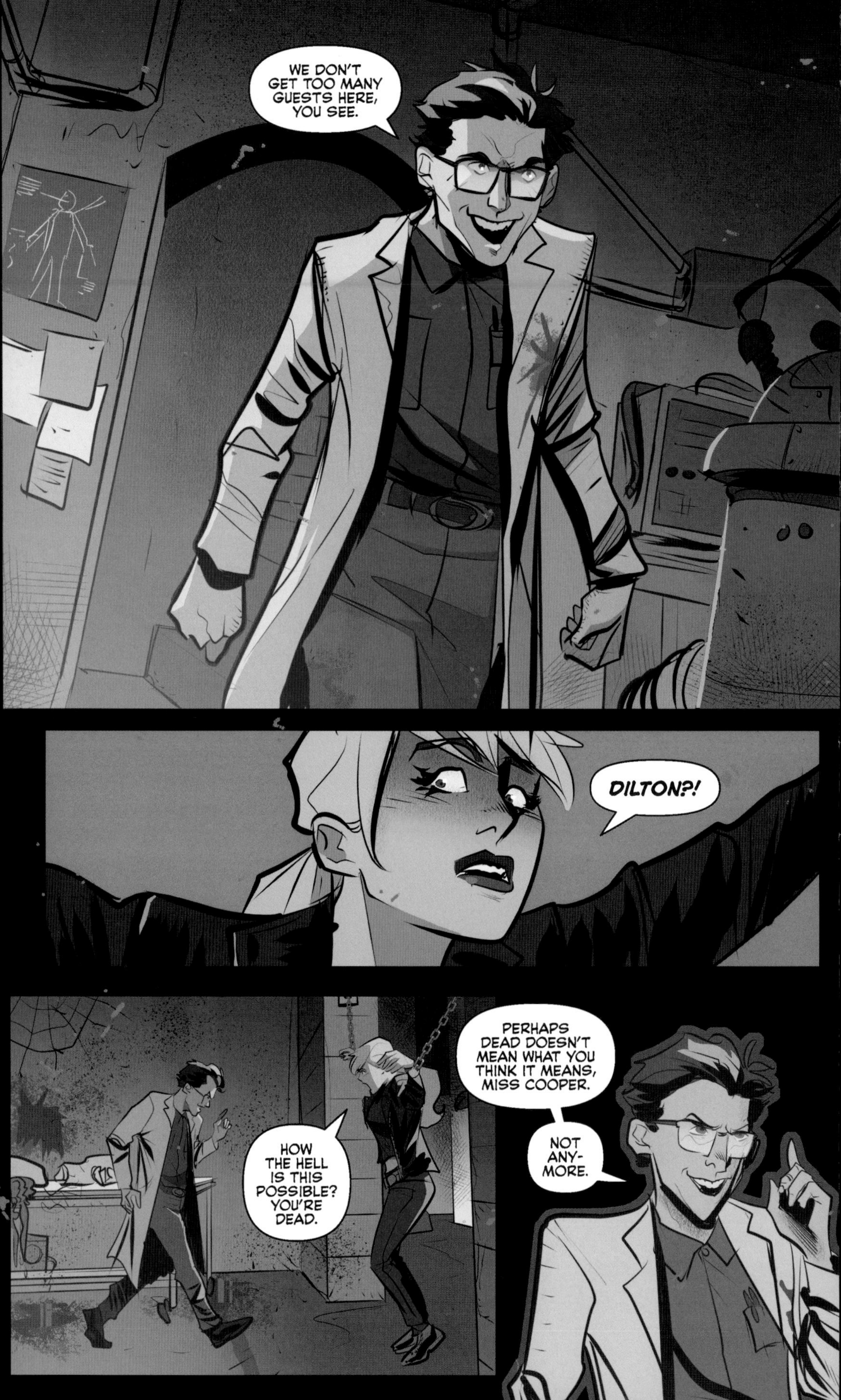
WE DON'T GET TOO MANY GUESTS HERE, YOU SEE.
DILTON?!
HOW THE HELL IS THIS POSSIBLE? YOU'RE DEAD.
PERHAPS DEAD DOESN'T MEAN WHAT YOU THINK IT MEANS, MISS COOPER.
NOT ANY-MORE.

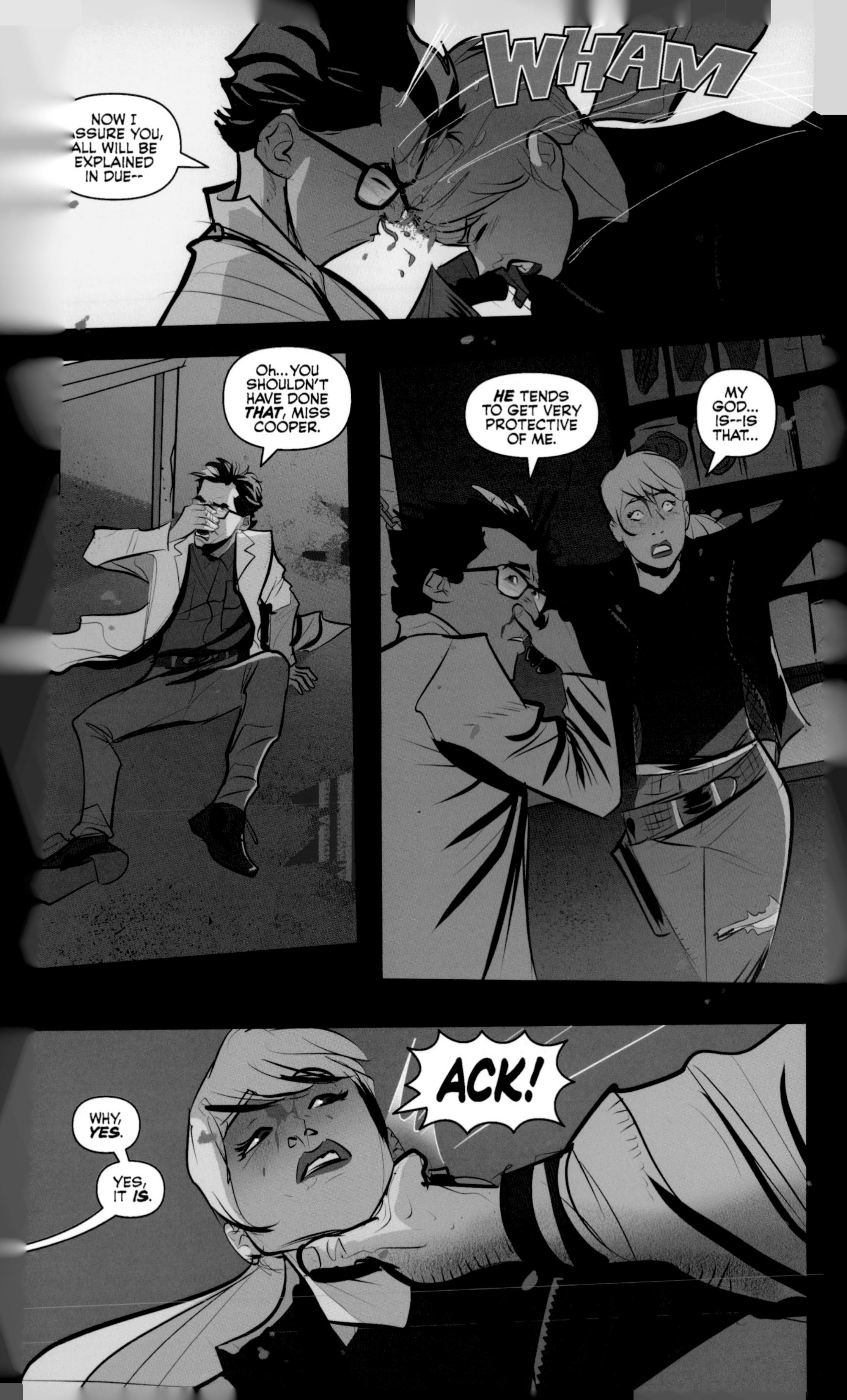
NOW I
ASSURE YOU,
ALL WILL BE
EXPLAINED
IN DUE--
WHAM
Oh...YOU SHOULDN'T HAVE DONE *THAT*, MISS COOPER.
HE TENDS TO GET VERY PROTECTIVE OF ME.
MY GOD... IS--IS THAT...
WHY, *YES*.
YES, IT *IS*.
ACK!

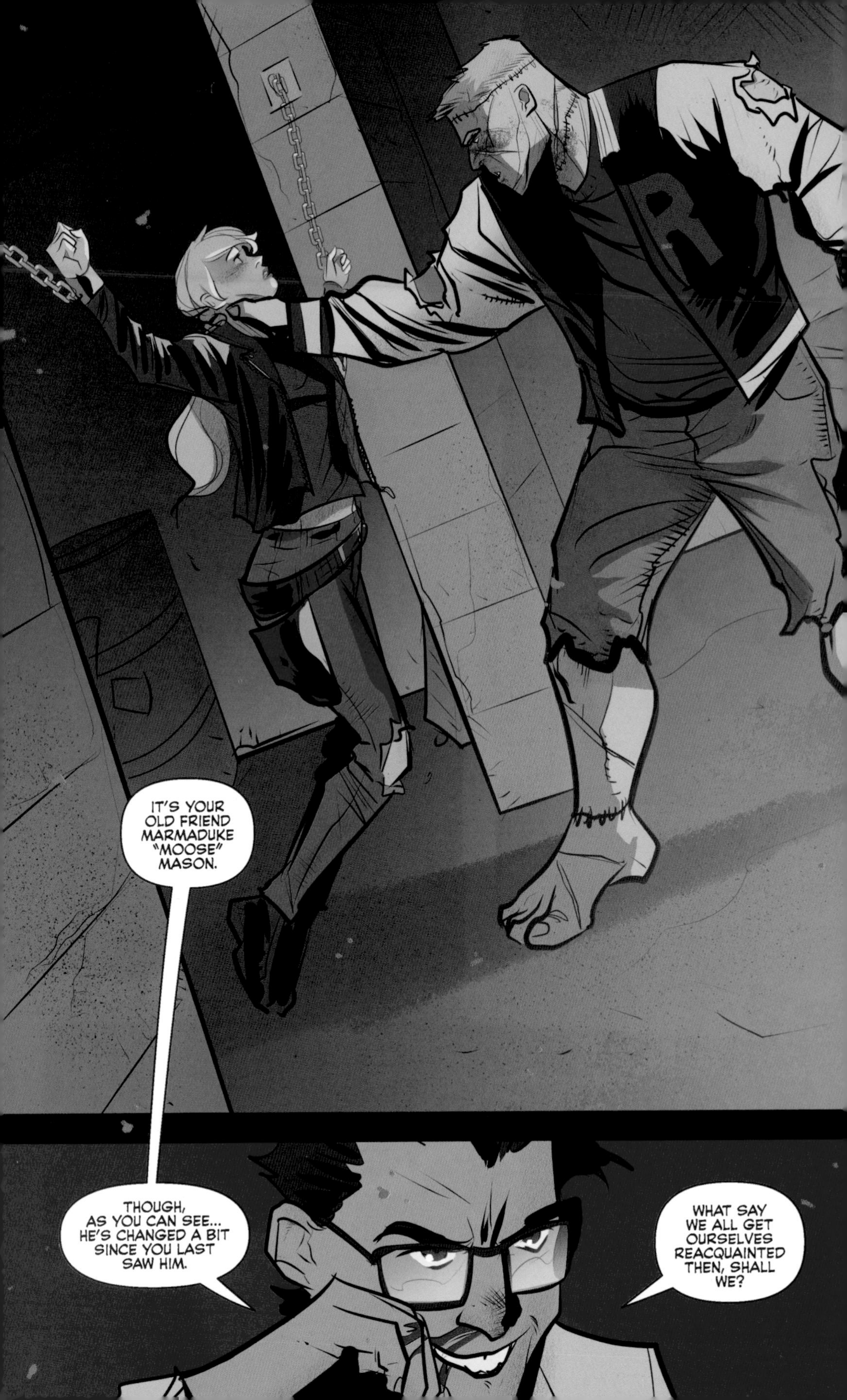
IT'S YOUR OLD FRIEND MARMADUKE "MOOSE" MASON.
THOUGH, AS YOU CAN SEE... HE'S CHANGED A BIT SINCE YOU LAST SAW HIM.
WHAT SAY WE ALL GET OURSELVES REACQUAINTED THEN, SHALL WE?

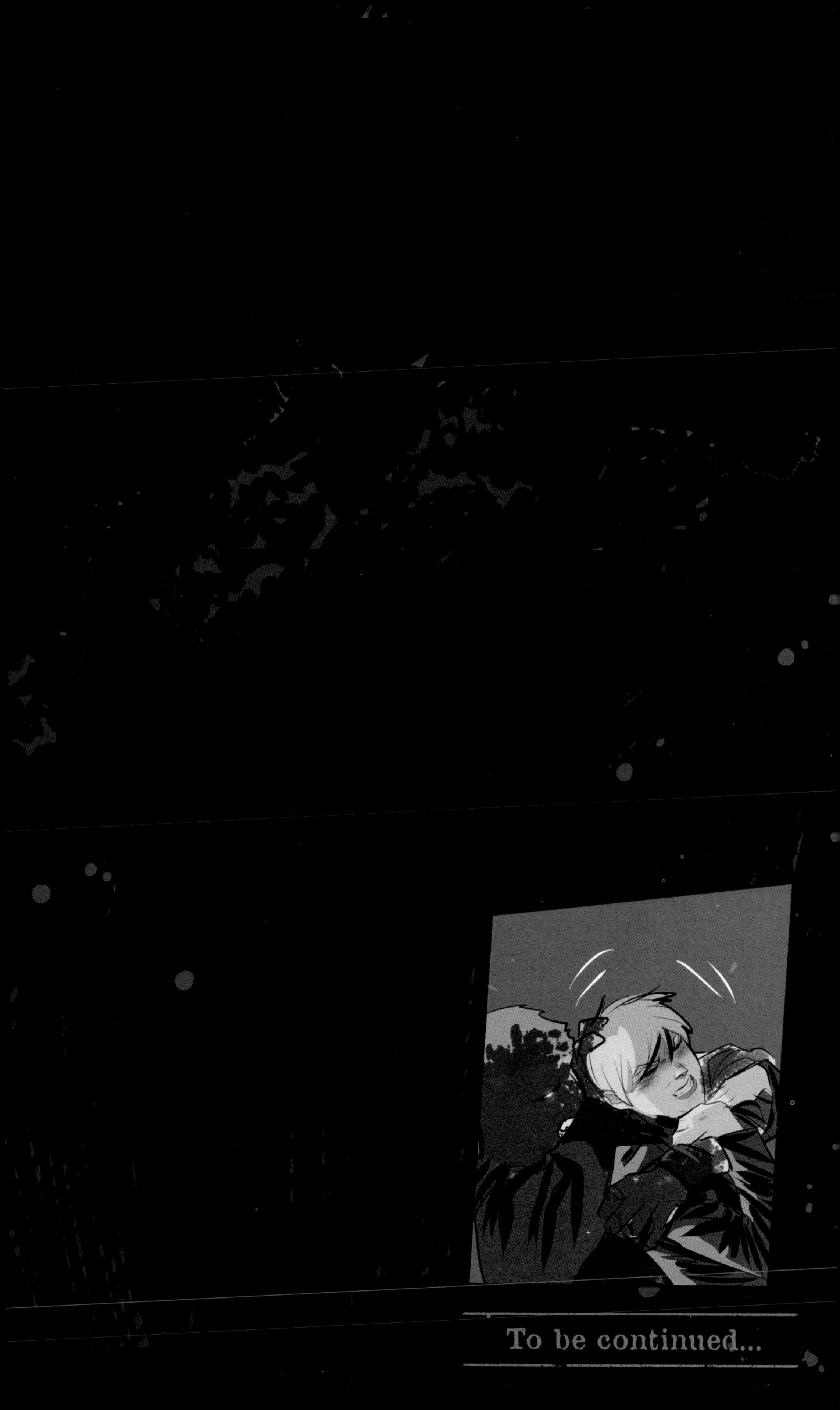
To be continued...

ISSUE TEN

FRANKENMOOSE MEETS WOLFJUG: PART 2

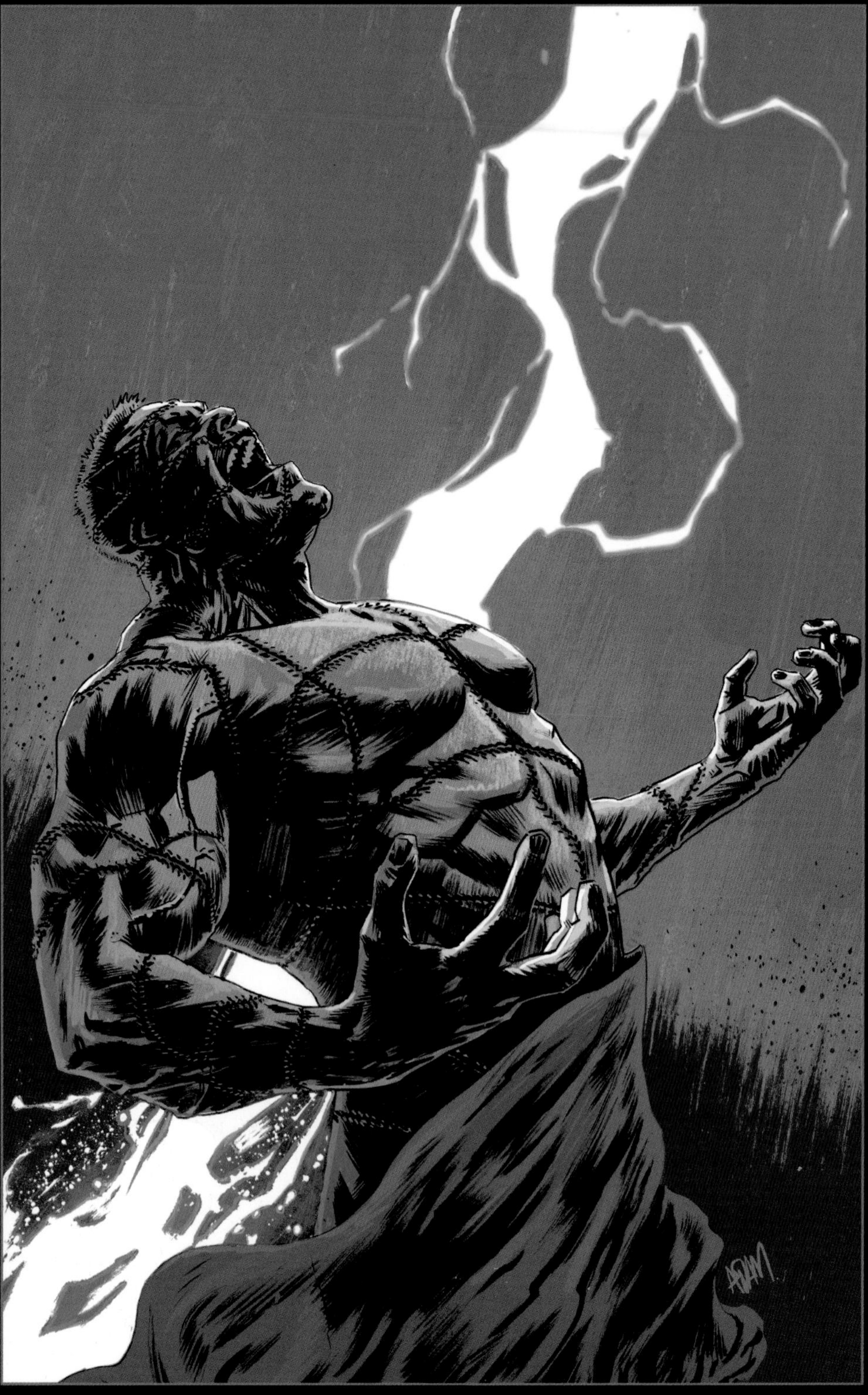

COVER ART **Adam Gorham**

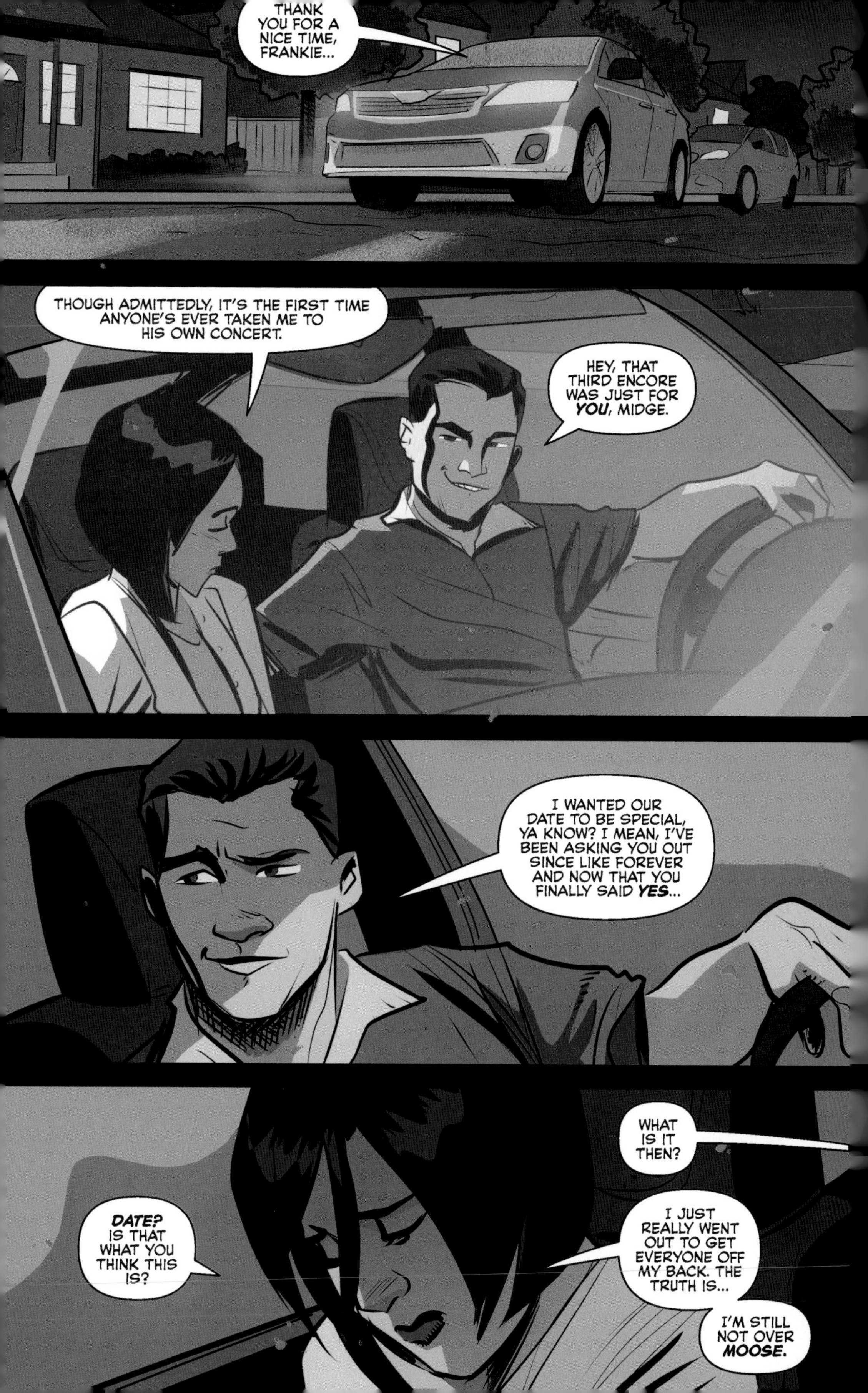

THANK YOU FOR A NICE TIME, FRANKIE...
THOUGH ADMITTEDLY, IT'S THE FIRST TIME ANYONE'S EVER TAKEN ME TO HIS OWN CONCERT.
HEY, THAT THIRD ENCORE WAS JUST FOR ***YOU***, MIDGE.
I WANTED OUR DATE TO BE SPECIAL, YA KNOW? I MEAN, I'VE BEEN ASKING YOU OUT SINCE LIKE FOREVER AND NOW THAT YOU FINALLY SAID ***YES***...
DATE? IS THAT WHAT YOU THINK THIS IS?
WHAT IS IT THEN?
I JUST REALLY WENT OUT TO GET EVERYONE OFF MY BACK. THE TRUTH IS...
I'M STILL NOT OVER ***MOOSE***.

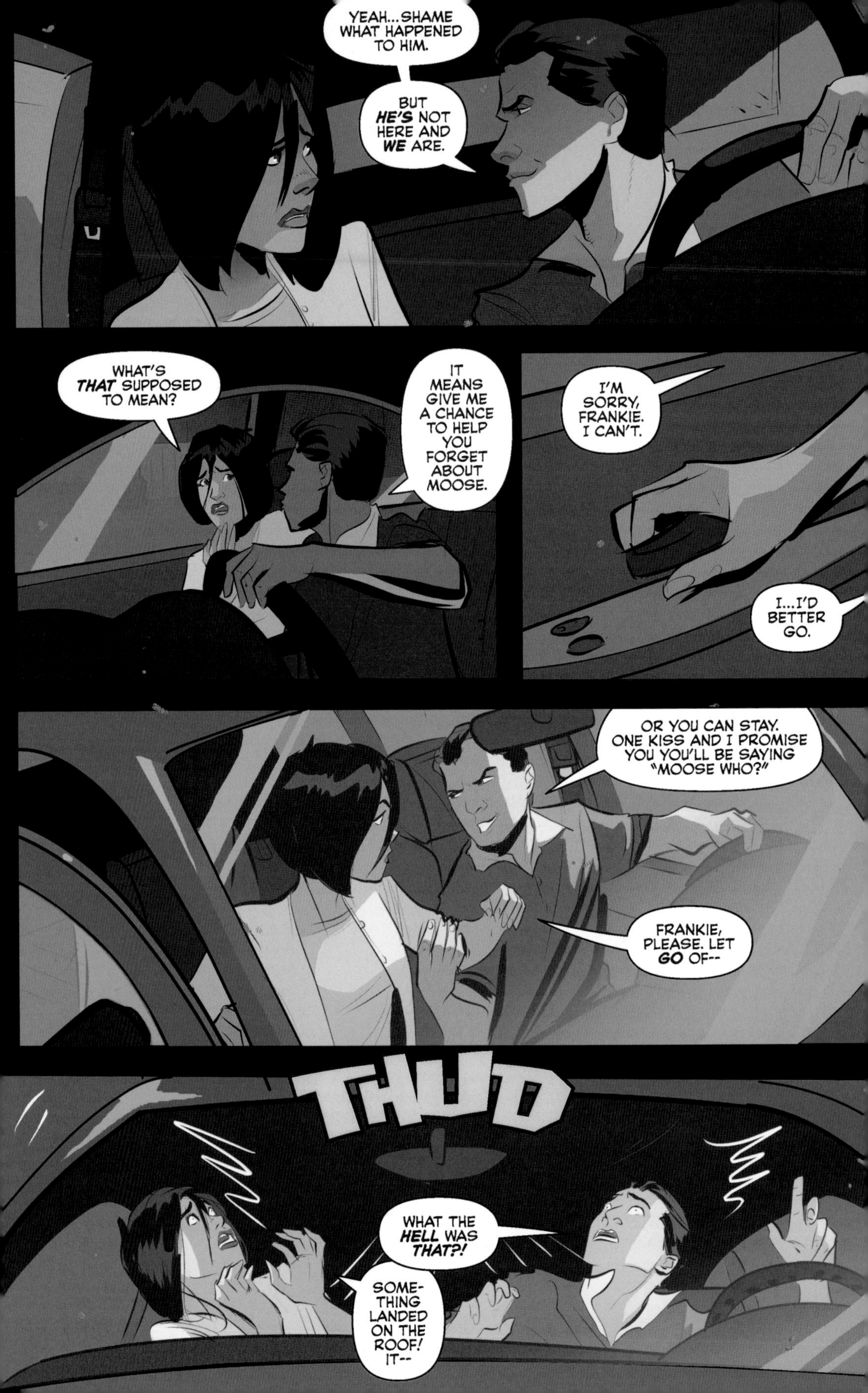
YEAH...SHAME WHAT HAPPENED TO HIM.
BUT HE'S NOT HERE AND WE ARE.
WHAT'S THAT SUPPOSED TO MEAN?
IT MEANS GIVE ME A CHANCE TO HELP YOU FORGET ABOUT MOOSE.
I'M SORRY, FRANKIE. I CAN'T.
I...I'D BETTER GO.
OR YOU CAN STAY. ONE KISS AND I PROMISE YOU YOU'LL BE SAYING "MOOSE WHO?"
FRANKIE, PLEASE. LET GO OF--
THUD
WHAT THE HELL WAS THAT?!
SOMETHING LANDED ON THE ROOF! IT--

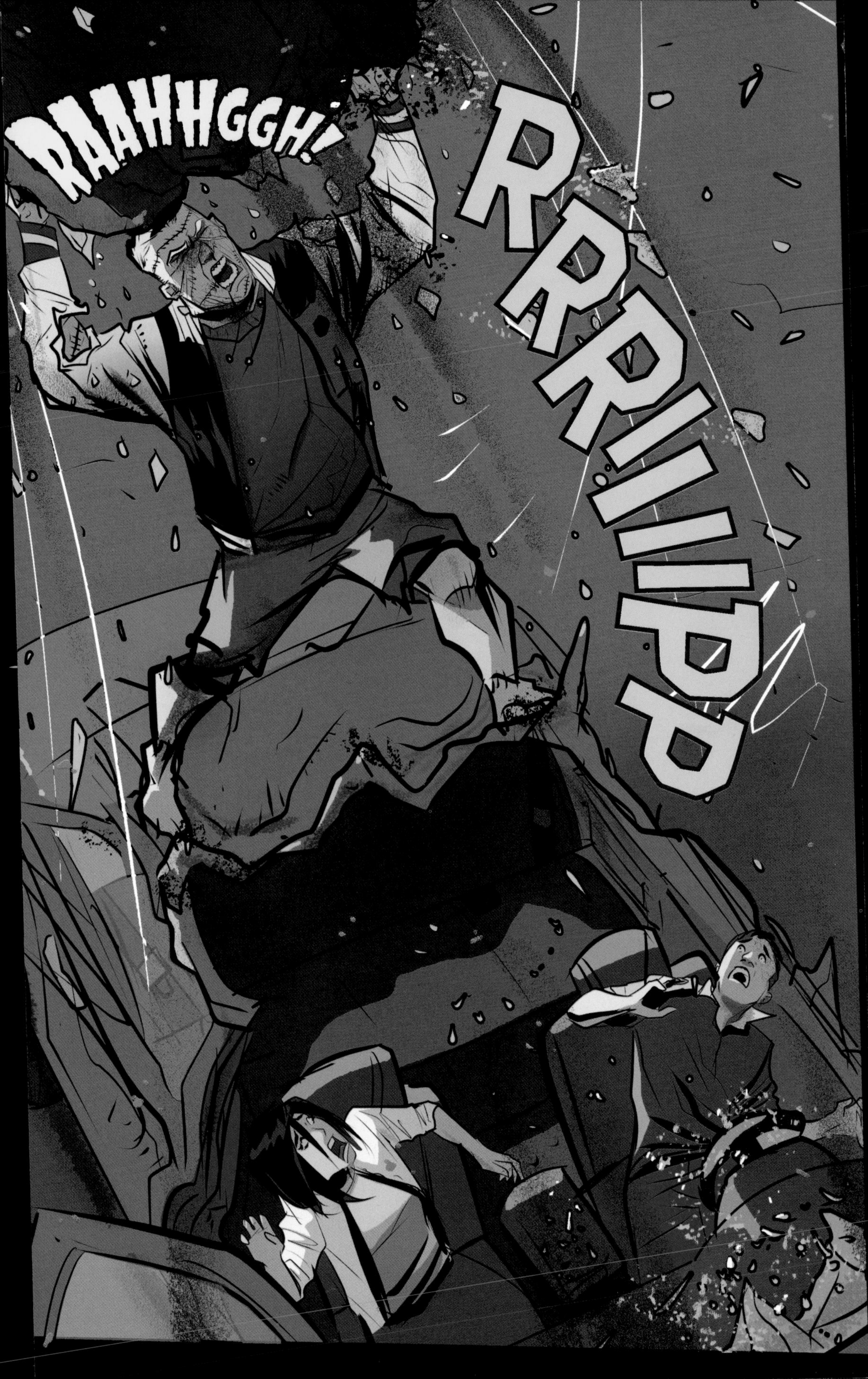
RAAHHGGH!
RRRIIIPP

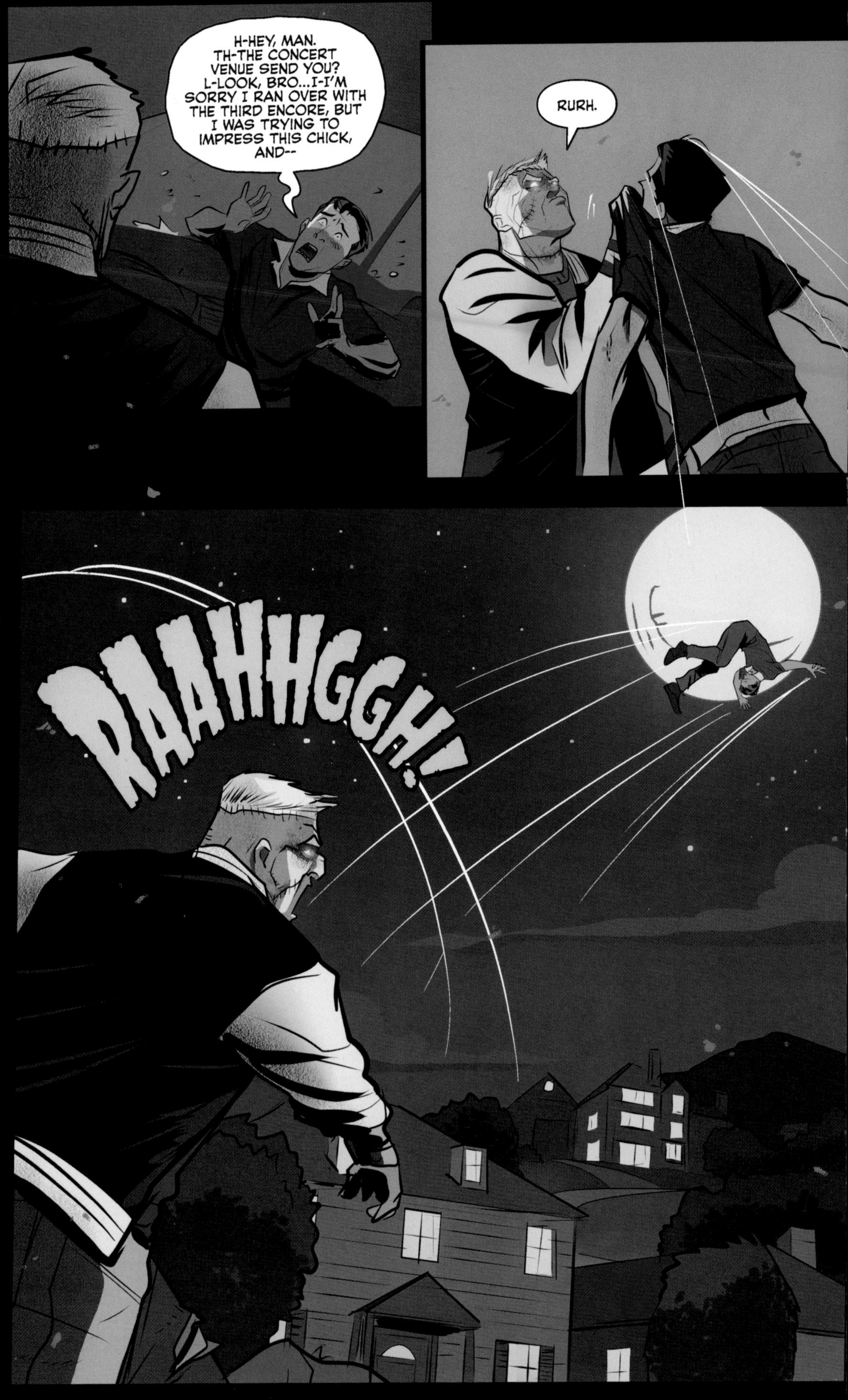
H-HEY, MAN. TH-THE CONCERT VENUE SEND YOU? L-LOOK, BRO...I-I'M SORRY I RAN OVER WITH THE THIRD ENCORE, BUT I WAS TRYING TO IMPRESS THIS CHICK, AND--
RURH.
RAAHHGGH!

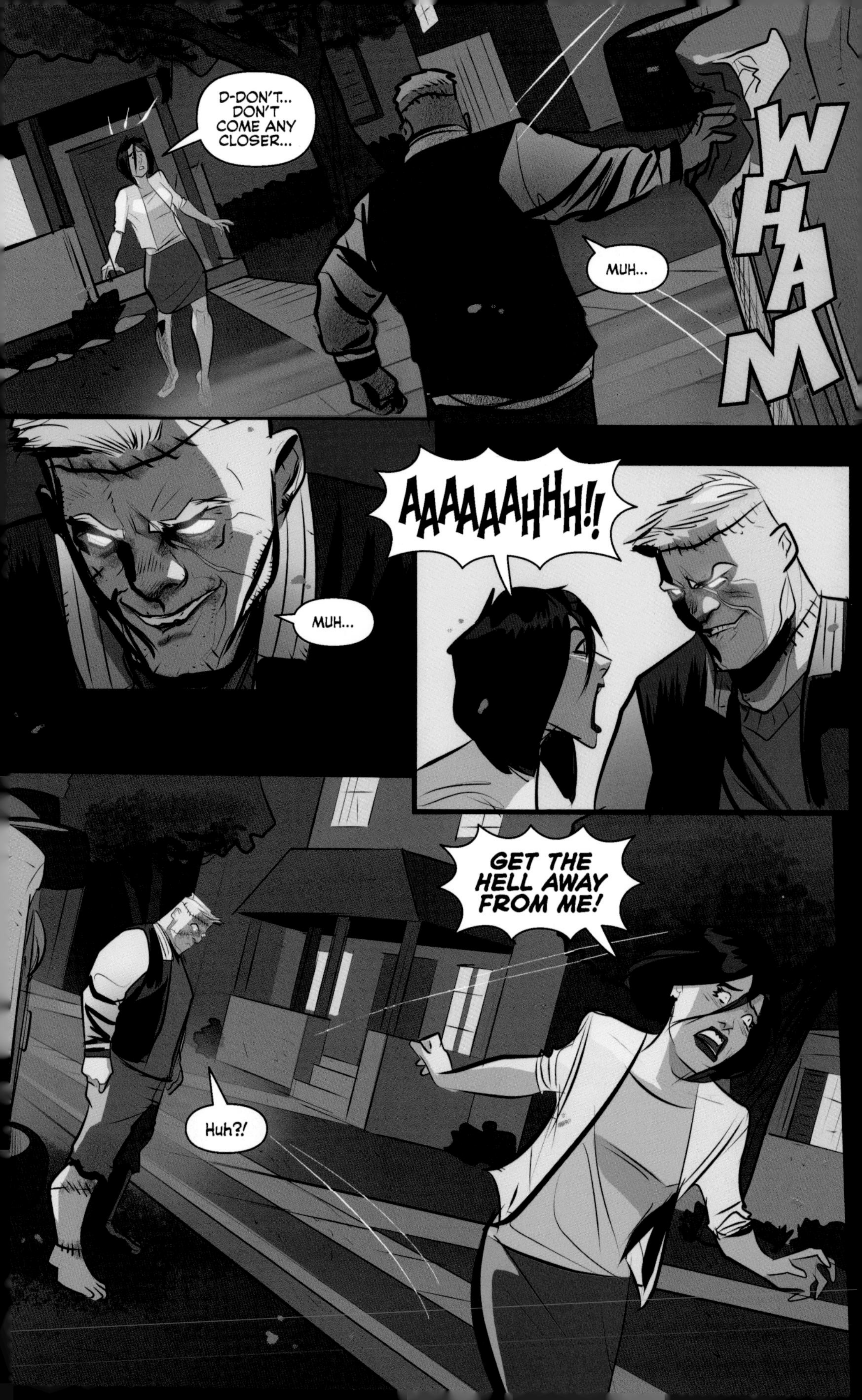
D-DON'T... DON'T COME ANY CLOSER...
MUH...
WHAM
MUH...
AAAAAAHHH!!
GET THE HELL AWAY FROM ME!
Huh?!

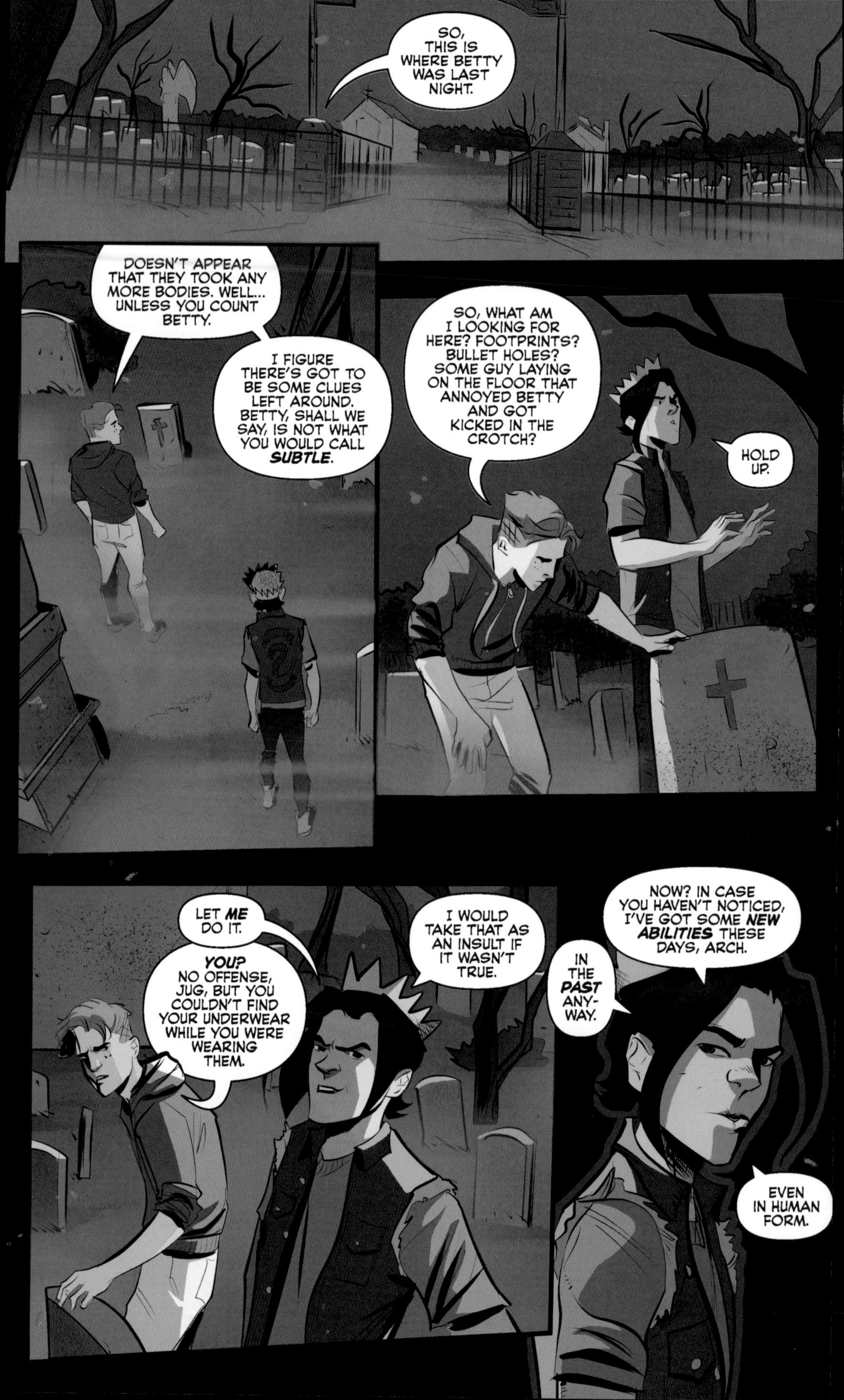
SO, THIS IS WHERE BETTY WAS LAST NIGHT.
DOESN'T APPEAR THAT THEY TOOK ANY MORE BODIES. WELL... UNLESS YOU COUNT BETTY.
I FIGURE THERE'S GOT TO BE SOME CLUES LEFT AROUND. BETTY, SHALL WE SAY, IS NOT WHAT YOU WOULD CALL **SUBTLE**.
SO, WHAT AM I LOOKING FOR HERE? FOOTPRINTS? BULLET HOLES? SOME GUY LAYING ON THE FLOOR THAT ANNOYED BETTY AND GOT KICKED IN THE CROTCH?
HOLD UP.
R.I.P.
LET **ME** DO IT.
YOU? NO OFFENSE, JUG, BUT YOU COULDN'T FIND YOUR UNDERWEAR WHILE YOU WERE WEARING THEM.
I WOULD TAKE THAT AS AN INSULT IF IT WASN'T TRUE.
IN THE **PAST** ANY-WAY.
NOW? IN CASE YOU HAVEN'T NOTICED, I'VE GOT SOME **NEW ABILITIES** THESE DAYS, ARCH.
EVEN IN HUMAN FORM.

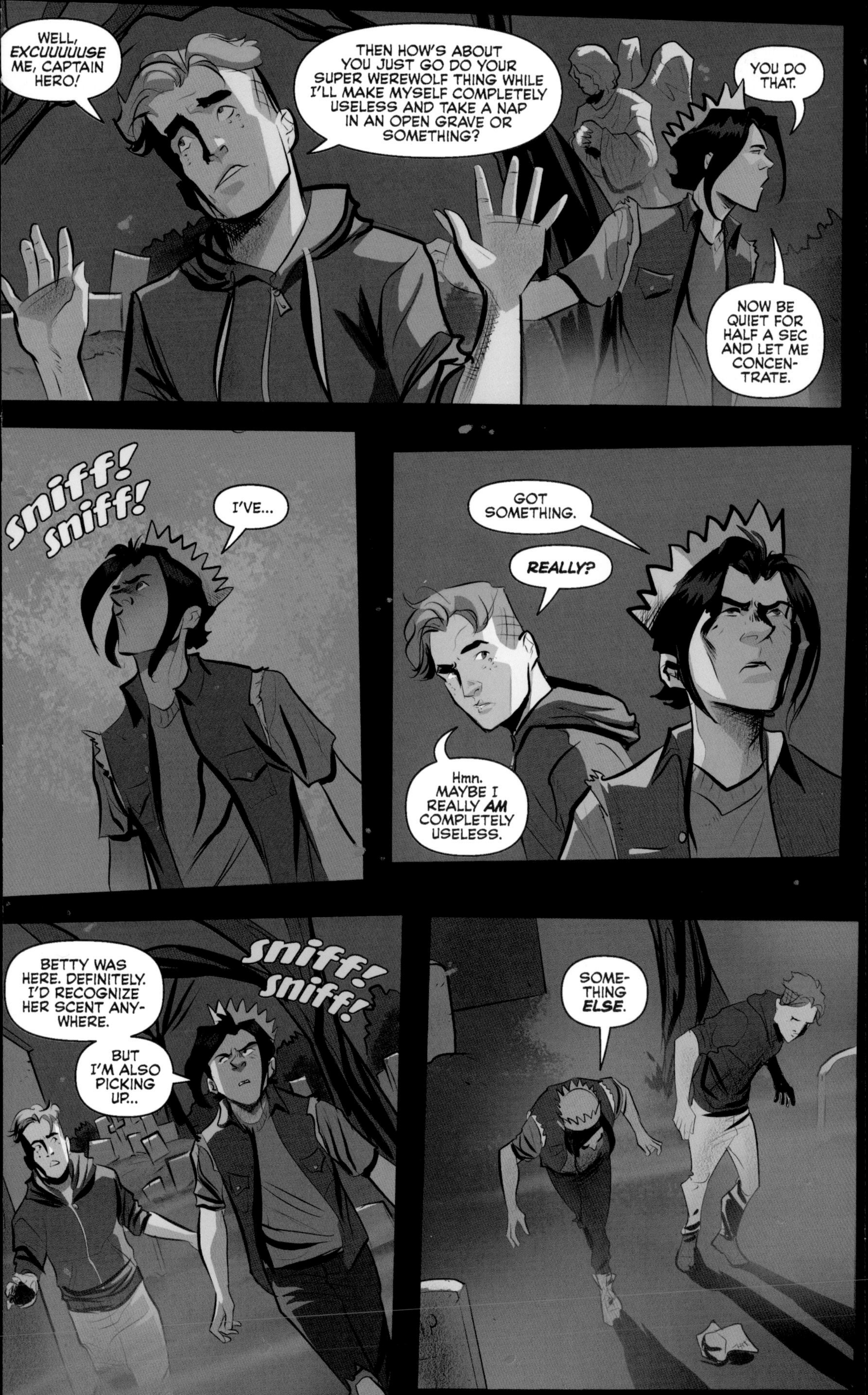
WELL, EXCUUUUUSE ME, CAPTAIN HERO!
THEN HOW'S ABOUT YOU JUST GO DO YOUR SUPER WEREWOLF THING WHILE I'LL MAKE MYSELF COMPLETELY USELESS AND TAKE A NAP IN AN OPEN GRAVE OR SOMETHING?
YOU DO THAT.
NOW BE QUIET FOR HALF A SEC AND LET ME CONCEN-TRATE.
sniff! sniff!
I'VE...
GOT SOMETHING.
REALLY?
Hmn. MAYBE I REALLY AM COMPLETELY USELESS.
BETTY WAS HERE. DEFINITELY. I'D RECOGNIZE HER SCENT ANY-WHERE.
sniff! sniff!
BUT I'M ALSO PICKING UP...
SOME-THING ELSE.

THIS KERCHIEF.

BETTY'S?

YEAH.

BUT THERE'S *ANOTHER* SCENT ON IT, TOO.

FAMILIAR, YET...

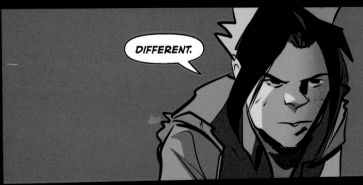

DIFFERENT.

DIFFERENT... LIKE *HOW?*

LIKE NOTHING I'VE EVER SMELLED BEFORE.

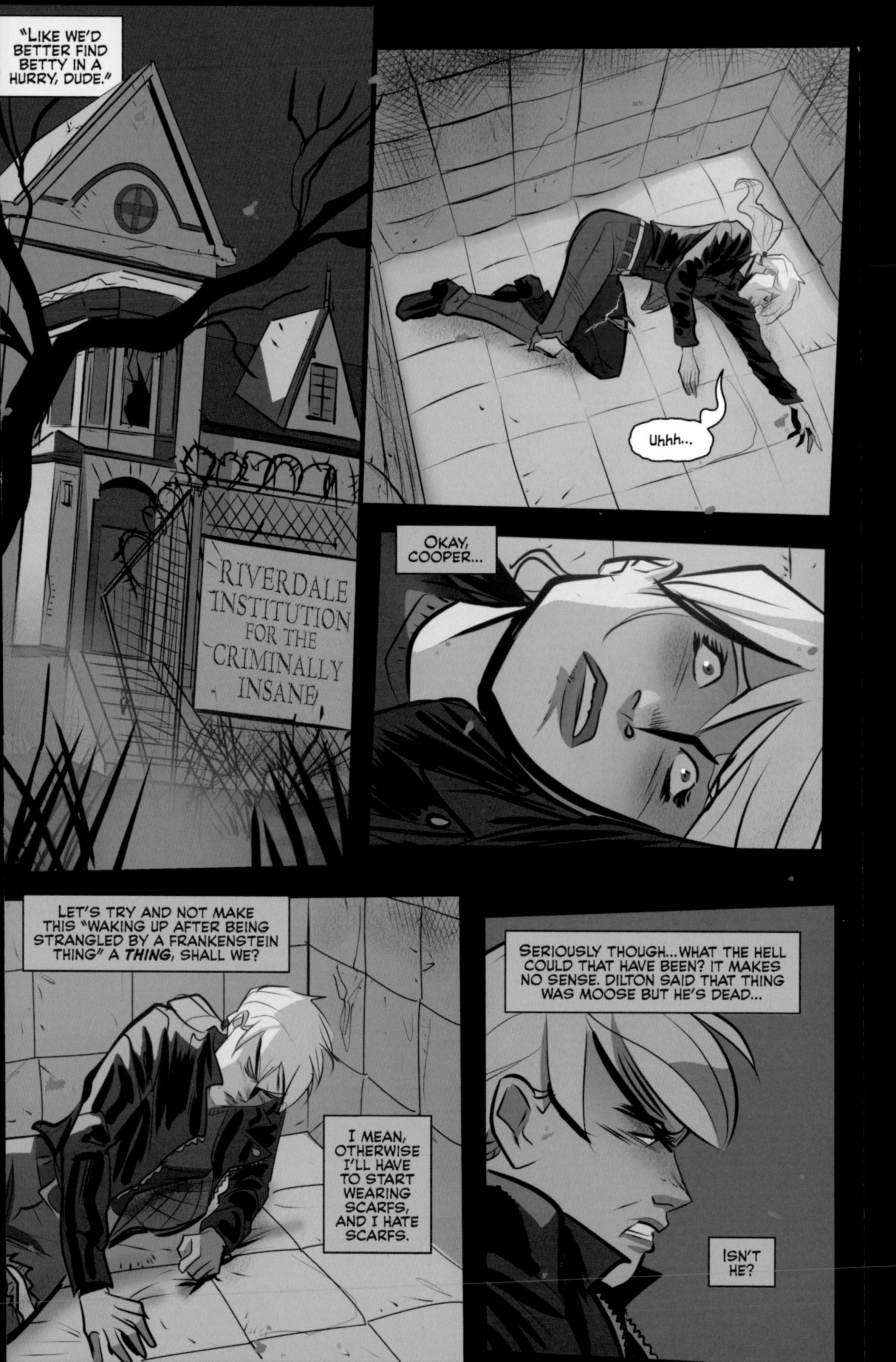
"LIKE WE'D BETTER FIND BETTY IN A HURRY, DUDE."
RIVERDALE INSTITUTION FOR THE CRIMINALLY INSANE
Uhhh...
OKAY, COOPER...
LET'S TRY AND NOT MAKE THIS "WAKING UP AFTER BEING STRANGLED BY A FRANKENSTEIN THING" A THING, SHALL WE?
I MEAN, OTHERWISE I'LL HAVE TO START WEARING SCARFS, AND I HATE SCARFS.
SERIOUSLY THOUGH...WHAT THE HELL COULD THAT HAVE BEEN? IT MAKES NO SENSE. DILTON SAID THAT THING WAS MOOSE BUT HE'S DEAD...
ISN'T HE?

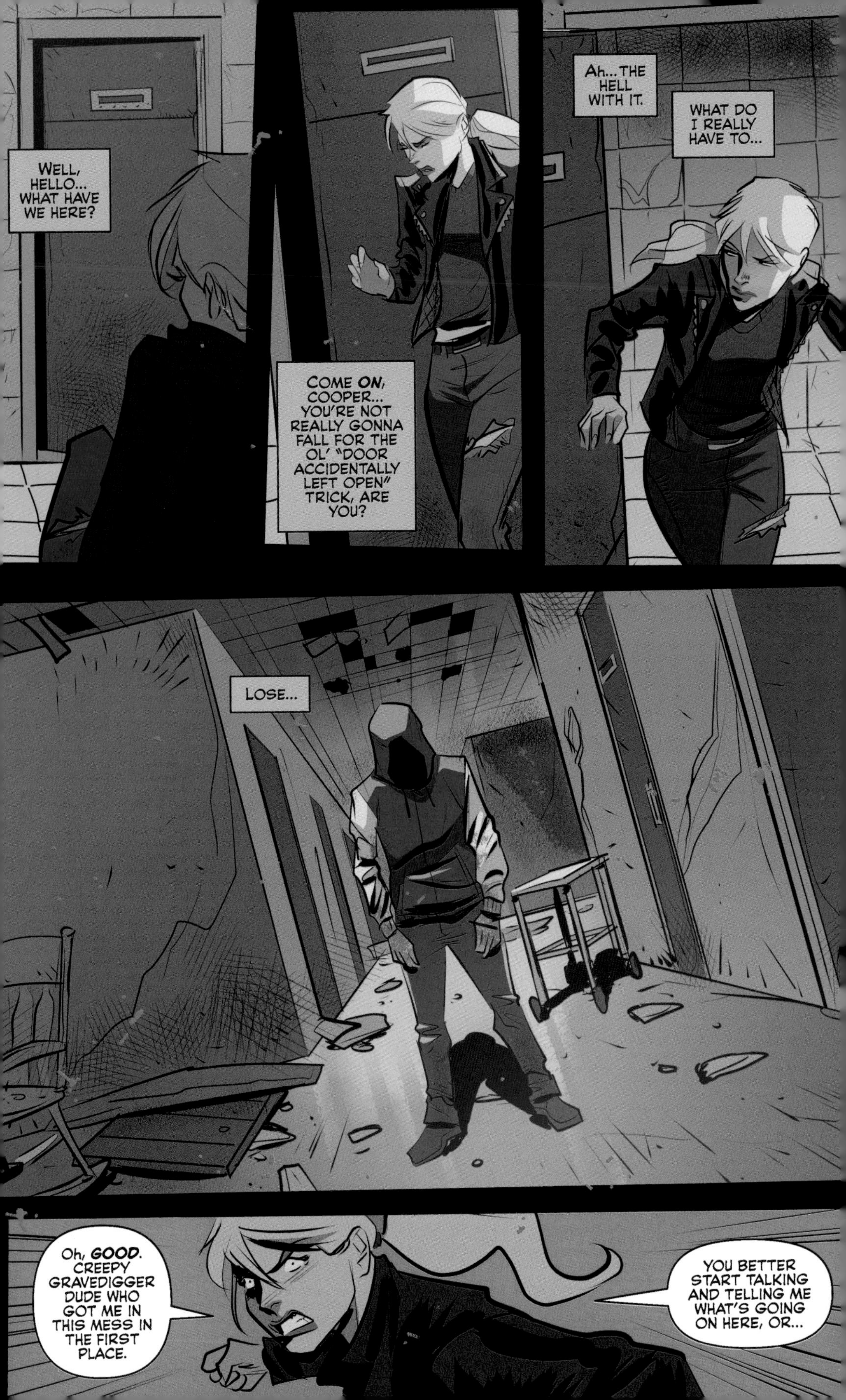
WELL, HELLO... WHAT HAVE WE HERE?
COME ON, COOPER... YOU'RE NOT REALLY GONNA FALL FOR THE OL' "DOOR ACCIDENTALLY LEFT OPEN" TRICK, ARE YOU?
Ah... THE HELL WITH IT.
WHAT DO I REALLY HAVE TO...
LOSE...
Oh, GOOD. CREEPY GRAVEDIGGER DUDE WHO GOT ME IN THIS MESS IN THE FIRST PLACE.
YOU BETTER START TALKING AND TELLING ME WHAT'S GOING ON HERE, OR...

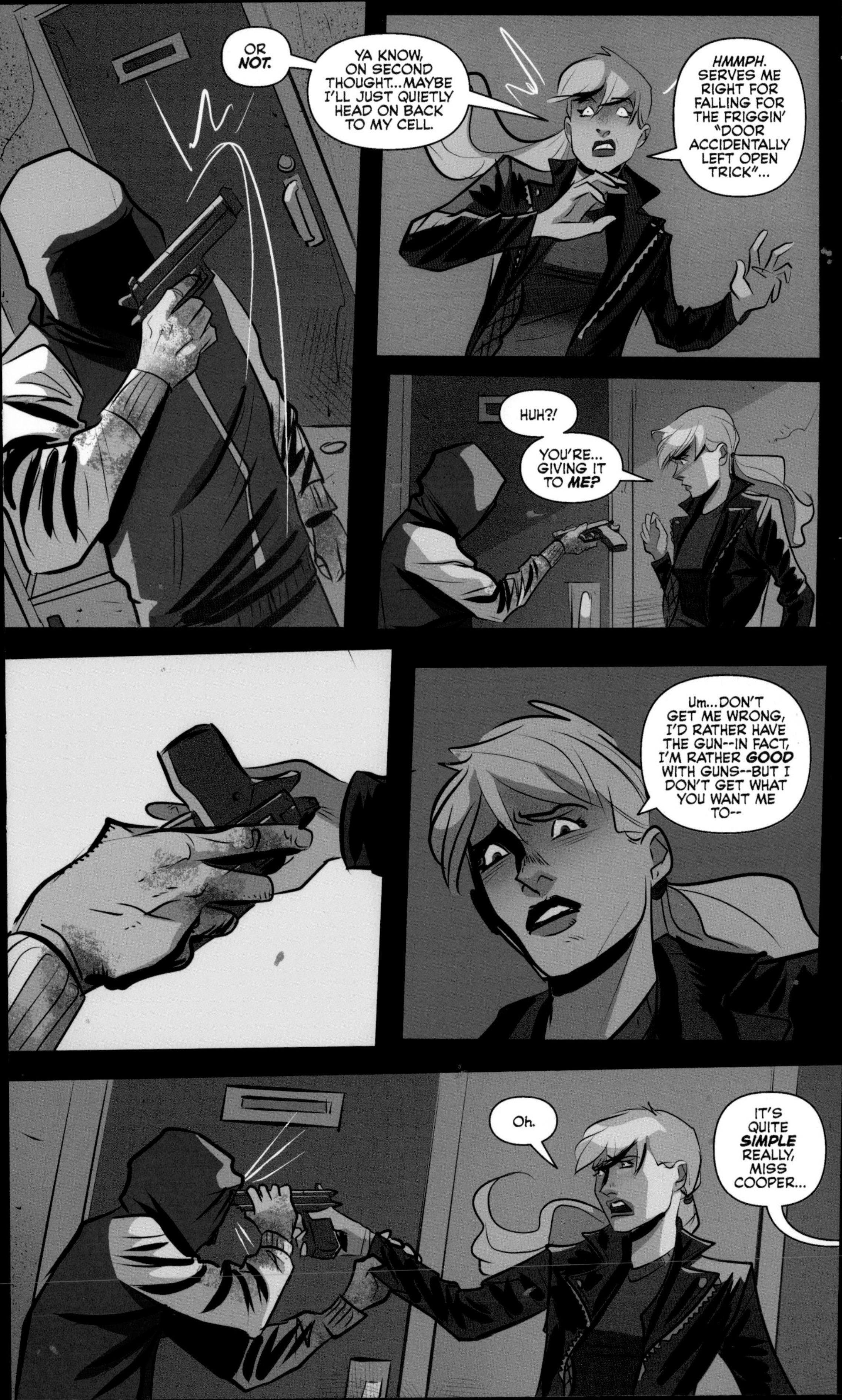
OR NOT.
YA KNOW, ON SECOND THOUGHT...MAYBE I'LL JUST QUIETLY HEAD ON BACK TO MY CELL.
HMMPH. SERVES ME RIGHT FOR FALLING FOR THE FRIGGIN' "DOOR ACCIDENTALLY LEFT OPEN TRICK"...
HUH?!
YOU'RE... GIVING IT TO ME?
Um...DON'T GET ME WRONG, I'D RATHER HAVE THE GUN--IN FACT, I'M RATHER GOOD WITH GUNS--BUT I DON'T GET WHAT YOU WANT ME TO--
Oh.
IT'S QUITE SIMPLE REALLY, MISS COOPER...

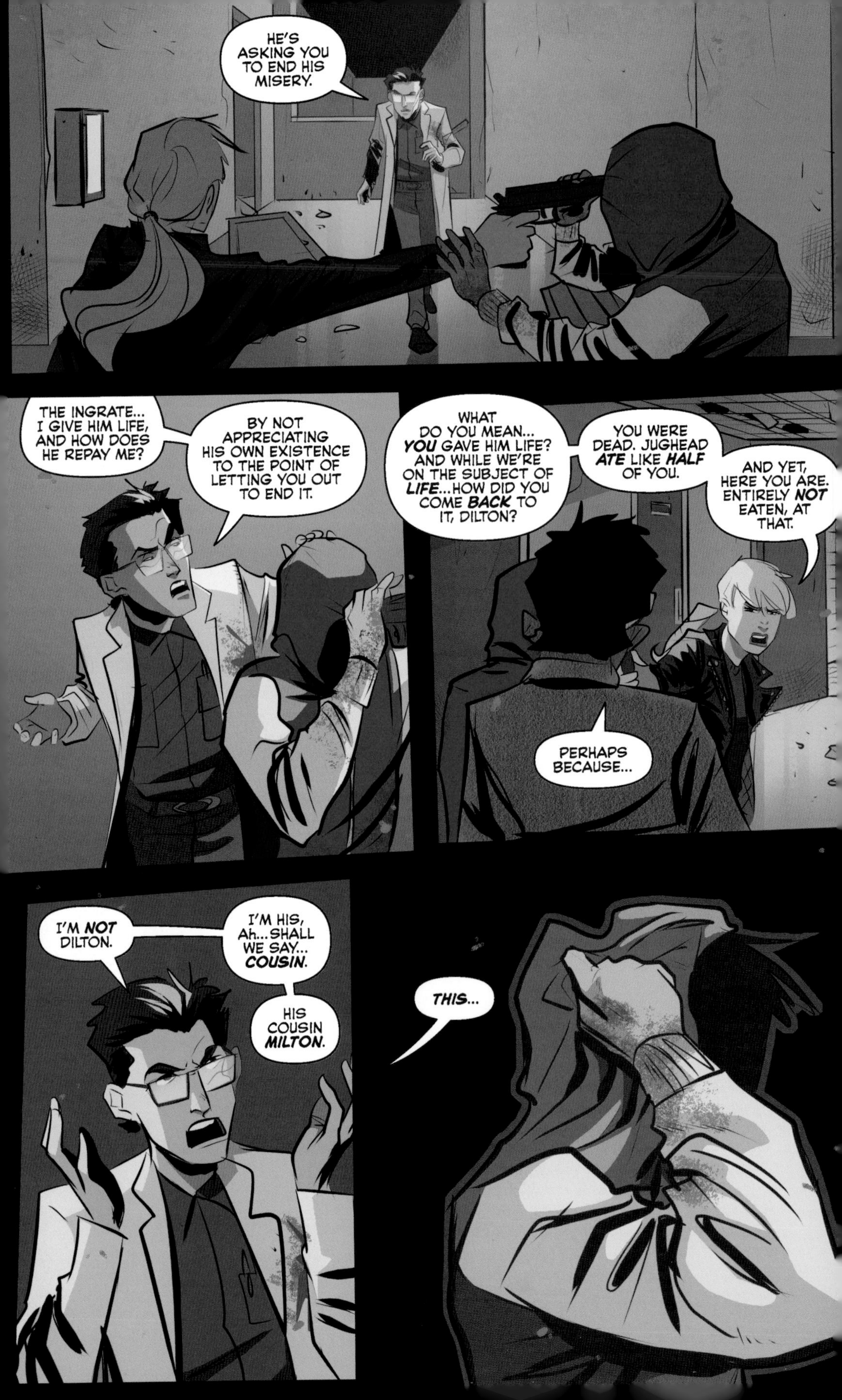
HE'S ASKING YOU TO END HIS MISERY.
THE INGRATE... I GIVE HIM LIFE, AND HOW DOES HE REPAY ME?
BY NOT APPRECIATING HIS OWN EXISTENCE TO THE POINT OF LETTING YOU OUT TO END IT.
WHAT DO YOU MEAN... YOU GAVE HIM LIFE? AND WHILE WE'RE ON THE SUBJECT OF LIFE...HOW DID YOU COME BACK TO IT, DILTON?
YOU WERE DEAD. JUGHEAD ATE LIKE HALF OF YOU.
AND YET, HERE YOU ARE. ENTIRELY NOT EATEN, AT THAT.
PERHAPS BECAUSE...
I'M NOT DILTON.
I'M HIS, Ah...SHALL WE SAY... COUSIN.
HIS COUSIN MILTON.
THIS...

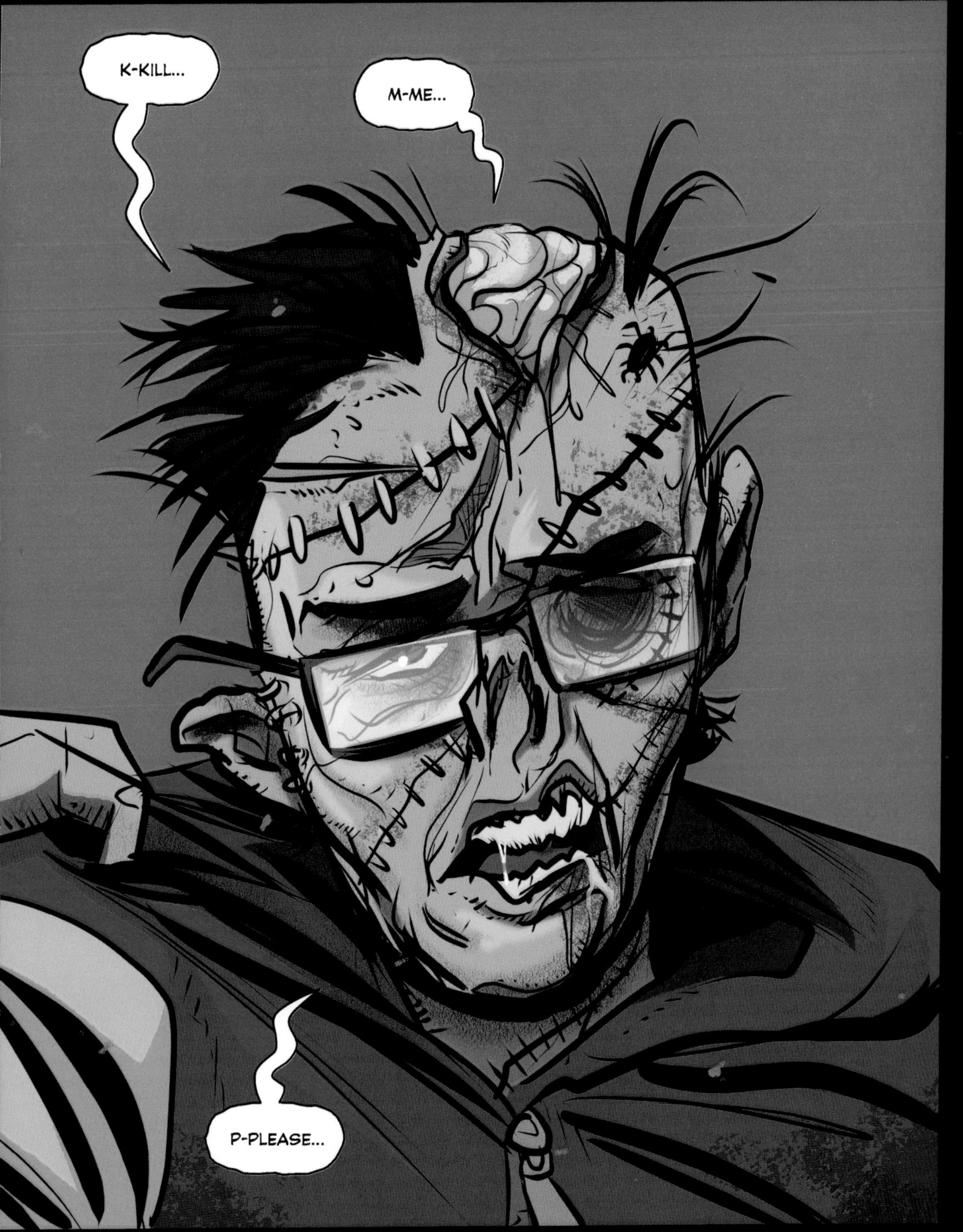
K-KILL...
M-ME...
P-PLEASE...
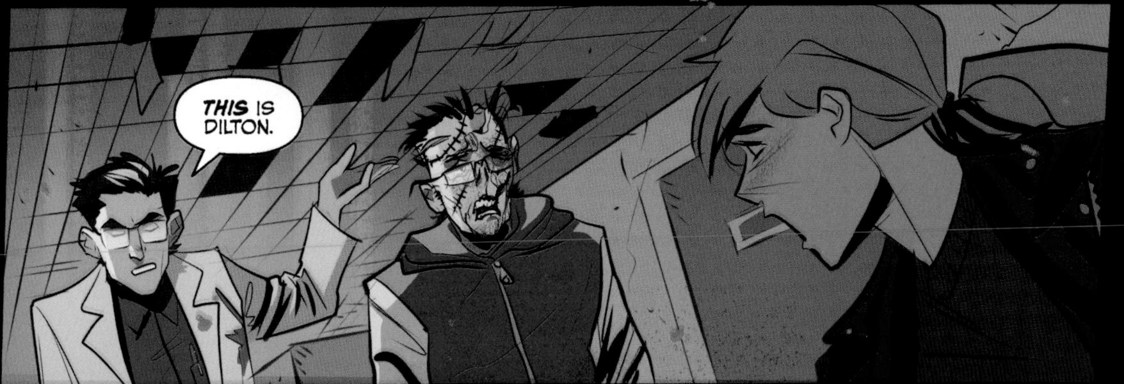
THIS IS DILTON.

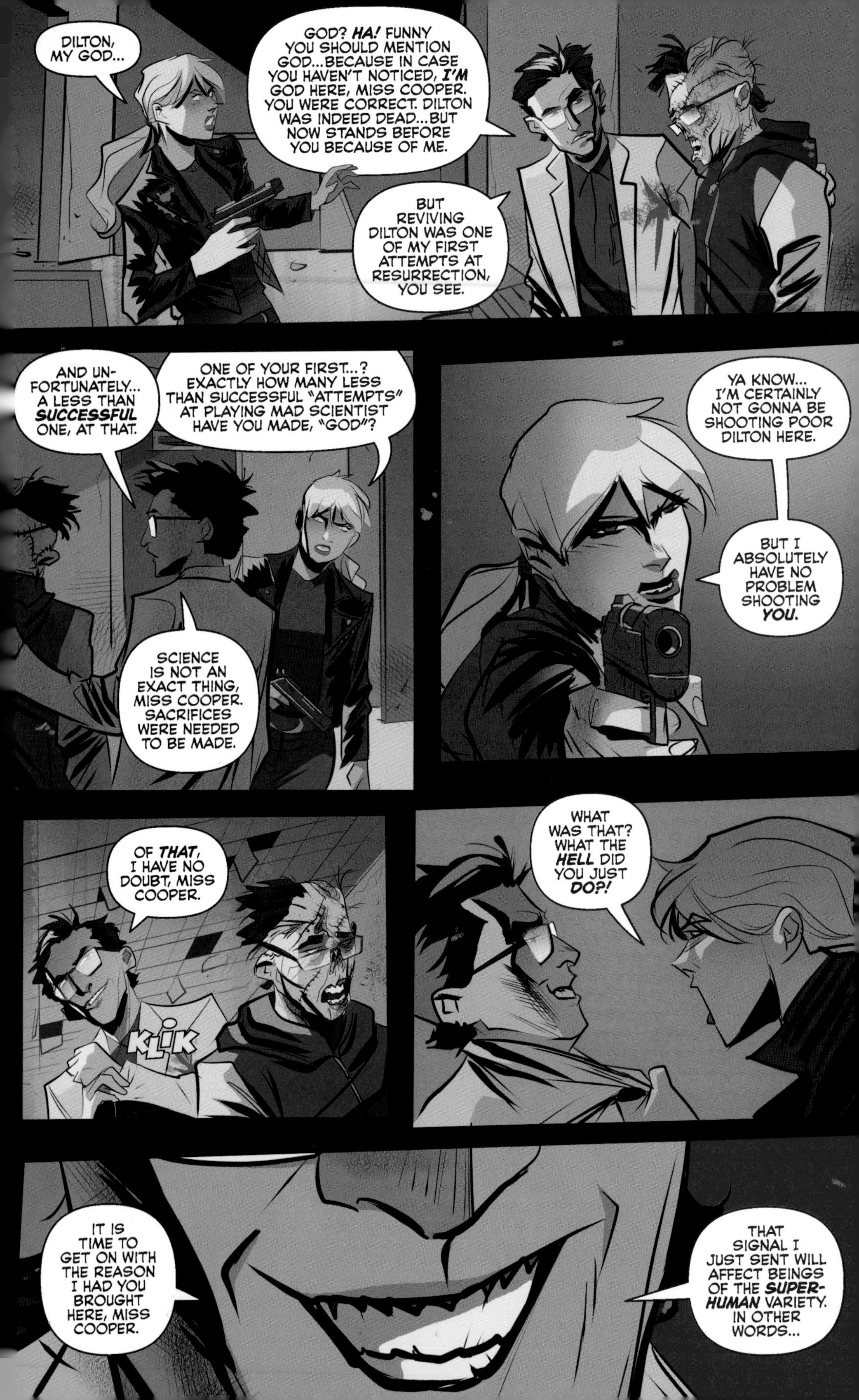

DILTON, MY GOD...
GOD? HA! FUNNY YOU SHOULD MENTION GOD...BECAUSE IN CASE YOU HAVEN'T NOTICED, I'M GOD HERE, MISS COOPER. YOU WERE CORRECT. DILTON WAS INDEED DEAD...BUT NOW STANDS BEFORE YOU BECAUSE OF ME.
BUT REVIVING DILTON WAS ONE OF MY FIRST ATTEMPTS AT RESURRECTION, YOU SEE.
AND UNFORTUNATELY... A LESS THAN SUCCESSFUL ONE, AT THAT.
ONE OF YOUR FIRST...? EXACTLY HOW MANY LESS THAN SUCCESSFUL "ATTEMPTS" AT PLAYING MAD SCIENTIST HAVE YOU MADE, "GOD"?
SCIENCE IS NOT AN EXACT THING, MISS COOPER. SACRIFICES WERE NEEDED TO BE MADE.
YA KNOW... I'M CERTAINLY NOT GONNA BE SHOOTING POOR DILTON HERE.
BUT I ABSOLUTELY HAVE NO PROBLEM SHOOTING YOU.
OF THAT, I HAVE NO DOUBT, MISS COOPER.
KLIK
WHAT WAS THAT? WHAT THE HELL DID YOU JUST DO?!
IT IS TIME TO GET ON WITH THE REASON I HAD YOU BROUGHT HERE, MISS COOPER.
THAT SIGNAL I JUST SENT WILL AFFECT BEINGS OF THE SUPER-HUMAN VARIETY. IN OTHER WORDS...

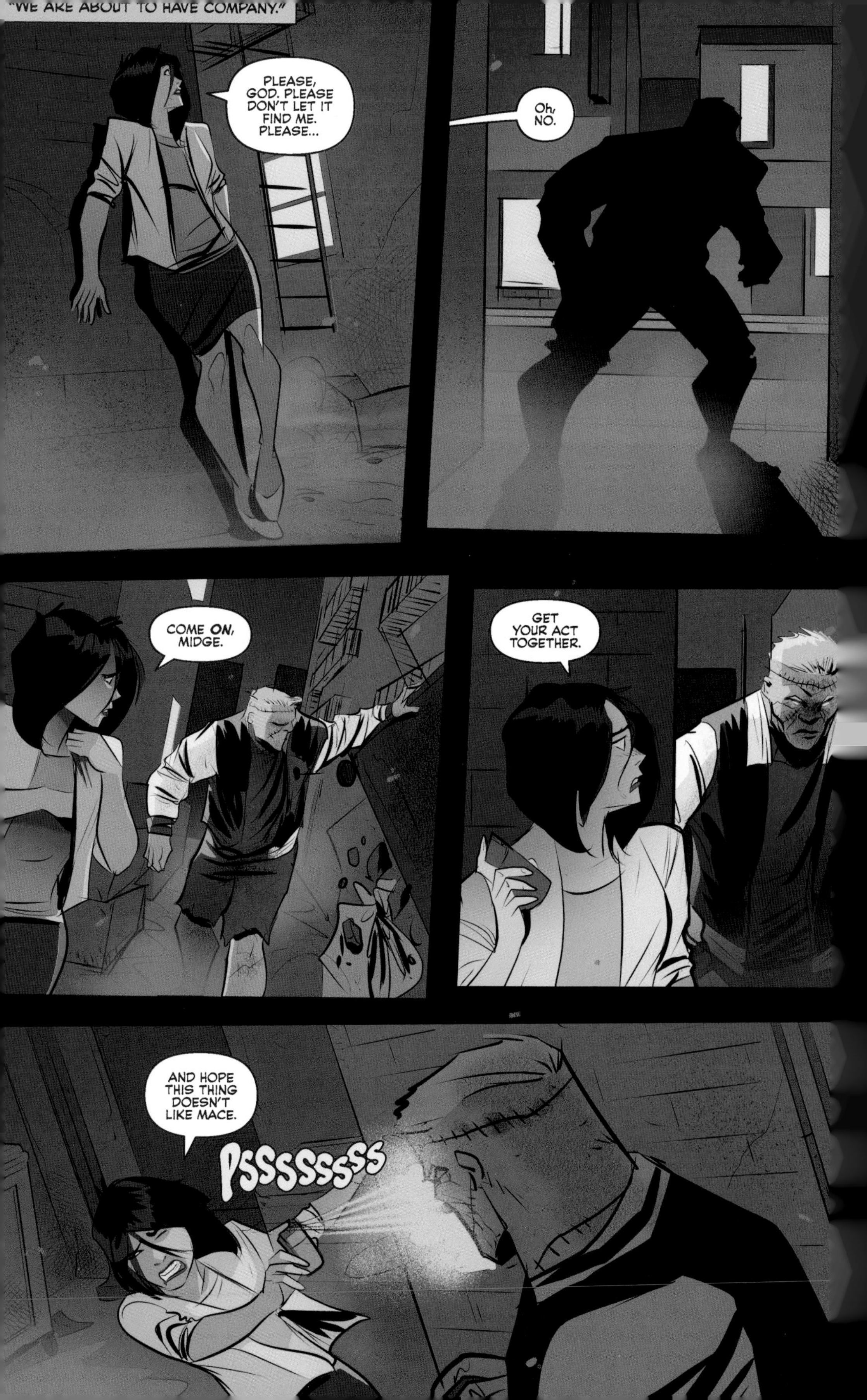
"WE ARE ABOUT TO HAVE COMPANY."
PLEASE, GOD. PLEASE DON'T LET IT FIND ME. PLEASE...
Oh, NO.
COME ON, MIDGE.
GET YOUR ACT TOGETHER.
AND HOPE THIS THING DOESN'T LIKE MACE.
PSSSSSSSS

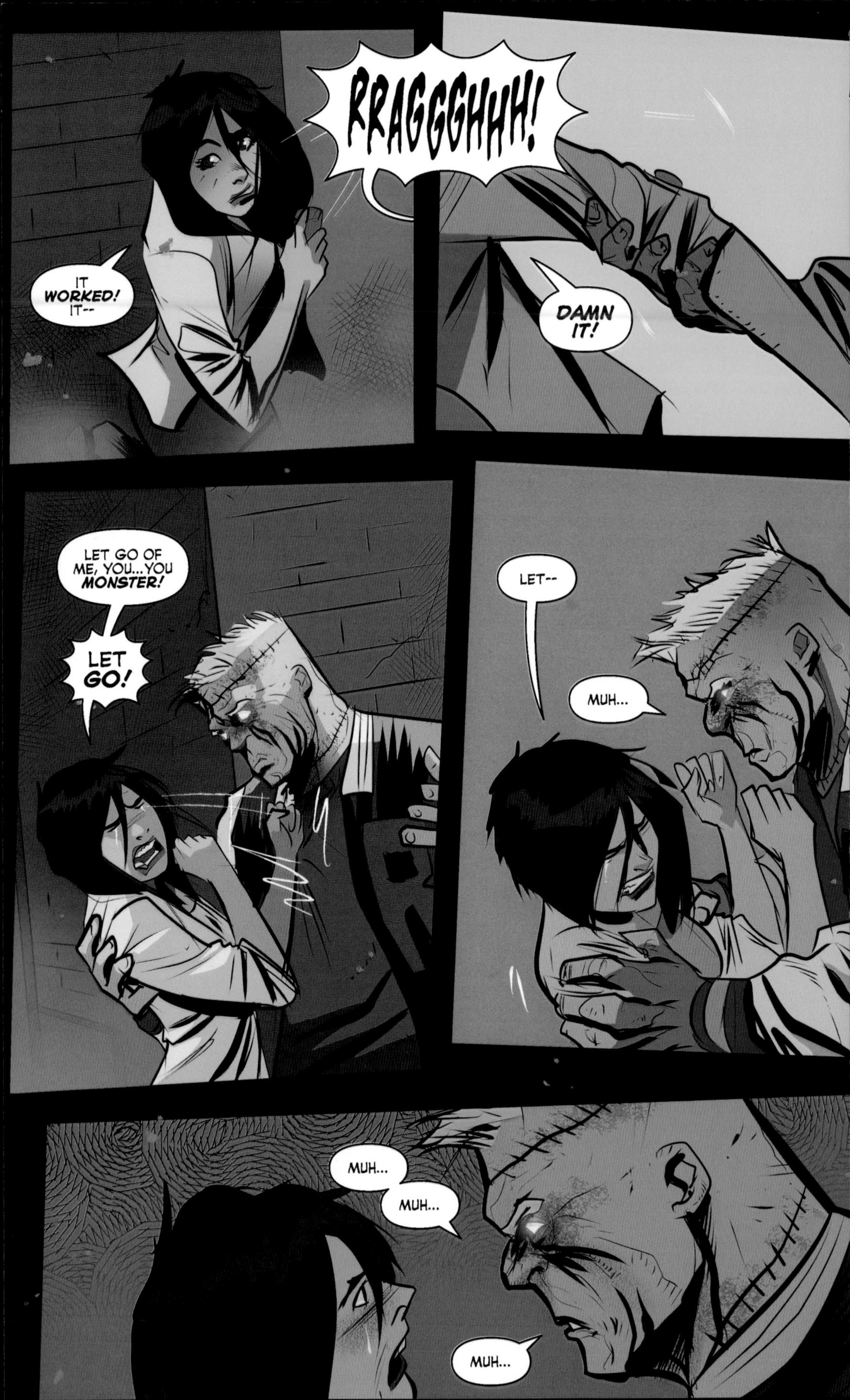
IT WORKED! IT--
RRAGGGHHH!
DAMN IT!
LET GO OF ME, YOU...YOU MONSTER!
LET GO!
LET--
MUH...
MUH...
MUH...
MUH...

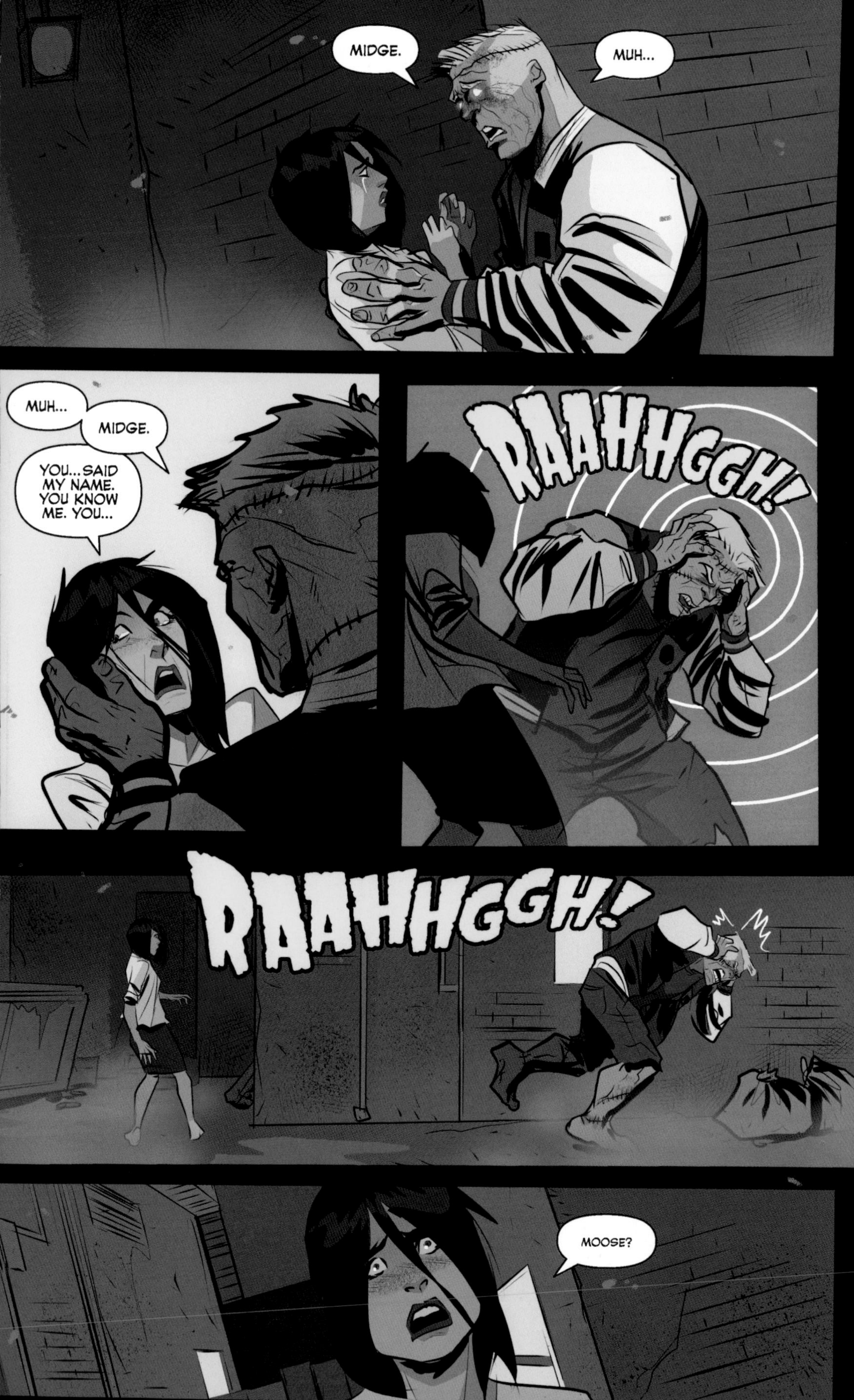

MIDGE.
MUH...
MUH...
MIDGE.
YOU...SAID MY NAME. YOU KNOW ME. YOU...
RAAHHGGH!
RAAHHGGH!
MOOSE?

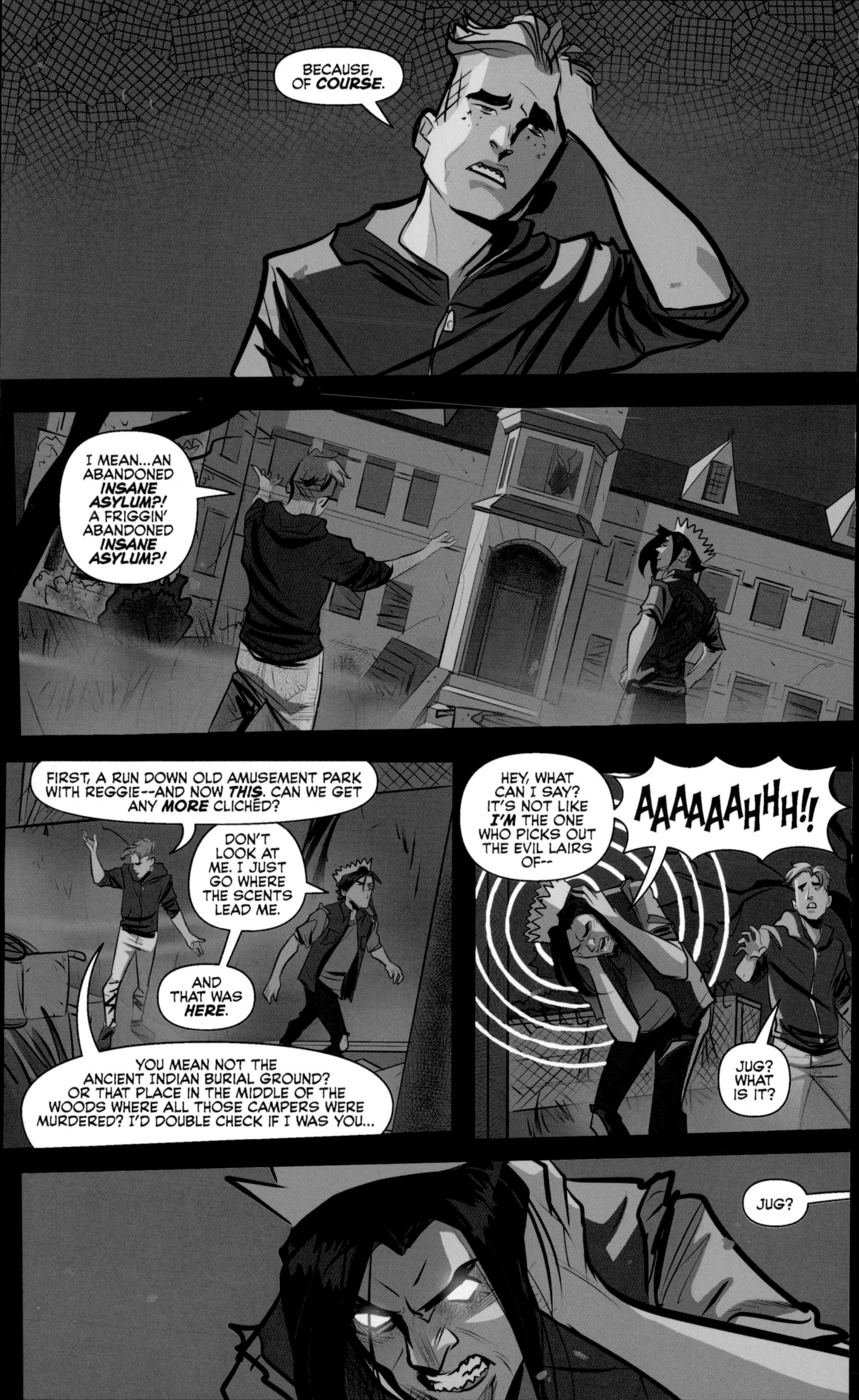
BECAUSE, OF COURSE.
I MEAN...AN ABANDONED INSANE ASYLUM?! A FRIGGIN' ABANDONED INSANE ASYLUM?!
FIRST, A RUN DOWN OLD AMUSEMENT PARK WITH REGGIE--AND NOW THIS. CAN WE GET ANY MORE CLICHED?
DON'T LOOK AT ME. I JUST GO WHERE THE SCENTS LEAD ME.
AND THAT WAS HERE.
YOU MEAN NOT THE ANCIENT INDIAN BURIAL GROUND? OR THAT PLACE IN THE MIDDLE OF THE WOODS WHERE ALL THOSE CAMPERS WERE MURDERED? I'D DOUBLE CHECK IF I WAS YOU...
HEY, WHAT CAN I SAY? IT'S NOT LIKE I'M THE ONE WHO PICKS OUT THE EVIL LAIRS OF--
AAAAAAHHH!!
JUG? WHAT IS IT?
JUG?

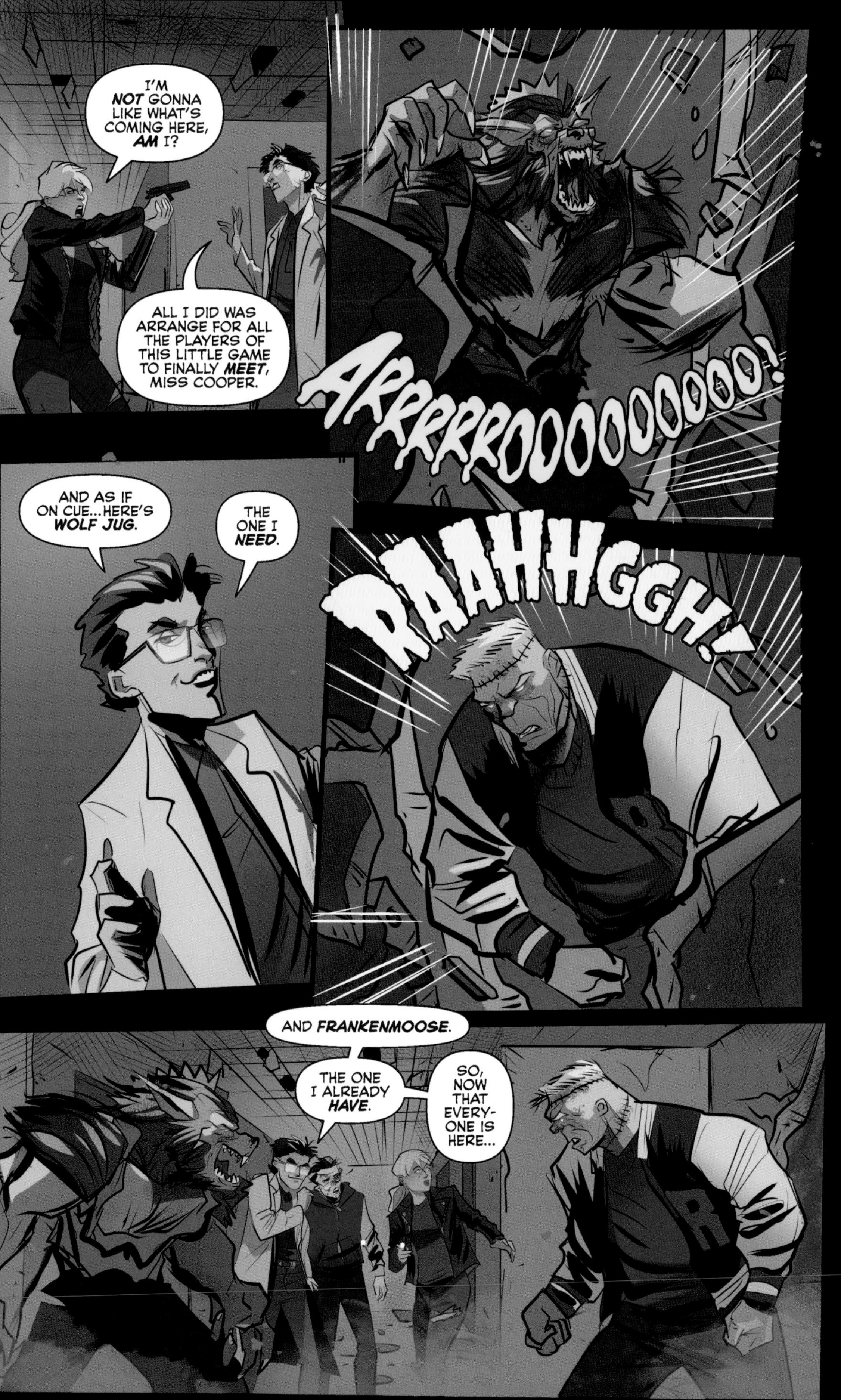
I'M NOT GONNA LIKE WHAT'S COMING HERE, AM I?
ALL I DID WAS ARRANGE FOR ALL THE PLAYERS OF THIS LITTLE GAME TO FINALLY MEET, MISS COOPER.
ARRRRROOOOOOOOOO!
AND AS IF ON CUE...HERE'S WOLF JUG.
THE ONE I NEED.
RAAHHGGH!
AND FRANKENMOOSE.
THE ONE I ALREADY HAVE.
SO, NOW THAT EVERYONE IS HERE...

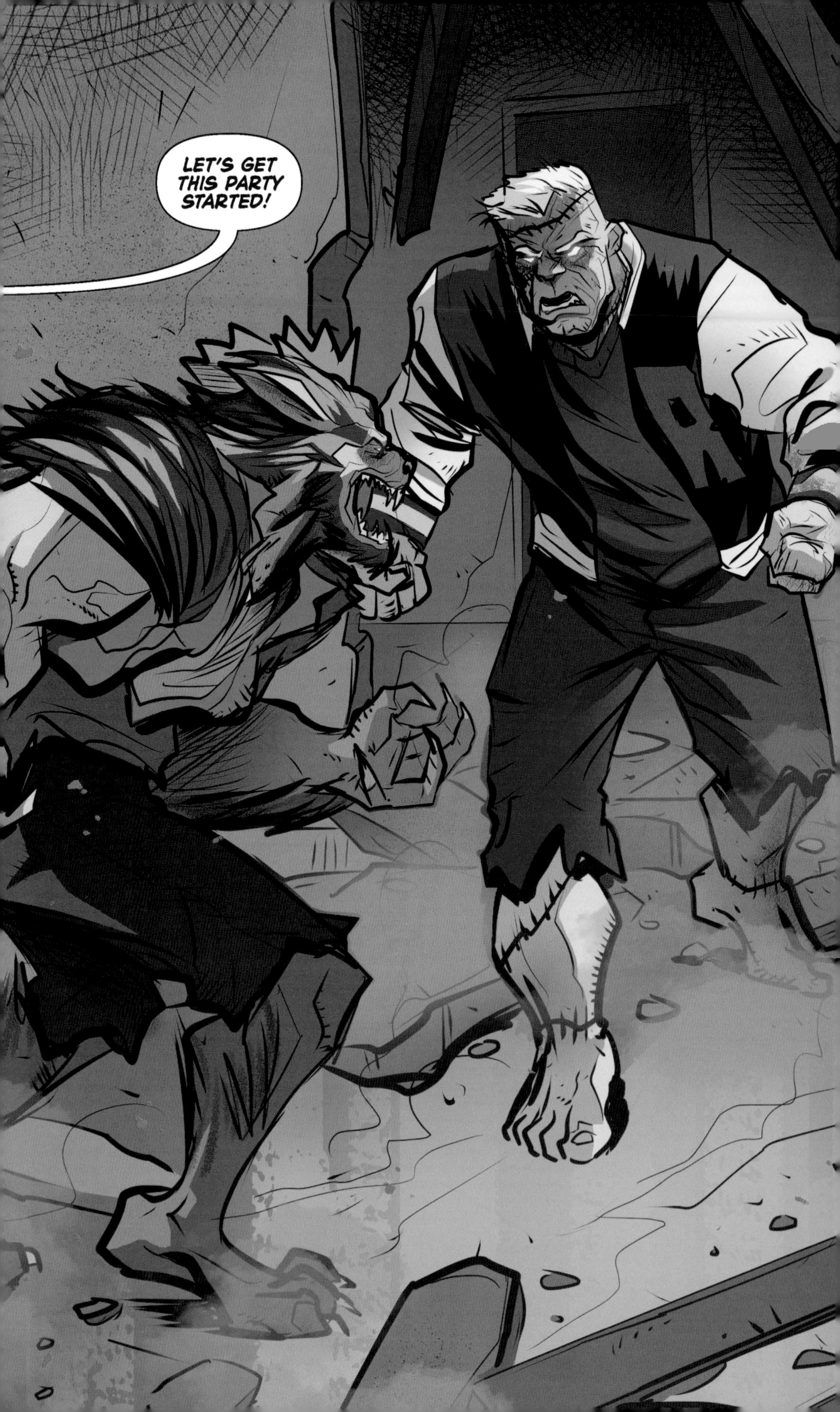
LET'S GET THIS PARTY STARTED!

To be continued...

ISSUE ELEVEN

FRANKENMOOSE MEETS WOLFJUG: PART 3

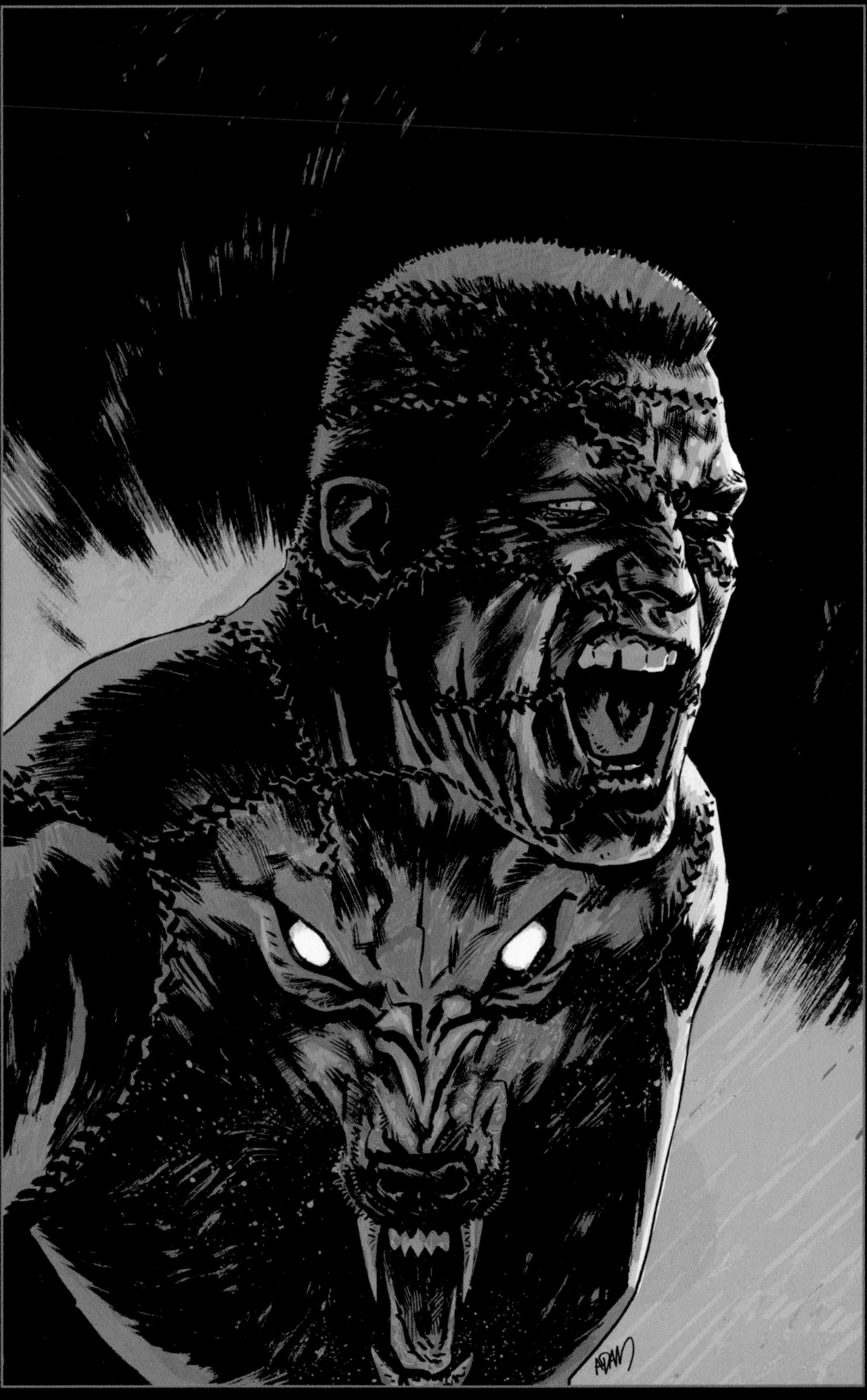
ADAM

COVER ART Adam Gorham

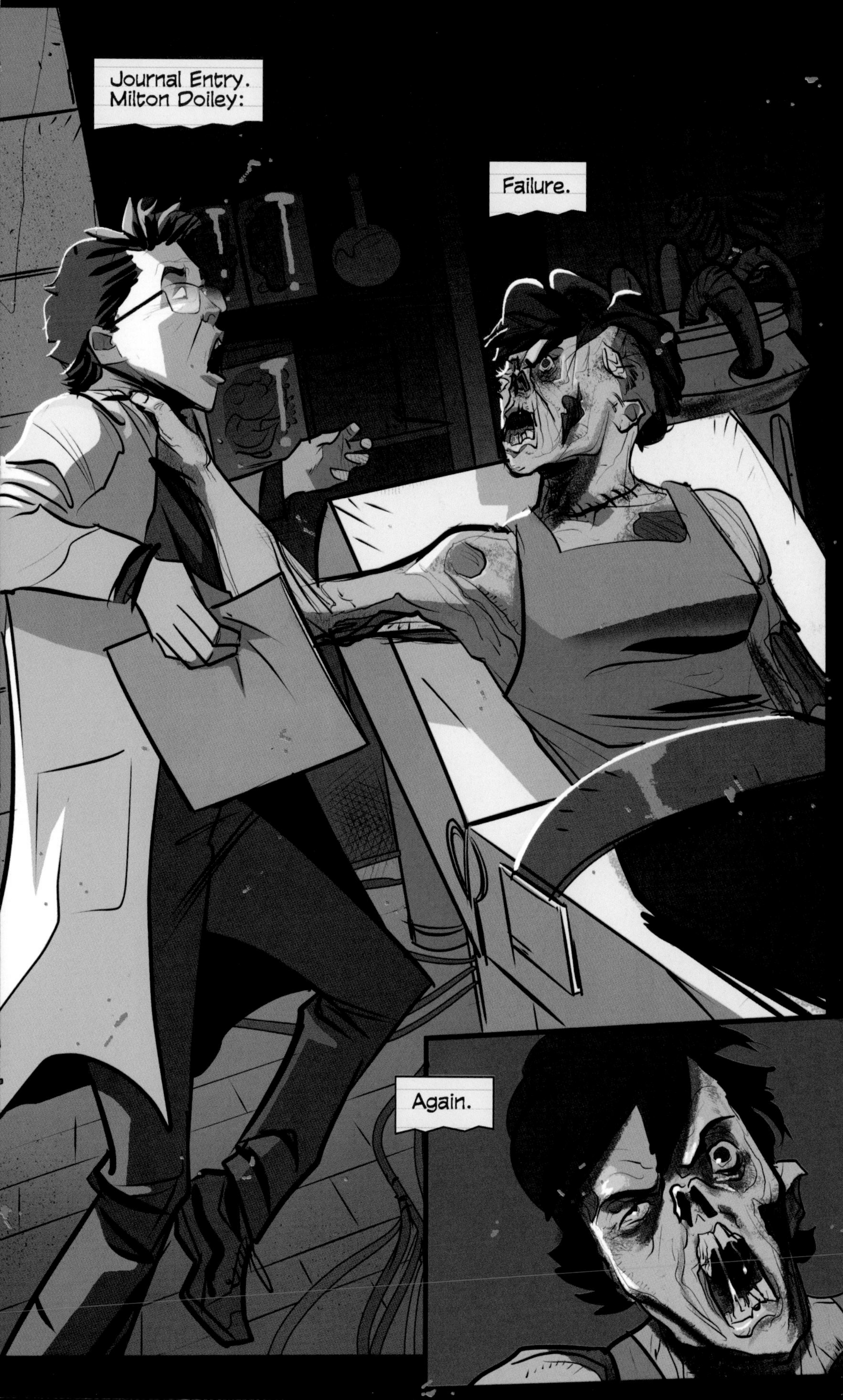
Journal Entry.
Milton Doiley:
Failure.
Again.

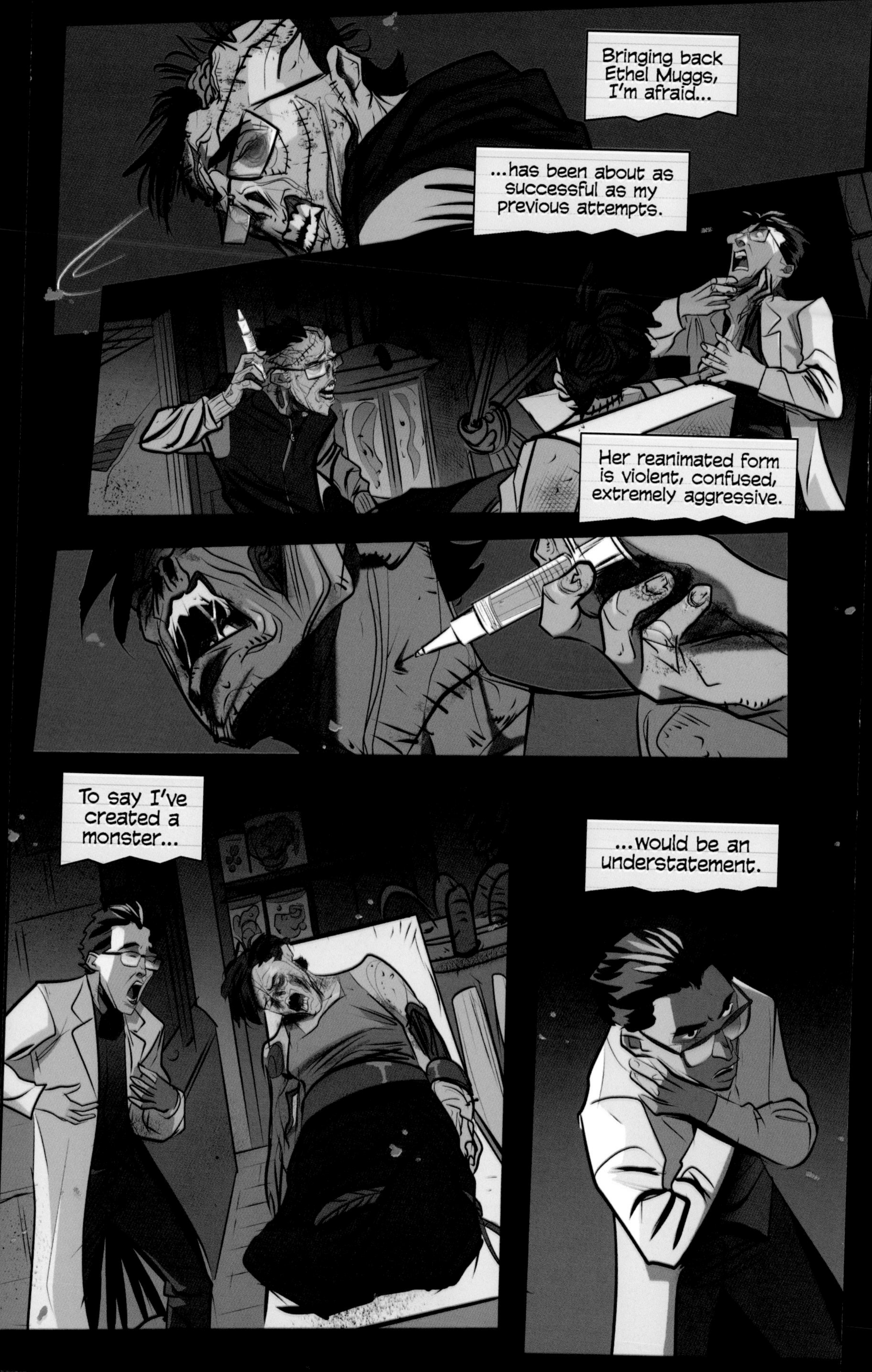
Bringing back Ethel Muggs, I'm afraid...
...has been about as successful as my previous attempts.
Her reanimated form is violent, confused, extremely aggressive.
To say I've created a monster...
...would be an understatement.

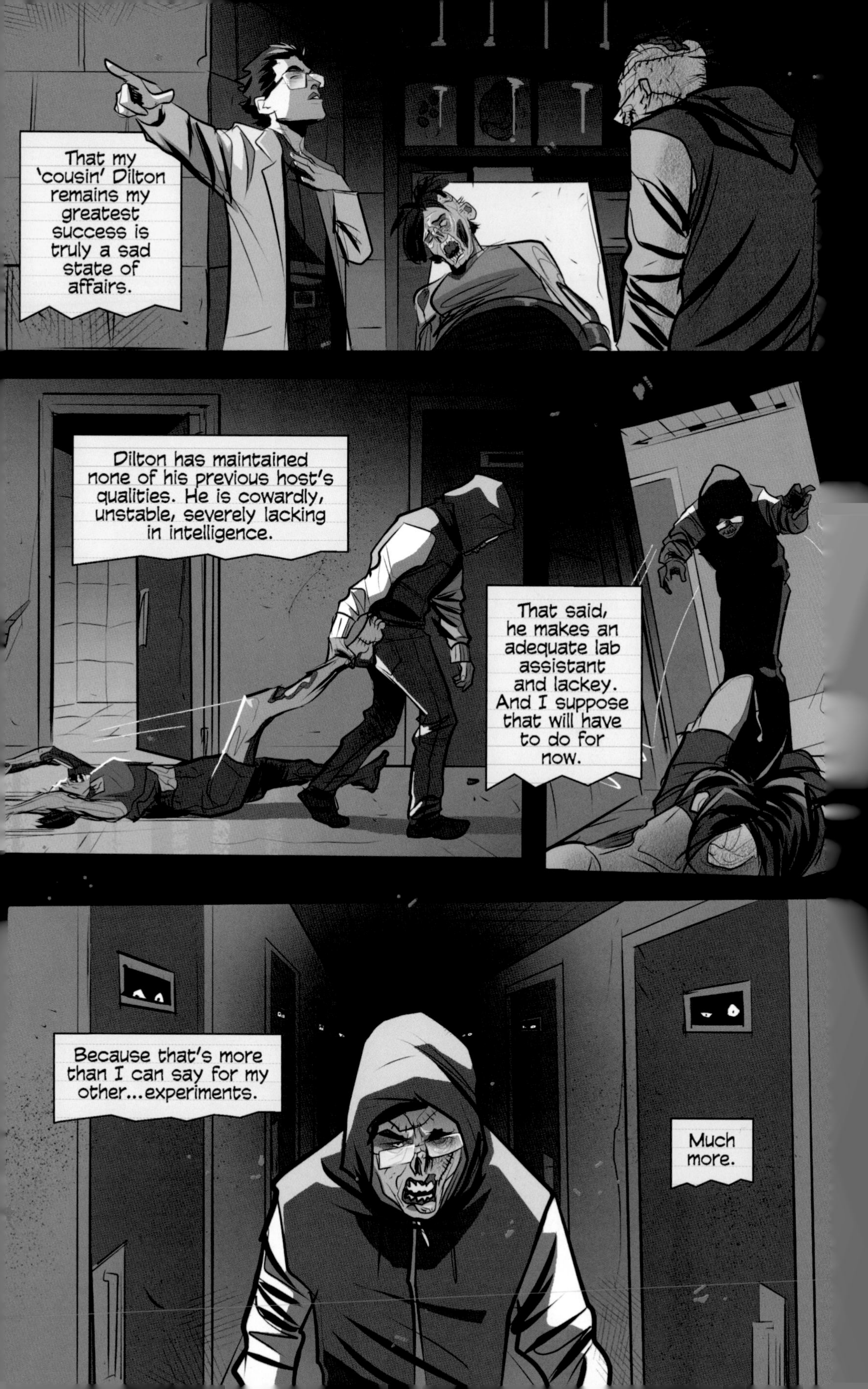
That my 'cousin' Dilton remains my greatest success is truly a sad state of affairs.
Dilton has maintained none of his previous host's qualities. He is cowardly, unstable, severely lacking in intelligence.
That said, he makes an adequate lab assistant and lackey. And I suppose that will have to do for now.
Because that's more than I can say for my other...experiments.
Much more.

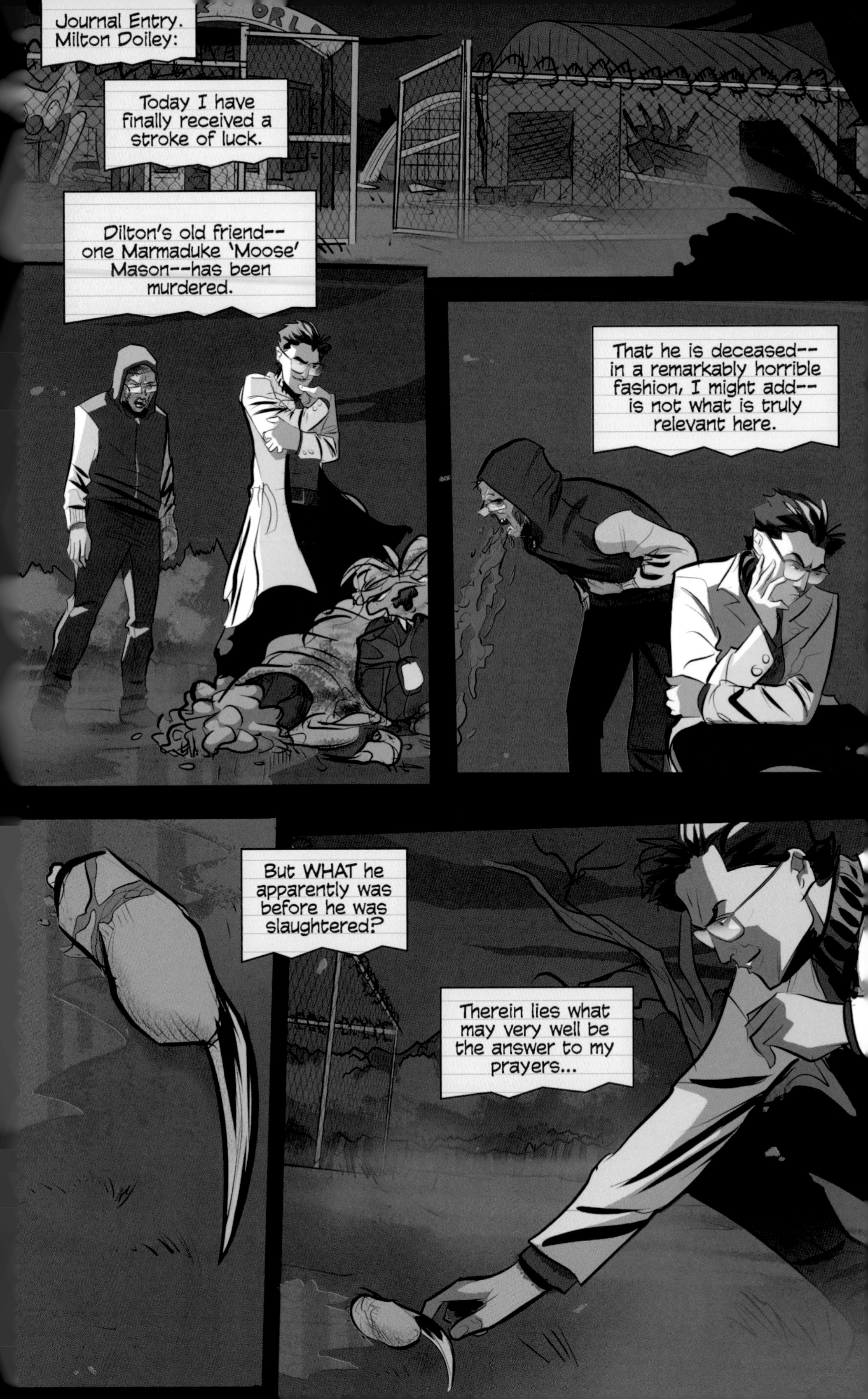
Journal Entry. Milton Doiley:
Today I have finally received a stroke of luck.
Dilton's old friend--one Marmaduke 'Moose' Mason--has been murdered.
That he is deceased--in a remarkably horrible fashion, I might add--is not what is truly relevant here.
But WHAT he apparently was before he was slaughtered?
Therein lies what may very well be the answer to my prayers...

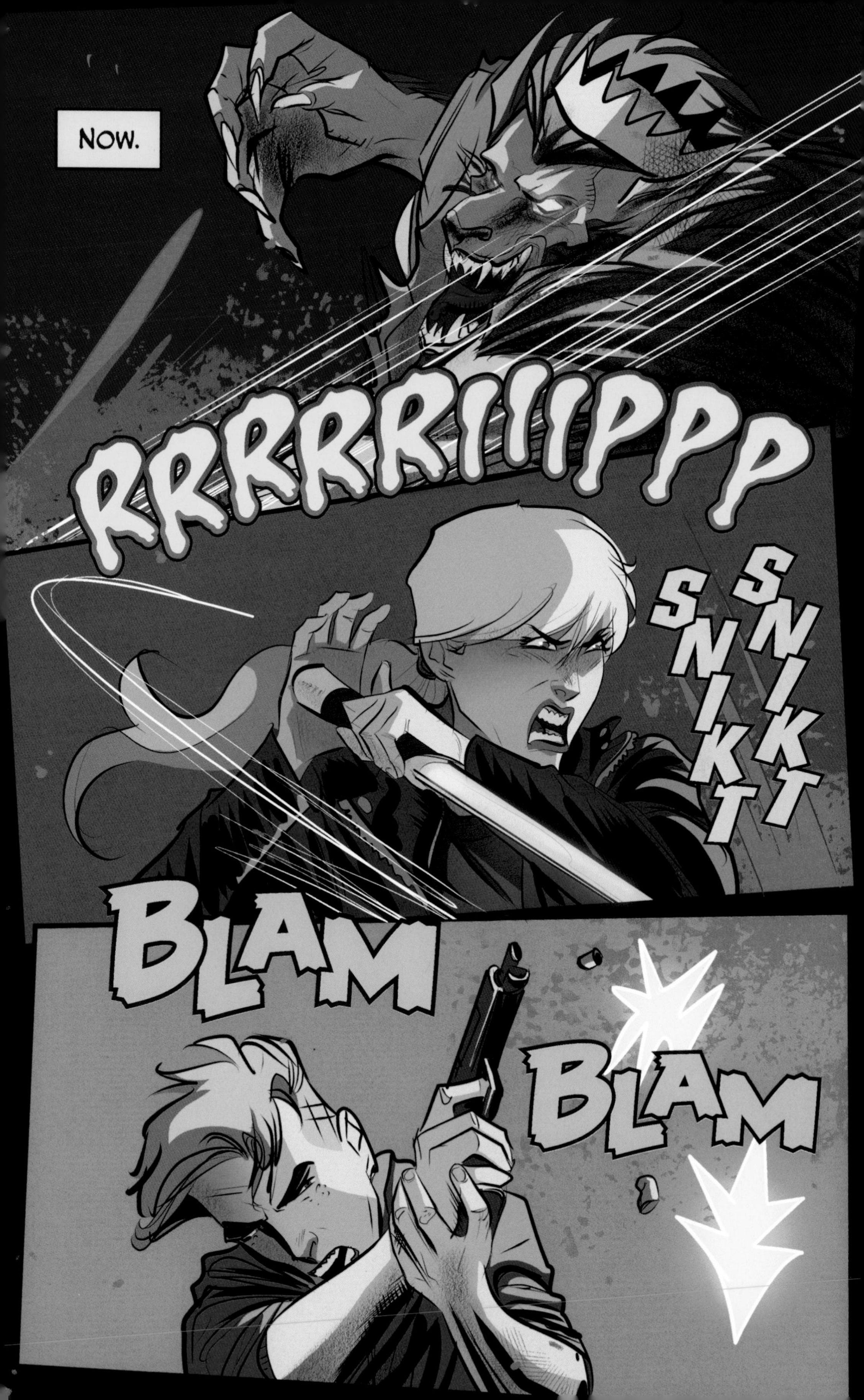
NOW.
RRRRRIIIPPP
SNIKT
SNIKT
BLAM
BLAM

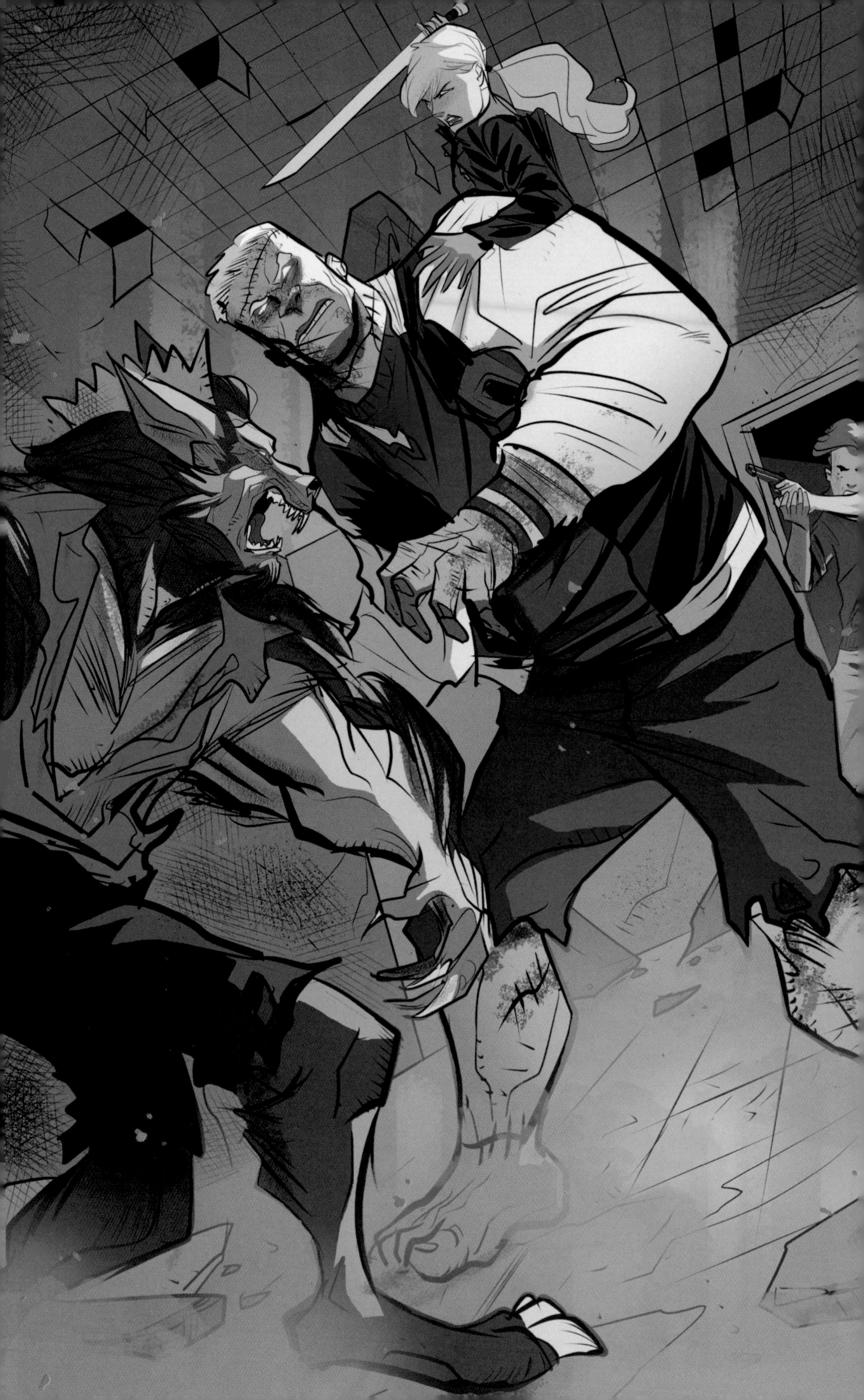

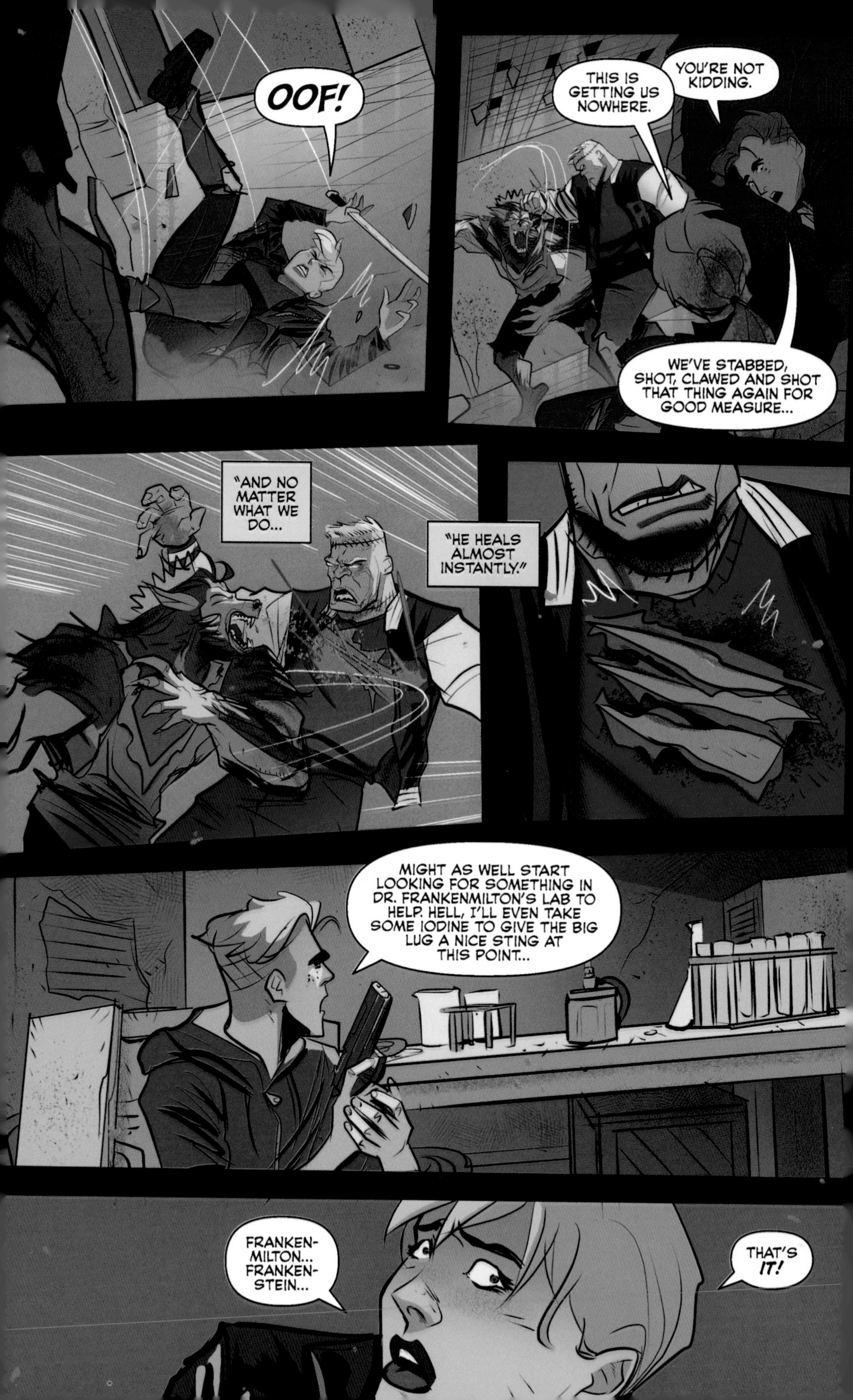
OOF!
THIS IS GETTING US NOWHERE.
YOU'RE NOT KIDDING.
WE'VE STABBED, SHOT, CLAWED AND SHOT THAT THING AGAIN FOR GOOD MEASURE...
"AND NO MATTER WHAT WE DO...
"HE HEALS ALMOST INSTANTLY."
MIGHT AS WELL START LOOKING FOR SOMETHING IN DR. FRANKENMILTON'S LAB TO HELP. HELL, I'LL EVEN TAKE SOME IODINE TO GIVE THE BIG LUG A NICE STING AT THIS POINT...
FRANKEN-MILTON... FRANKEN-STEIN...
THAT'S *IT!*

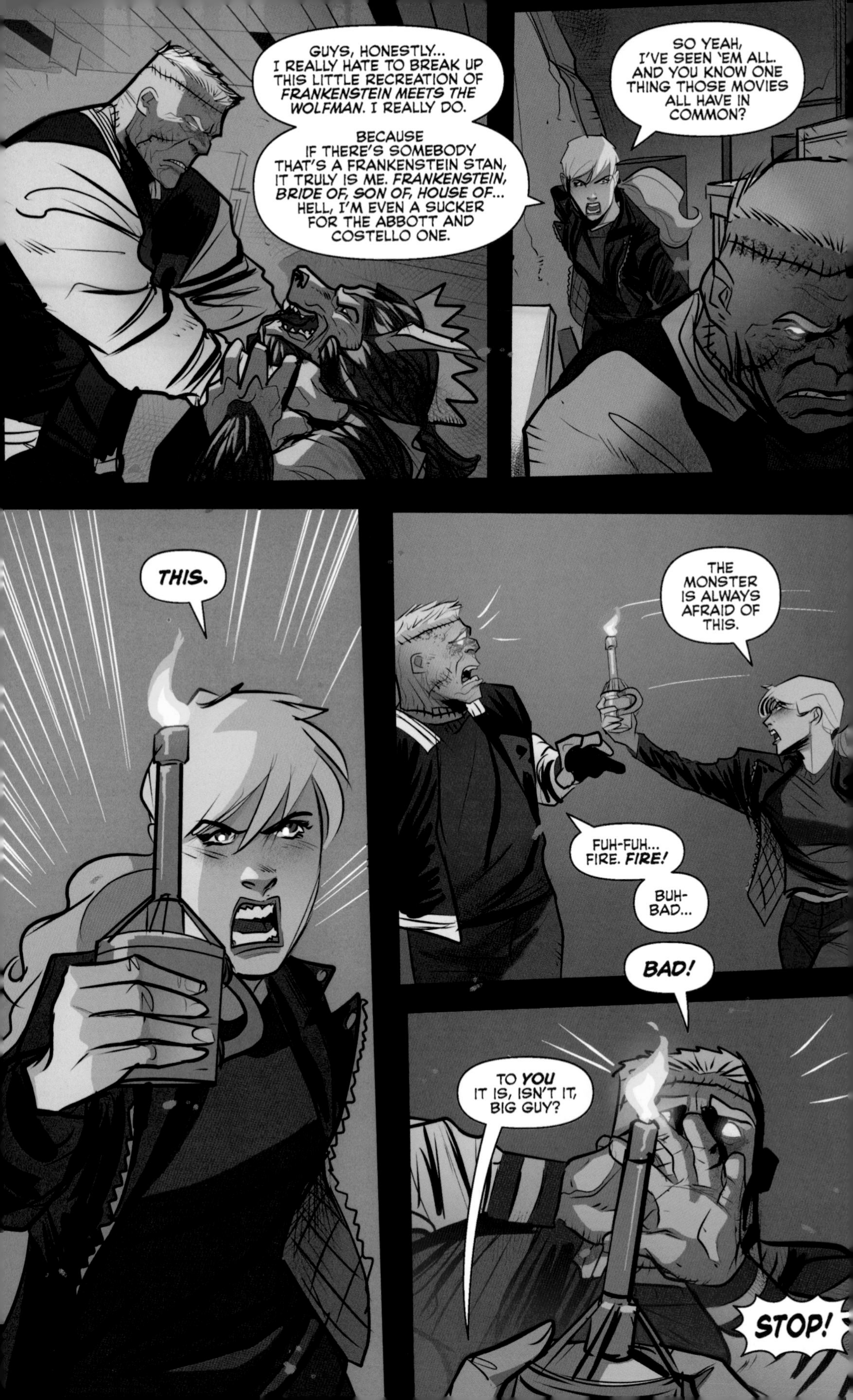
GUYS, HONESTLY... I REALLY HATE TO BREAK UP THIS LITTLE RECREATION OF *FRANKENSTEIN MEETS THE WOLFMAN*. I REALLY DO.
BECAUSE IF THERE'S SOMEBODY THAT'S A FRANKENSTEIN STAN, IT TRULY IS ME. *FRANKENSTEIN, BRIDE OF, SON OF, HOUSE OF*... HELL, I'M EVEN A SUCKER FOR THE ABBOTT AND COSTELLO ONE.
SO YEAH, I'VE SEEN 'EM ALL. AND YOU KNOW ONE THING THOSE MOVIES ALL HAVE IN COMMON?
THIS.
THE MONSTER IS ALWAYS AFRAID OF THIS.
FUH-FUH... FIRE. *FIRE!*
BUH-BAD...
BAD!
TO *YOU* IT IS, ISN'T IT, BIG GUY?
STOP!

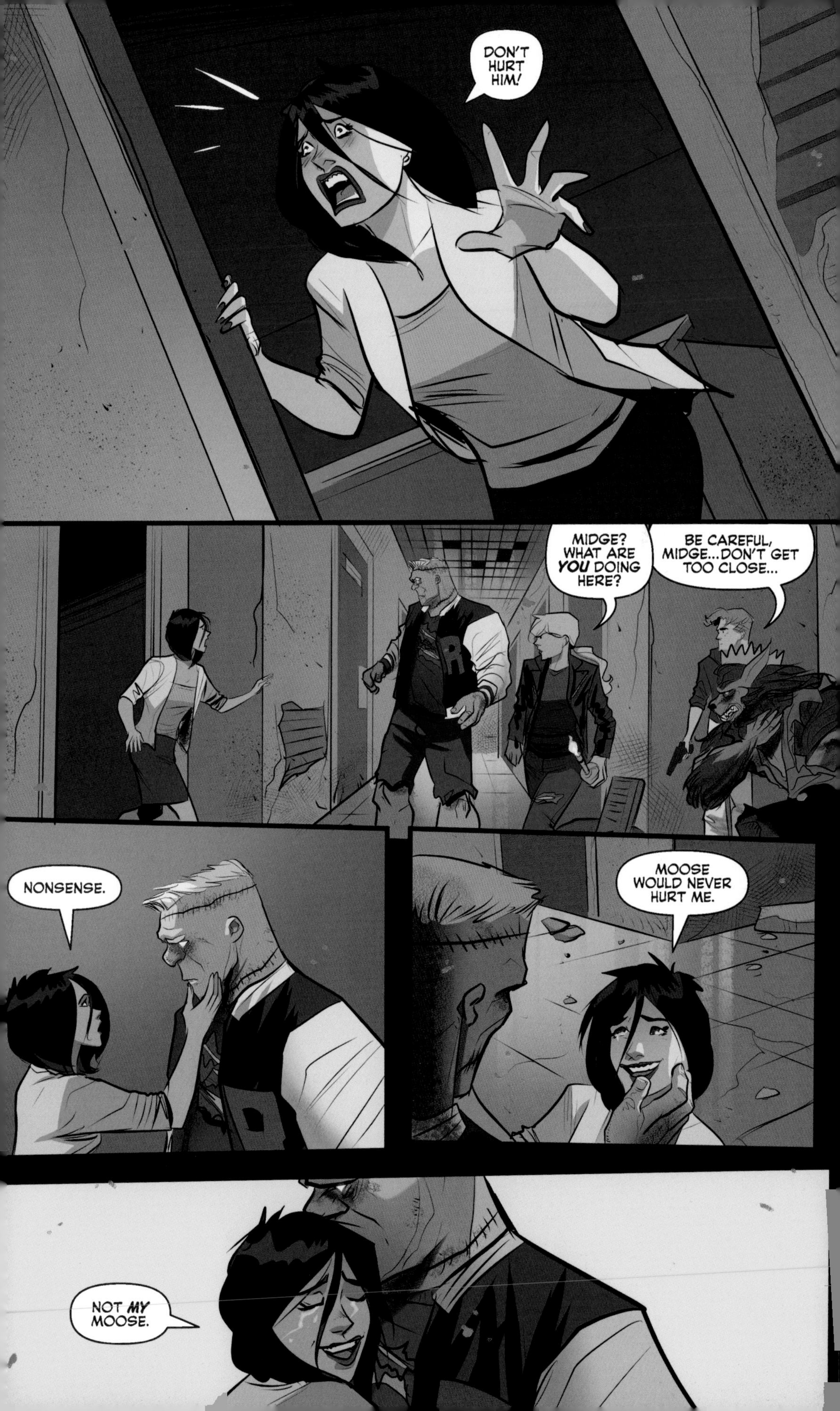
DON'T HURT HIM!
MIDGE? WHAT ARE *YOU* DOING HERE?
BE CAREFUL, MIDGE...DON'T GET TOO CLOSE...
NONSENSE.
MOOSE WOULD NEVER HURT ME.
NOT *MY* MOOSE.

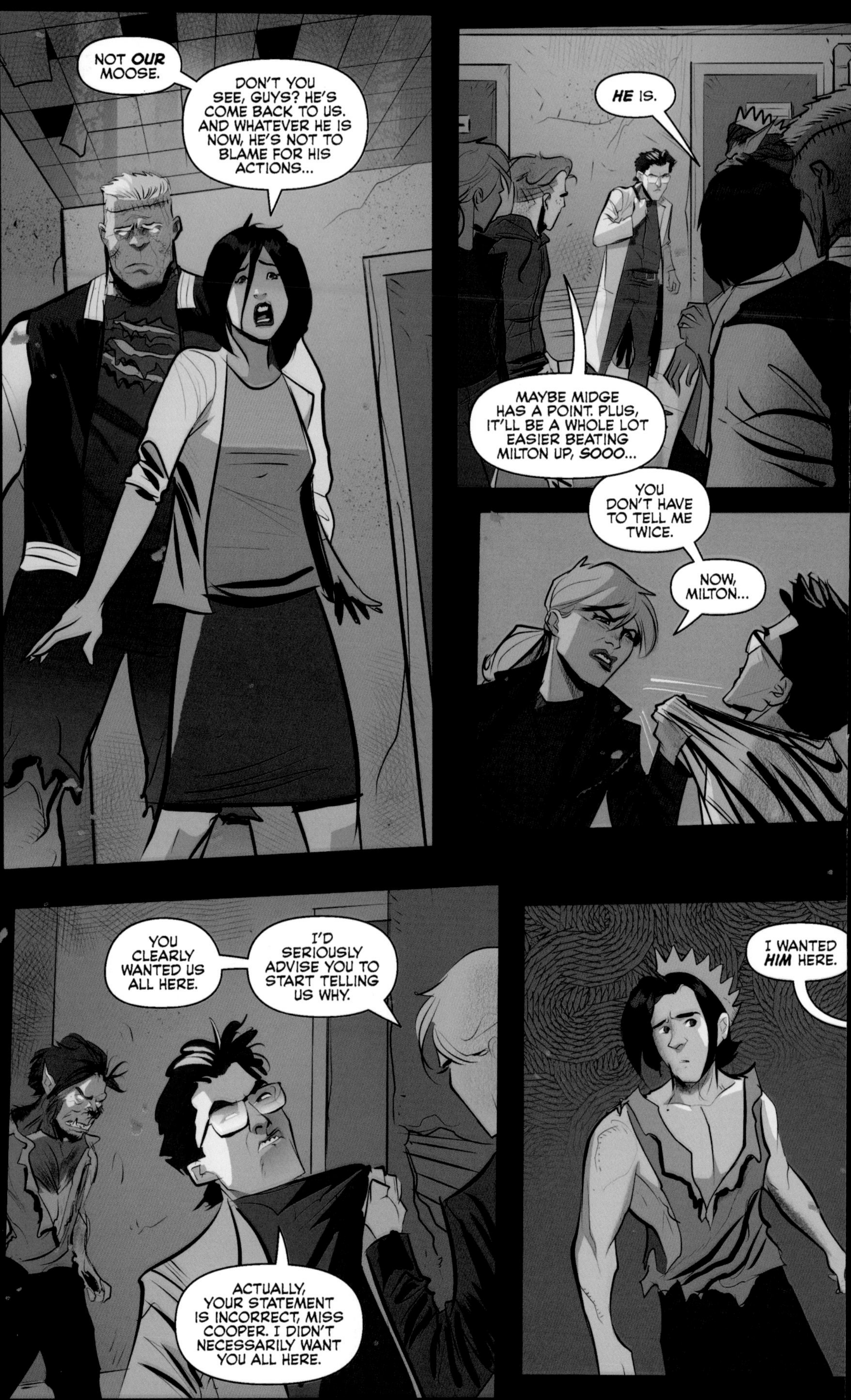
NOT **OUR** MOOSE.
DON'T YOU SEE, GUYS? HE'S COME BACK TO US. AND WHATEVER HE IS NOW, HE'S NOT TO BLAME FOR HIS ACTIONS...
HE IS.
MAYBE MIDGE HAS A POINT. PLUS, IT'LL BE A WHOLE LOT EASIER BEATING MILTON UP, **SOOO**...
YOU DON'T HAVE TO TELL ME TWICE.
NOW, MILTON...
YOU CLEARLY WANTED US ALL HERE.
I'D SERIOUSLY ADVISE YOU TO START TELLING US WHY.
ACTUALLY, YOUR STATEMENT IS INCORRECT, MISS COOPER. I DIDN'T NECESSARILY WANT YOU ALL HERE.
I WANTED **HIM** HERE.

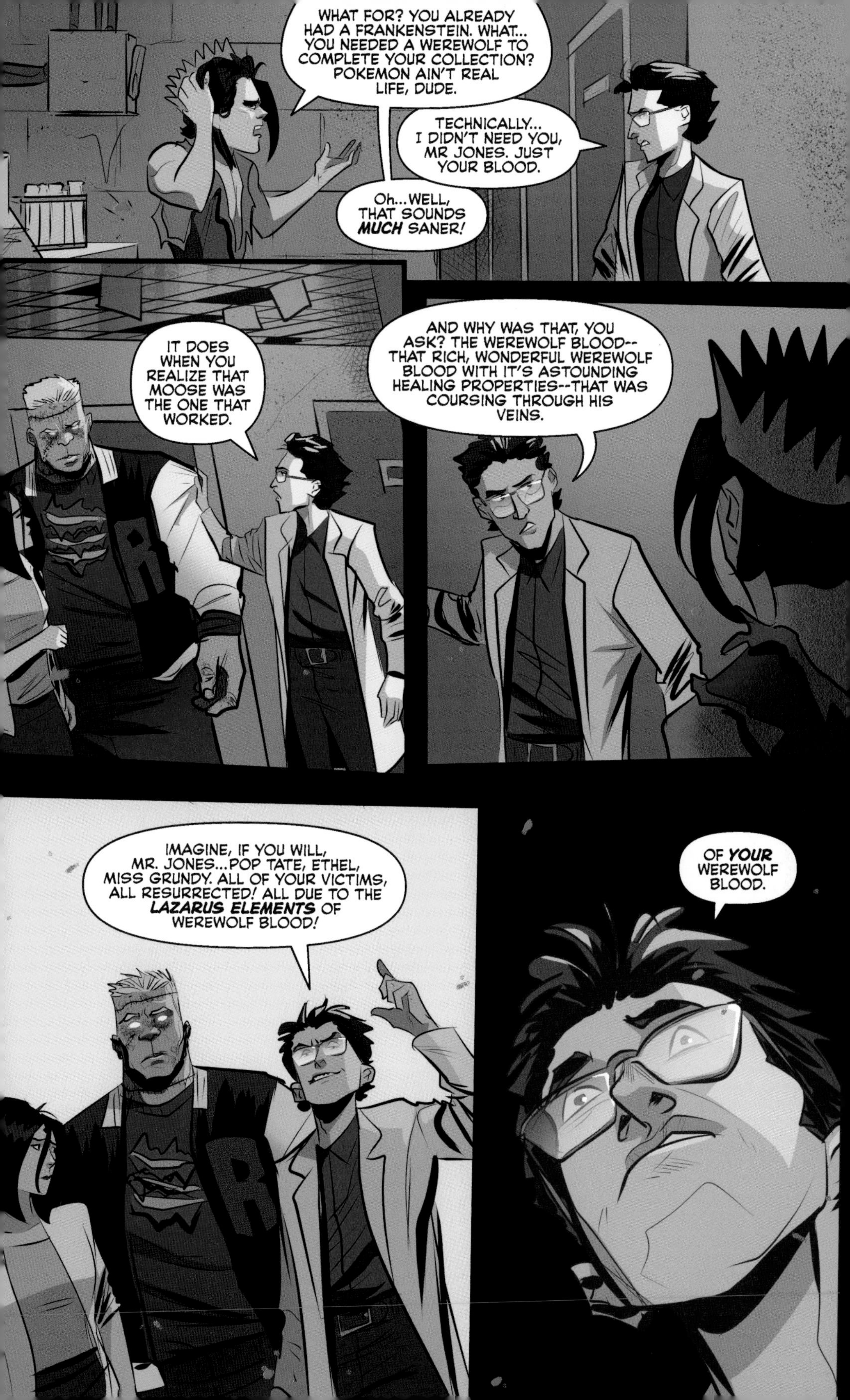
WHAT FOR? YOU ALREADY HAD A FRANKENSTEIN. WHAT... YOU NEEDED A WEREWOLF TO COMPLETE YOUR COLLECTION? POKEMON AIN'T REAL LIFE, DUDE.
TECHNICALLY... I DIDN'T NEED YOU, MR JONES. JUST YOUR BLOOD.
Oh...WELL, THAT SOUNDS *MUCH* SANER!
IT DOES WHEN YOU REALIZE THAT MOOSE WAS THE ONE THAT WORKED.
AND WHY WAS THAT, YOU ASK? THE WEREWOLF BLOOD--THAT RICH, WONDERFUL WEREWOLF BLOOD WITH IT'S ASTOUNDING HEALING PROPERTIES--THAT WAS COURSING THROUGH HIS VEINS.
IMAGINE, IF YOU WILL, MR. JONES...POP TATE, ETHEL, MISS GRUNDY. ALL OF YOUR VICTIMS, ALL RESURRECTED! ALL DUE TO THE ***LAZARUS ELEMENTS*** OF WEREWOLF BLOOD!
OF ***YOUR*** WEREWOLF BLOOD.

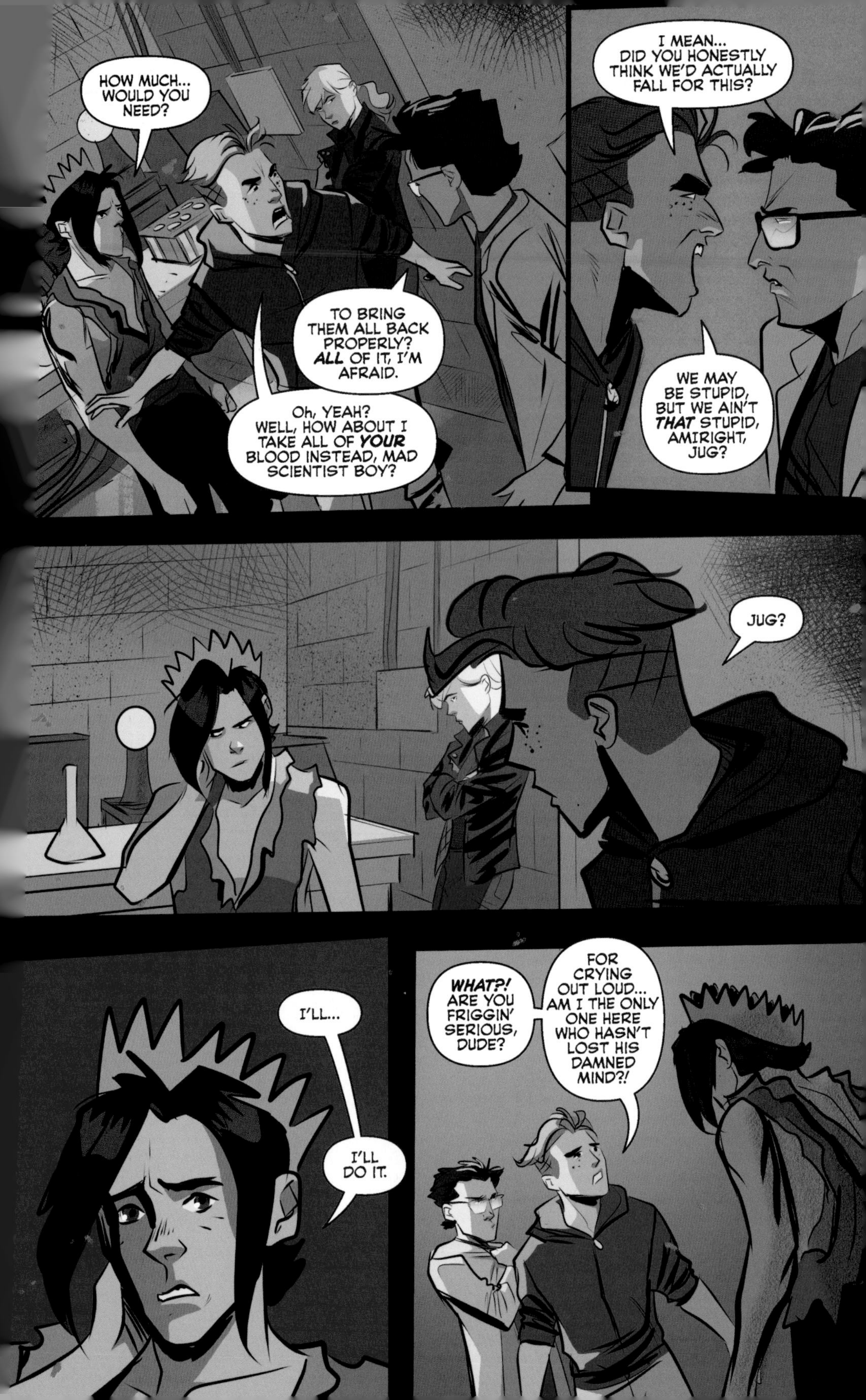
HOW MUCH... WOULD YOU NEED?
TO BRING THEM ALL BACK PROPERLY? ALL OF IT, I'M AFRAID.
Oh, YEAH? WELL, HOW ABOUT I TAKE ALL OF YOUR BLOOD INSTEAD, MAD SCIENTIST BOY?
I MEAN... DID YOU HONESTLY THINK WE'D ACTUALLY FALL FOR THIS?
WE MAY BE STUPID, BUT WE AIN'T THAT STUPID, AMIRIGHT, JUG?
JUG?
I'LL...
I'LL DO IT.
WHAT?! ARE YOU FRIGGIN' SERIOUS, DUDE?
FOR CRYING OUT LOUD... AM I THE ONLY ONE HERE WHO HASN'T LOST HIS DAMNED MIND?!

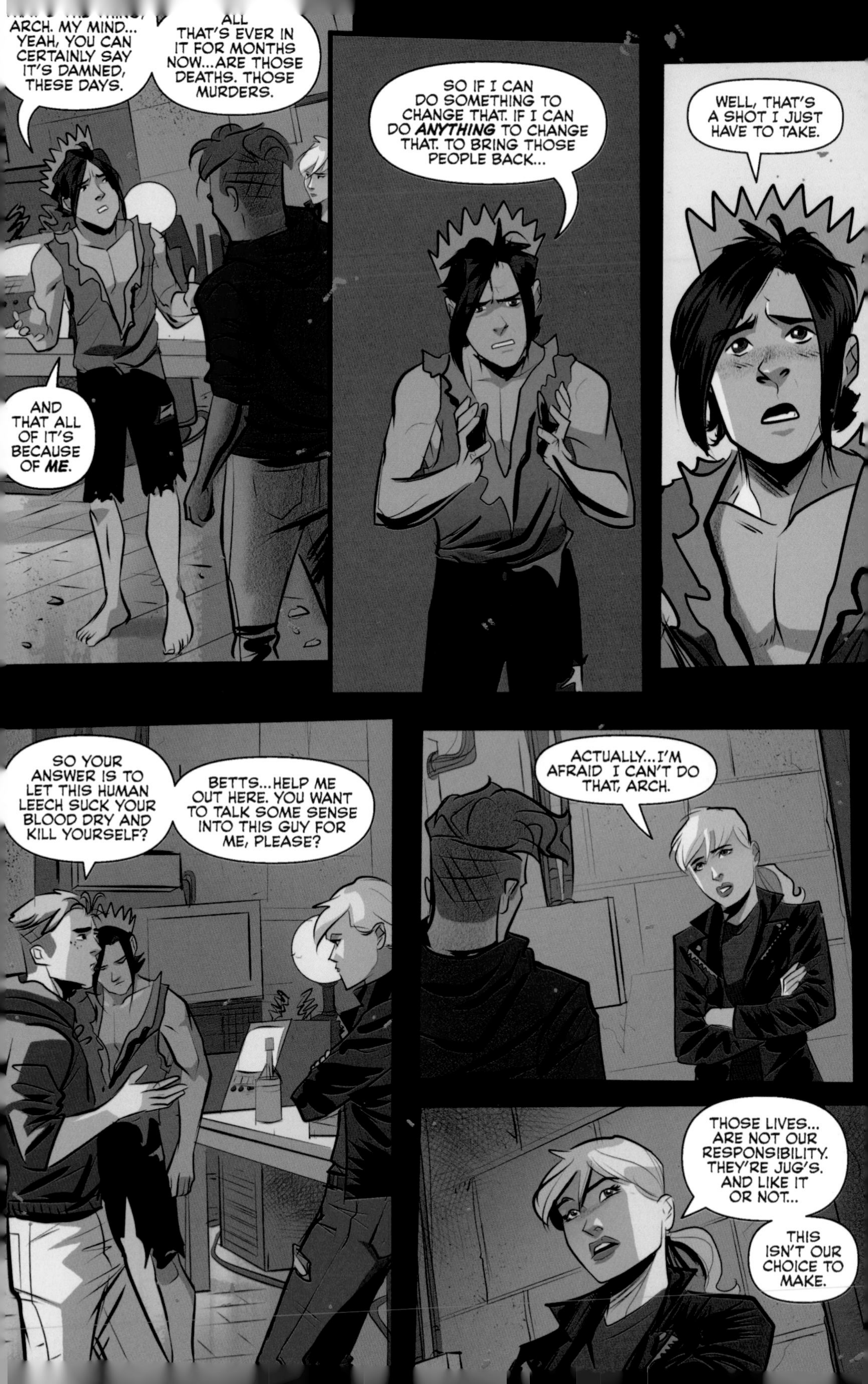
ARCH. MY MIND... YEAH, YOU CAN CERTAINLY SAY IT'S DAMNED, THESE DAYS.
ALL THAT'S EVER IN IT FOR MONTHS NOW...ARE THOSE DEATHS. THOSE MURDERS.
AND THAT ALL OF IT'S BECAUSE OF ME.
SO IF I CAN DO SOMETHING TO CHANGE THAT. IF I CAN DO ANYTHING TO CHANGE THAT. TO BRING THOSE PEOPLE BACK...
WELL, THAT'S A SHOT I JUST HAVE TO TAKE.
SO YOUR ANSWER IS TO LET THIS HUMAN LEECH SUCK YOUR BLOOD DRY AND KILL YOURSELF?
BETTS...HELP ME OUT HERE. YOU WANT TO TALK SOME SENSE INTO THIS GUY FOR ME, PLEASE?
ACTUALLY...I'M AFRAID I CAN'T DO THAT, ARCH.
THOSE LIVES... ARE NOT OUR RESPONSIBILITY. THEY'RE JUG'S. AND LIKE IT OR NOT...
THIS ISN'T OUR CHOICE TO MAKE.

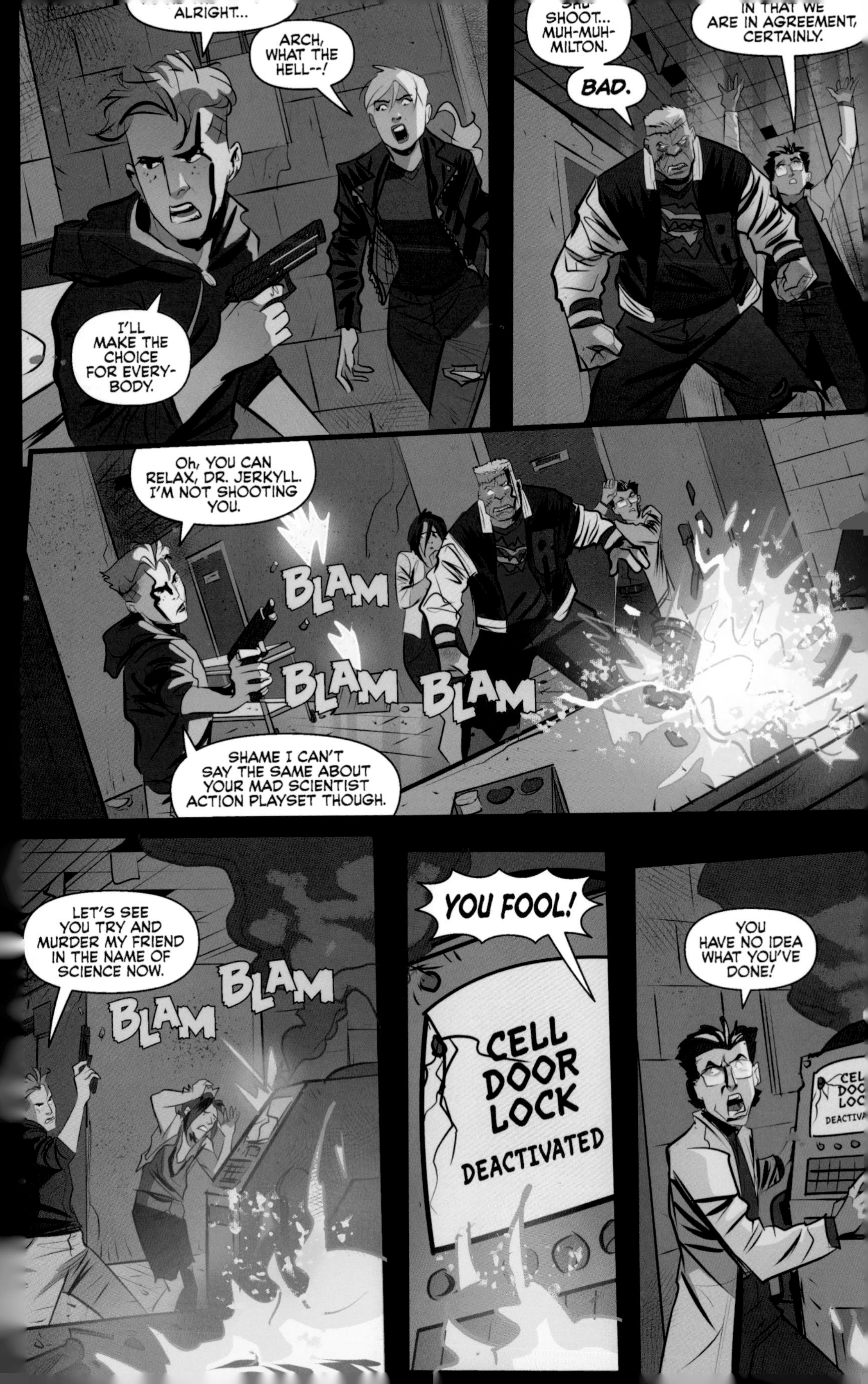
ALRIGHT...
ARCH, WHAT THE HELL--!
I'LL MAKE THE CHOICE FOR EVERY-BODY.
SHOOT... MUH-MUH-MILTON.
BAD.
IN THAT WE ARE IN AGREEMENT, CERTAINLY.
Oh, YOU CAN RELAX, DR. JERKYLL. I'M NOT SHOOTING YOU.
BLAM
BLAM
BLAM
SHAME I CAN'T SAY THE SAME ABOUT YOUR MAD SCIENTIST ACTION PLAYSET THOUGH.
LET'S SEE YOU TRY AND MURDER MY FRIEND IN THE NAME OF SCIENCE NOW.
BLAM
BLAM
YOU FOOL!
CELL DOOR LOCK
DEACTIVATED
YOU HAVE NO IDEA WHAT YOU'VE DONE!

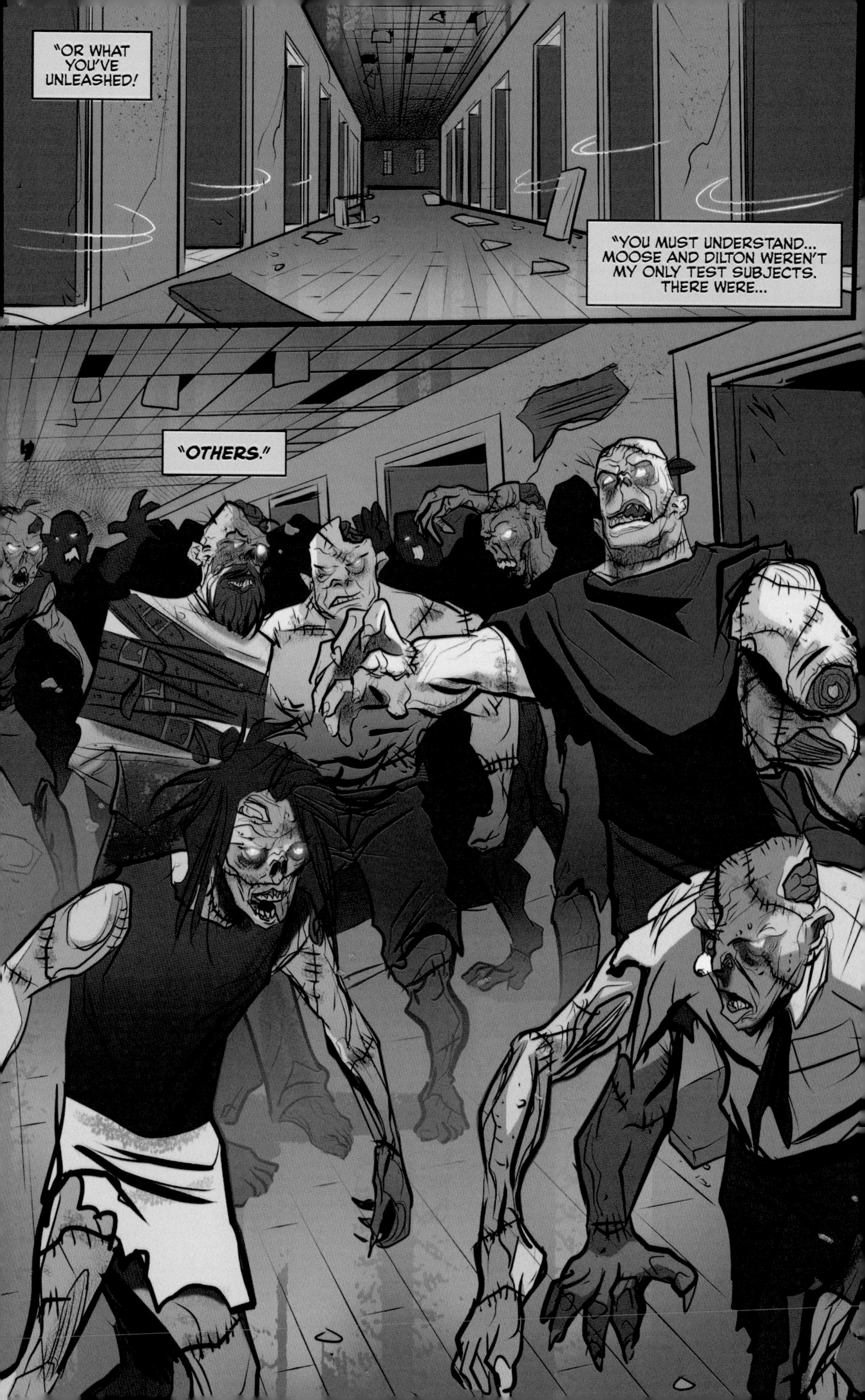
"OR WHAT YOU'VE UNLEASHED!
"YOU MUST UNDERSTAND... MOOSE AND DILTON WEREN'T MY ONLY TEST SUBJECTS. THERE WERE...
"OTHERS."

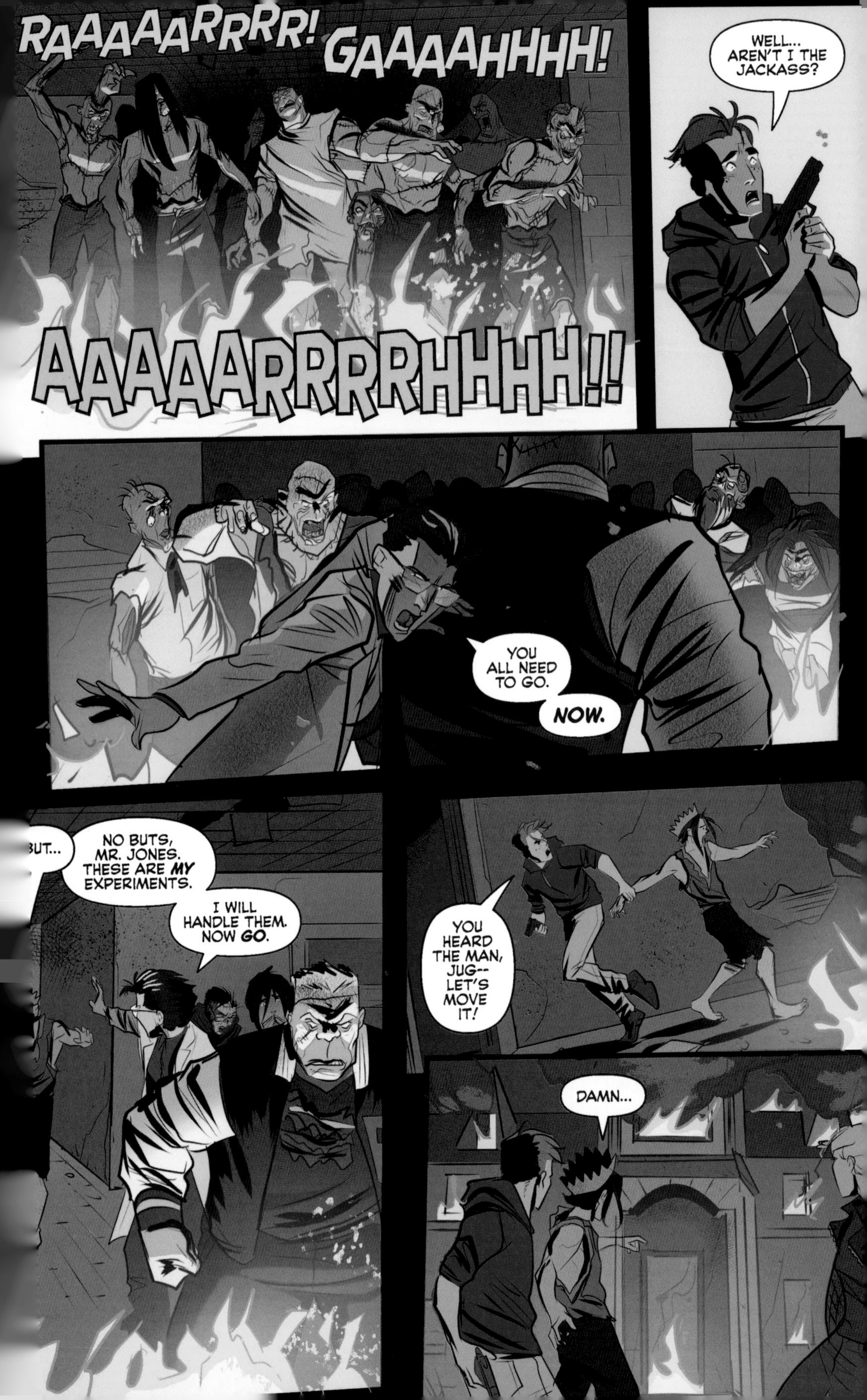
RAAAAARRRR!
GAAAAHHHH!
AAAAARRRRHHHH!!
WELL... AREN'T I THE JACKASS?
YOU ALL NEED TO GO.
NOW.
BUT...
NO BUTS, MR. JONES. THESE ARE MY EXPERIMENTS.
I WILL HANDLE THEM. NOW GO.
YOU HEARD THE MAN, JUG-- LET'S MOVE IT!
DAMN...

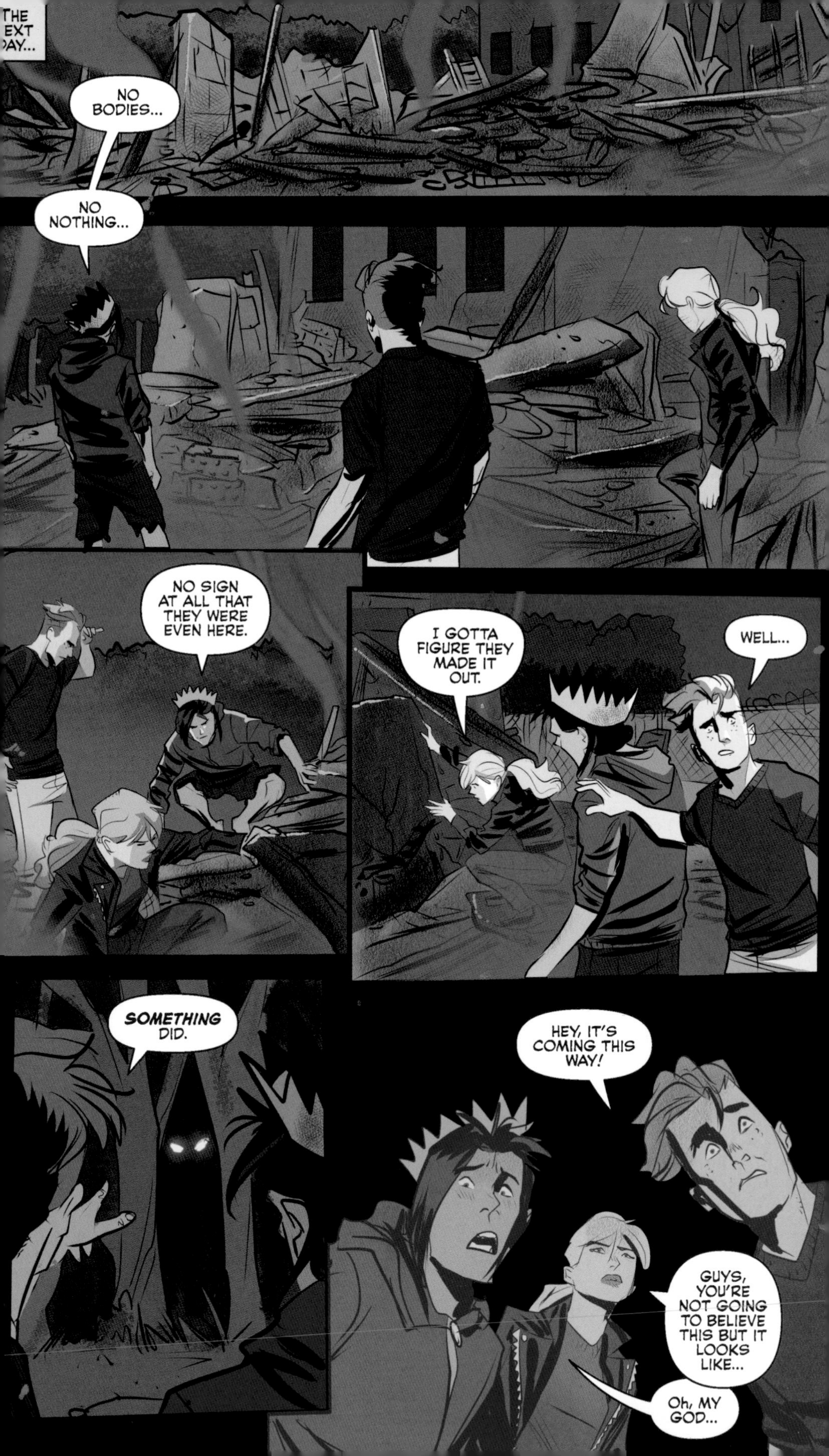
THE
EXT
DAY...
NO BODIES...
NO NOTHING...
NO SIGN AT ALL THAT THEY WERE EVEN HERE.
I GOTTA FIGURE THEY MADE IT OUT.
WELL...
SOMETHING DID.
HEY, IT'S COMING THIS WAY!
GUYS, YOU'RE NOT GOING TO BELIEVE THIS BUT IT LOOKS LIKE...
Oh, MY GOD...

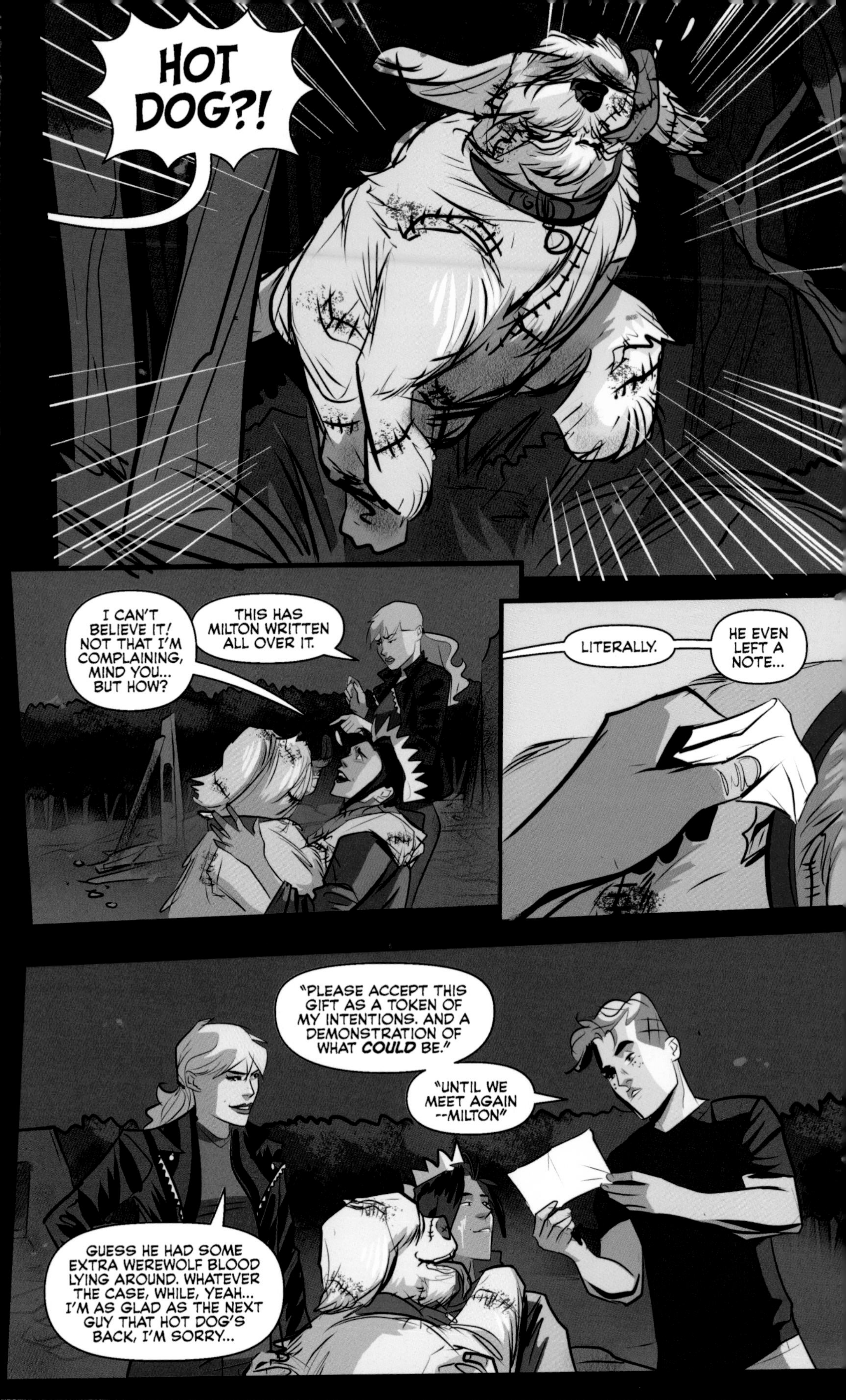
HOT DOG?!
I CAN'T BELIEVE IT! NOT THAT I'M COMPLAINING, MIND YOU... BUT HOW?
THIS HAS MILTON WRITTEN ALL OVER IT.
LITERALLY.
HE EVEN LEFT A NOTE...
"PLEASE ACCEPT THIS GIFT AS A TOKEN OF MY INTENTIONS. AND A DEMONSTRATION OF WHAT COULD BE."
"UNTIL WE MEET AGAIN --MILTON"
GUESS HE HAD SOME EXTRA WEREWOLF BLOOD LYING AROUND. WHATEVER THE CASE, WHILE, YEAH... I'M AS GLAD AS THE NEXT GUY THAT HOT DOG'S BACK, I'M SORRY...

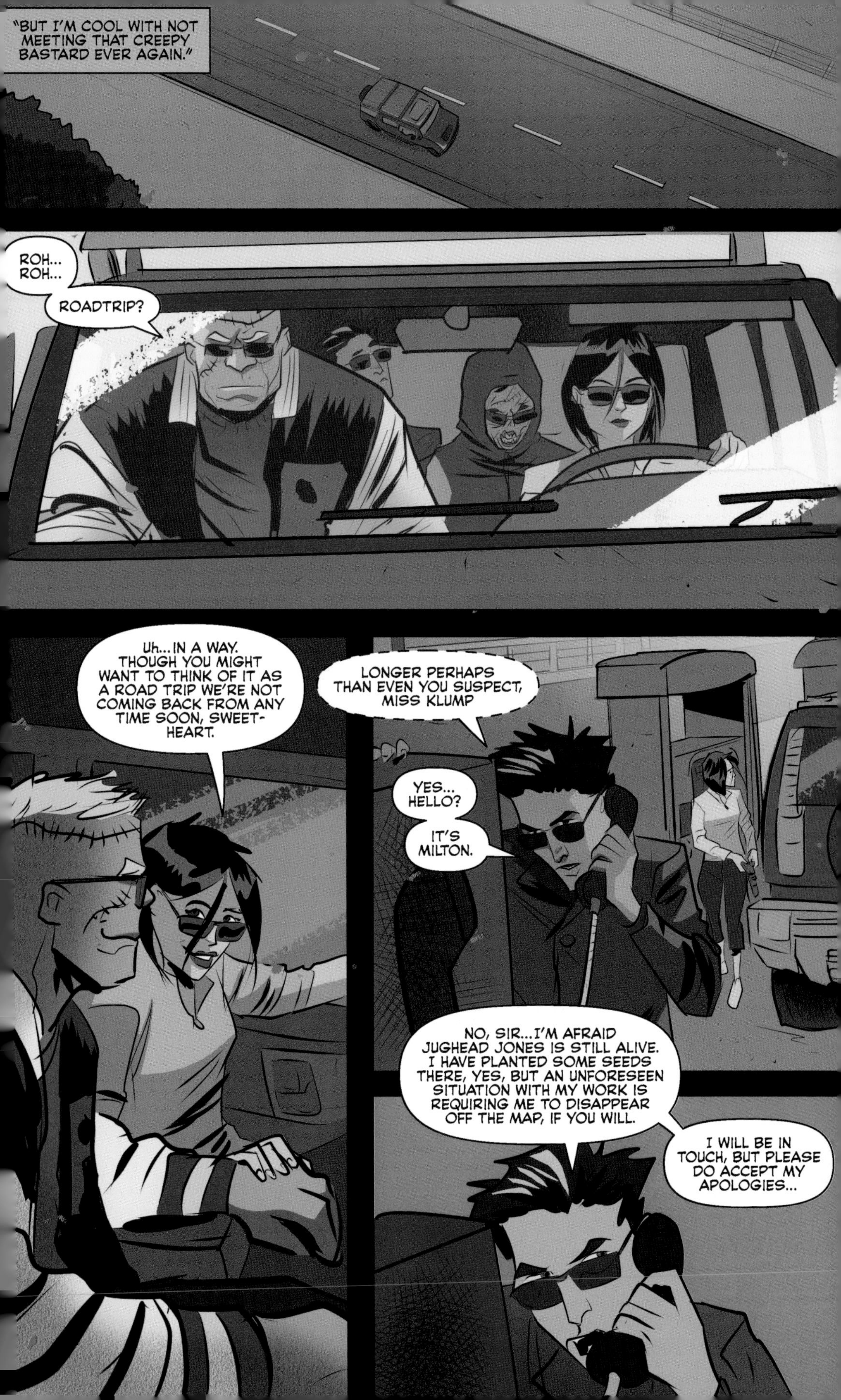
"BUT I'M COOL WITH NOT MEETING THAT CREEPY BASTARD EVER AGAIN."
ROH... ROH...
ROADTRIP?
Uh...IN A WAY. THOUGH YOU MIGHT WANT TO THINK OF IT AS A ROAD TRIP WE'RE NOT COMING BACK FROM ANY TIME SOON, SWEET-HEART.
LONGER PERHAPS THAN EVEN YOU SUSPECT, MISS KLUMP
YES... HELLO?
IT'S MILTON.
NO, SIR...I'M AFRAID JUGHEAD JONES IS STILL ALIVE. I HAVE PLANTED SOME SEEDS THERE, YES, BUT AN UNFORESEEN SITUATION WITH MY WORK IS REQUIRING ME TO DISAPPEAR OFF THE MAP, IF YOU WILL.
I WILL BE IN TOUCH, BUT PLEASE DO ACCEPT MY APOLOGIES...

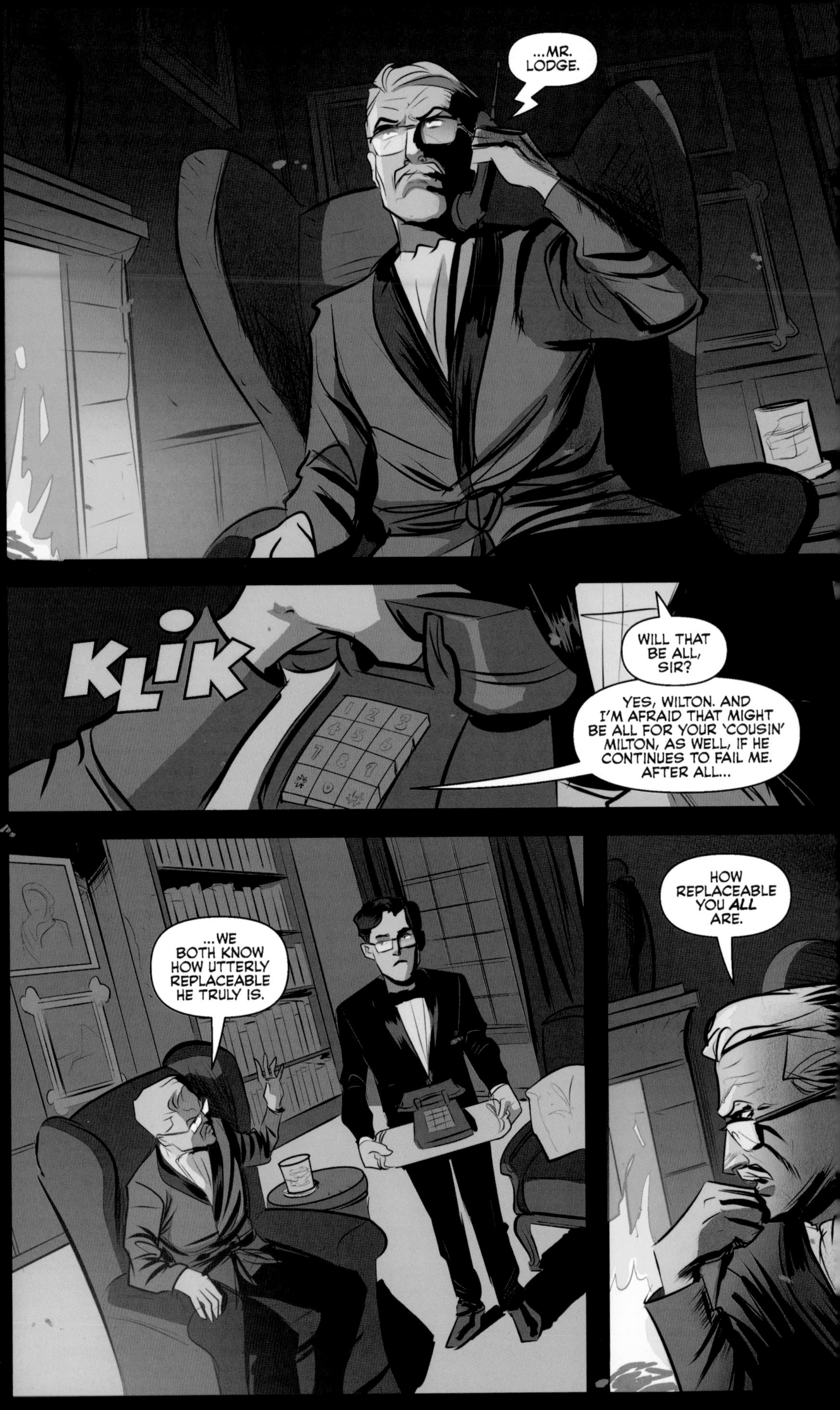
...MR. LODGE.
KLIK
WILL THAT BE ALL, SIR?
YES, WILTON. AND I'M AFRAID THAT MIGHT BE ALL FOR YOUR 'COUSIN' MILTON, AS WELL, IF HE CONTINUES TO FAIL ME. AFTER ALL...
...WE BOTH KNOW HOW UTTERLY REPLACEABLE HE TRULY IS.
HOW REPLACEABLE YOU *ALL* ARE.

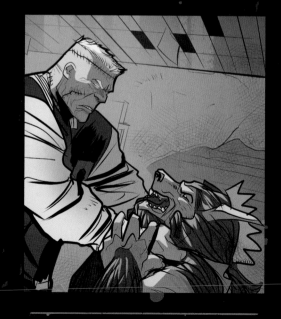

To be continued...

ISSUE TWELVE

BINGO WAS HIS NAME, OH NO: PART 1

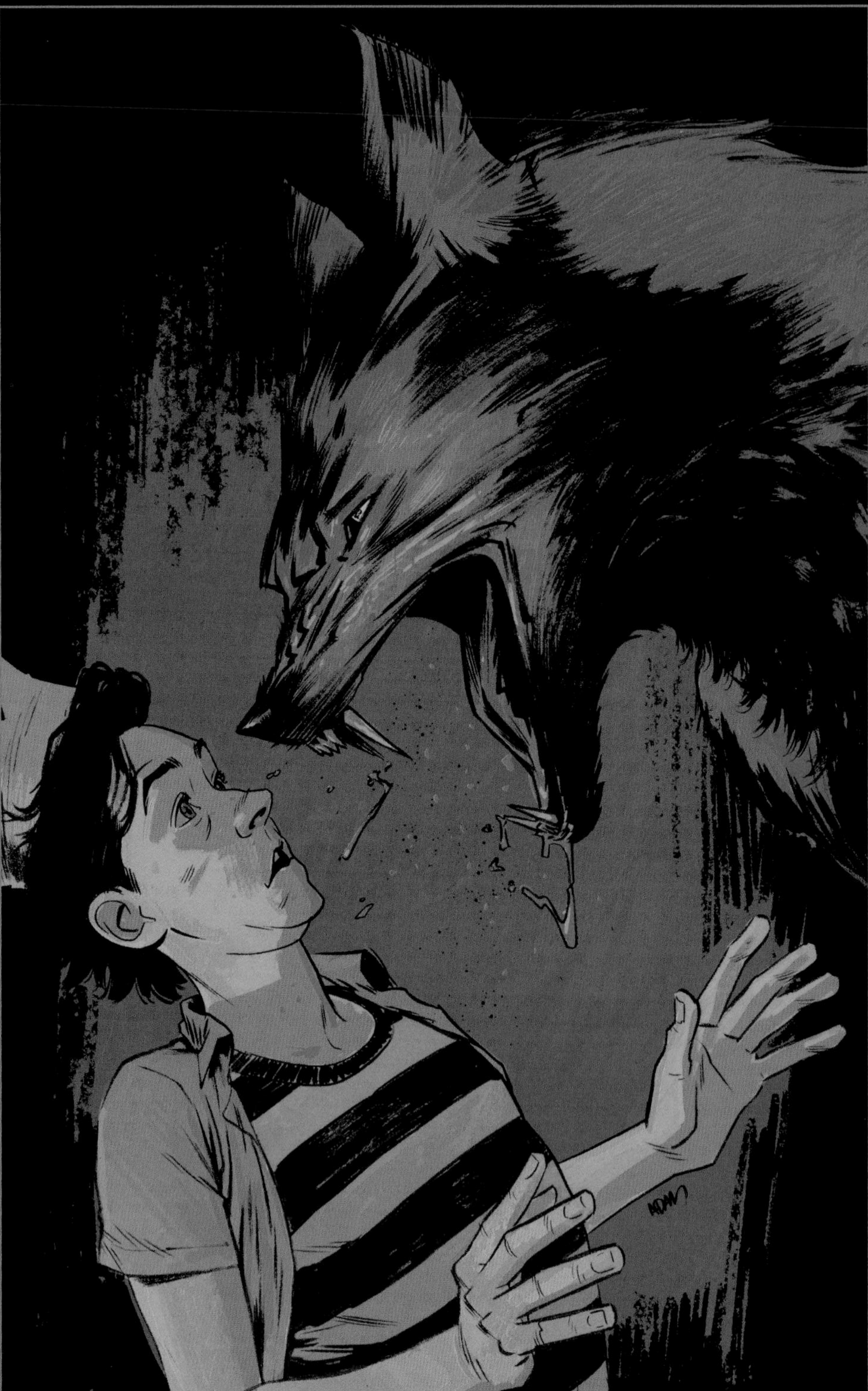

COVER ART **Adam Gorham**

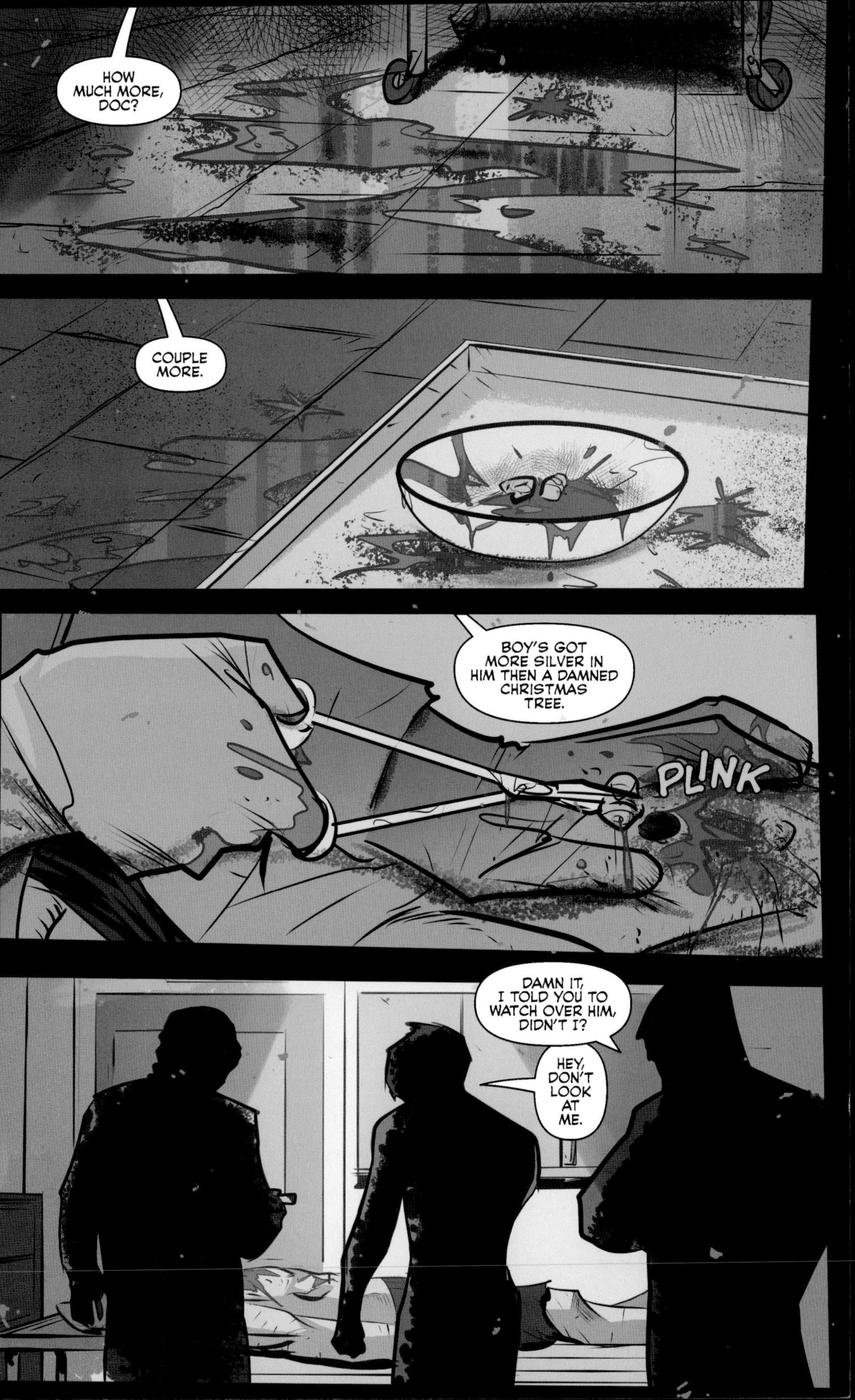
HOW MUCH MORE, DOC?
COUPLE MORE.
BOY'S GOT MORE SILVER IN HIM THEN A DAMNED CHRISTMAS TREE.
PLINK
DAMN IT, I TOLD YOU TO WATCH OVER HIM, DIDN'T I?
HEY, DON'T LOOK AT ME.

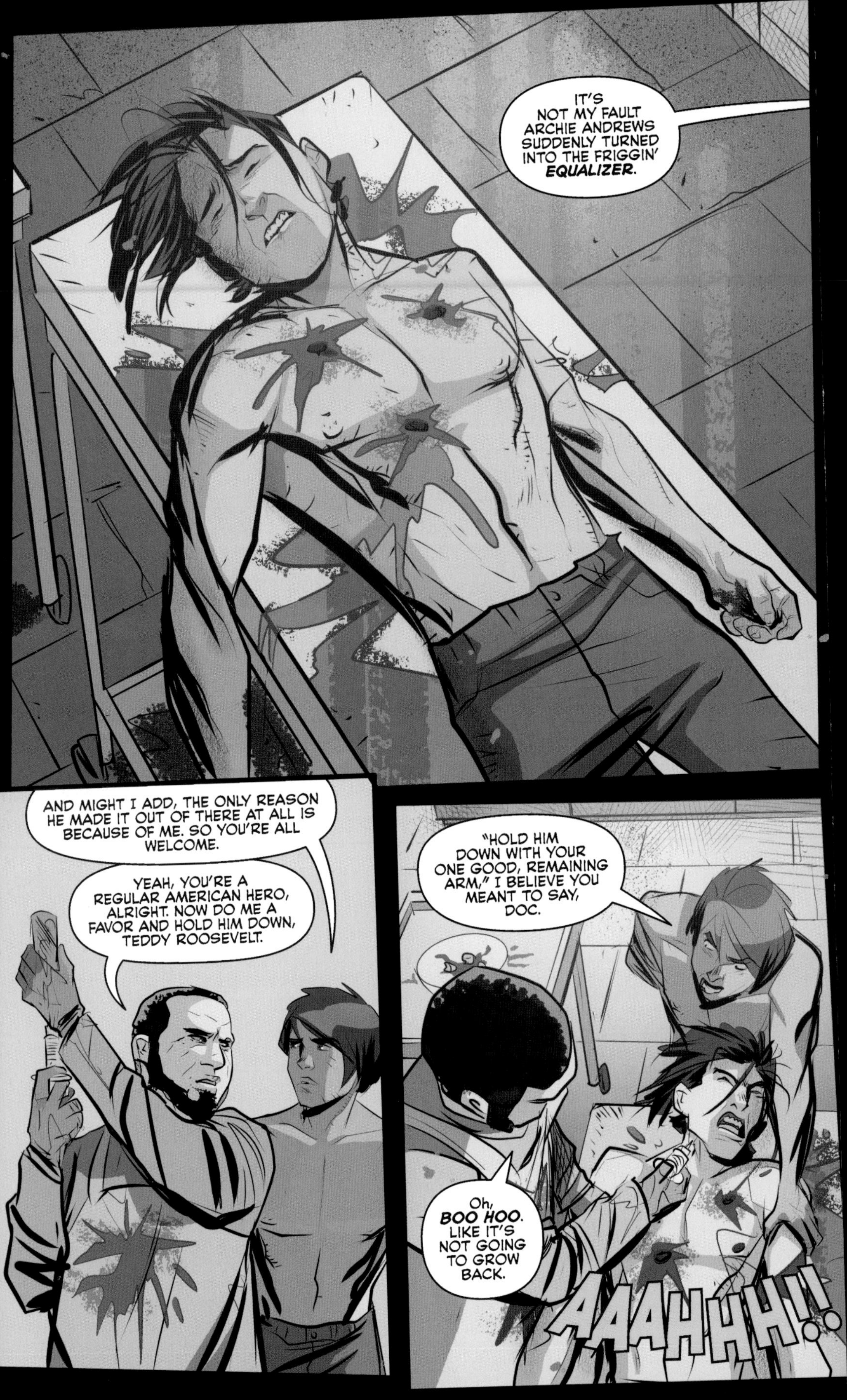
IT'S NOT MY FAULT ARCHIE ANDREWS SUDDENLY TURNED INTO THE FRIGGIN' *EQUALIZER*.
AND MIGHT I ADD, THE ONLY REASON HE MADE IT OUT OF THERE AT ALL IS BECAUSE OF ME. SO YOU'RE ALL WELCOME.
YEAH, YOU'RE A REGULAR AMERICAN HERO, ALRIGHT. NOW DO ME A FAVOR AND HOLD HIM DOWN, TEDDY ROOSEVELT.
"HOLD HIM DOWN WITH YOUR ONE GOOD, REMAINING ARM," I BELIEVE YOU MEANT TO SAY, DOC.
Oh, **BOO HOO**. LIKE IT'S NOT GOING TO GROW BACK.
AAAHHH!!

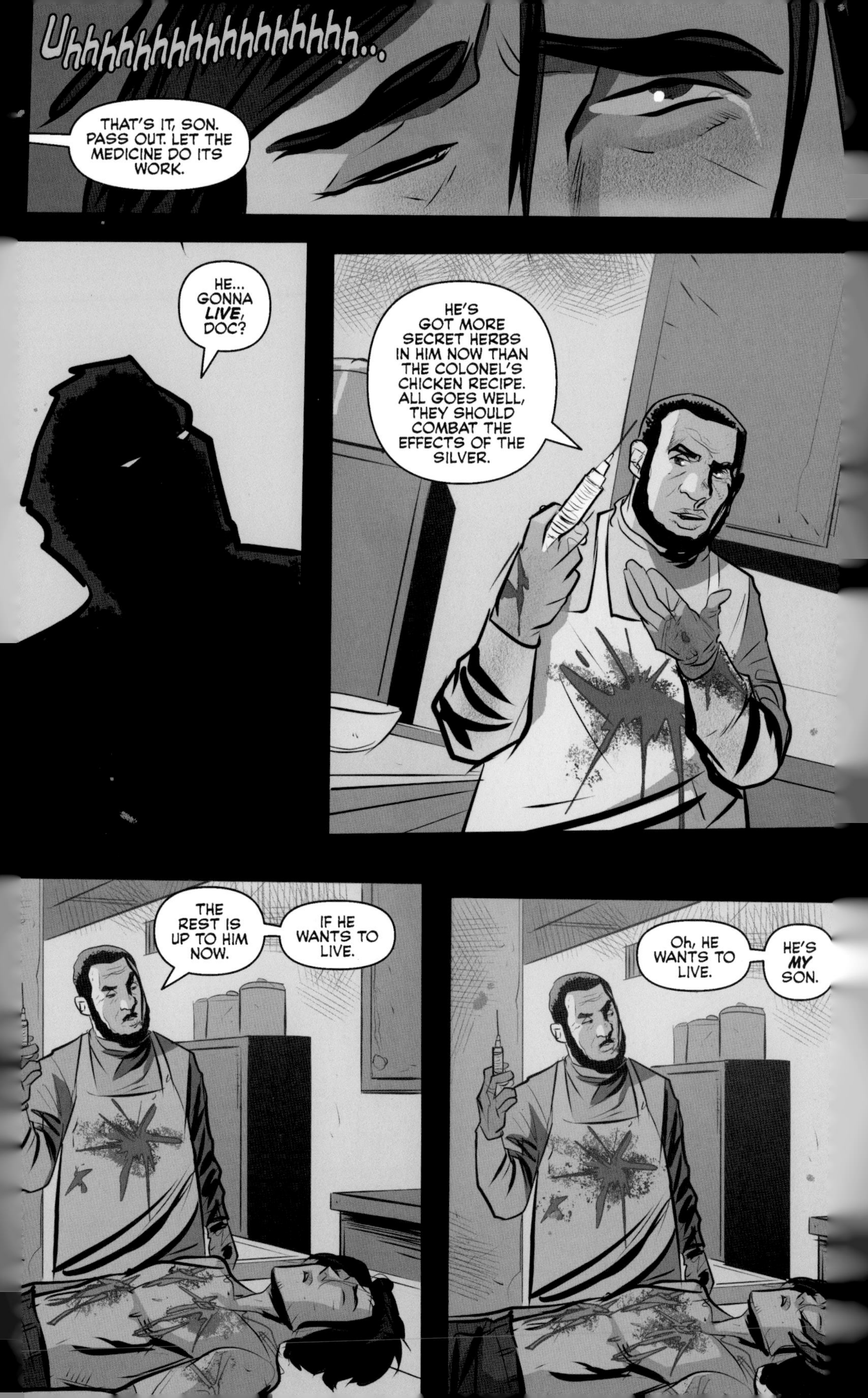
Uhhhhhhhhhhhhhhhhh...
THAT'S IT, SON. PASS OUT. LET THE MEDICINE DO ITS WORK.
HE... GONNA LIVE, DOC?
HE'S GOT MORE SECRET HERBS IN HIM NOW THAN THE COLONEL'S CHICKEN RECIPE. ALL GOES WELL, THEY SHOULD COMBAT THE EFFECTS OF THE SILVER.
THE REST IS UP TO HIM NOW.
IF HE WANTS TO LIVE.
Oh, HE WANTS TO LIVE.
HE'S MY SON.

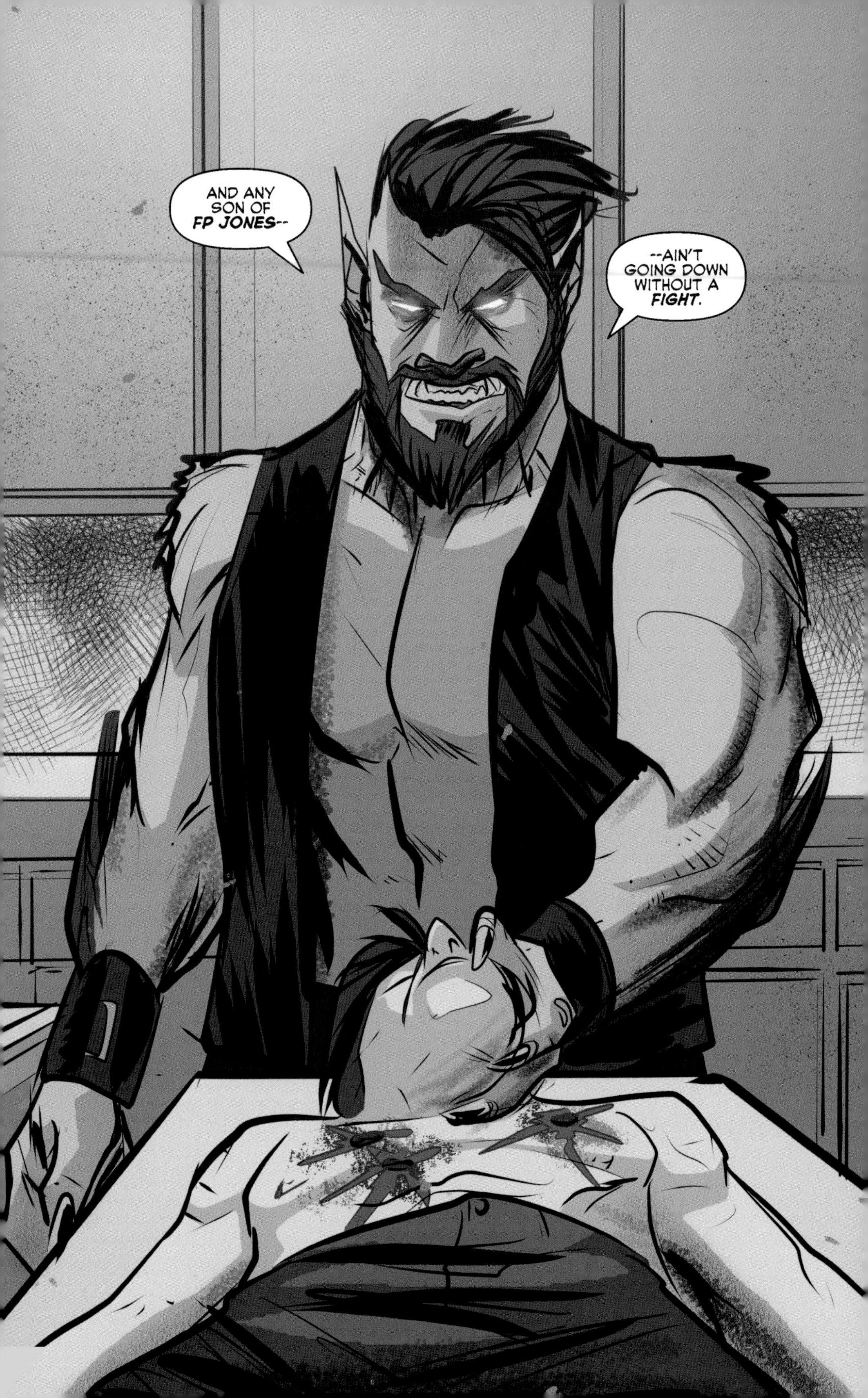
AND ANY SON OF *FP JONES*--
--AIN'T GOING DOWN WITHOUT A *FIGHT*.

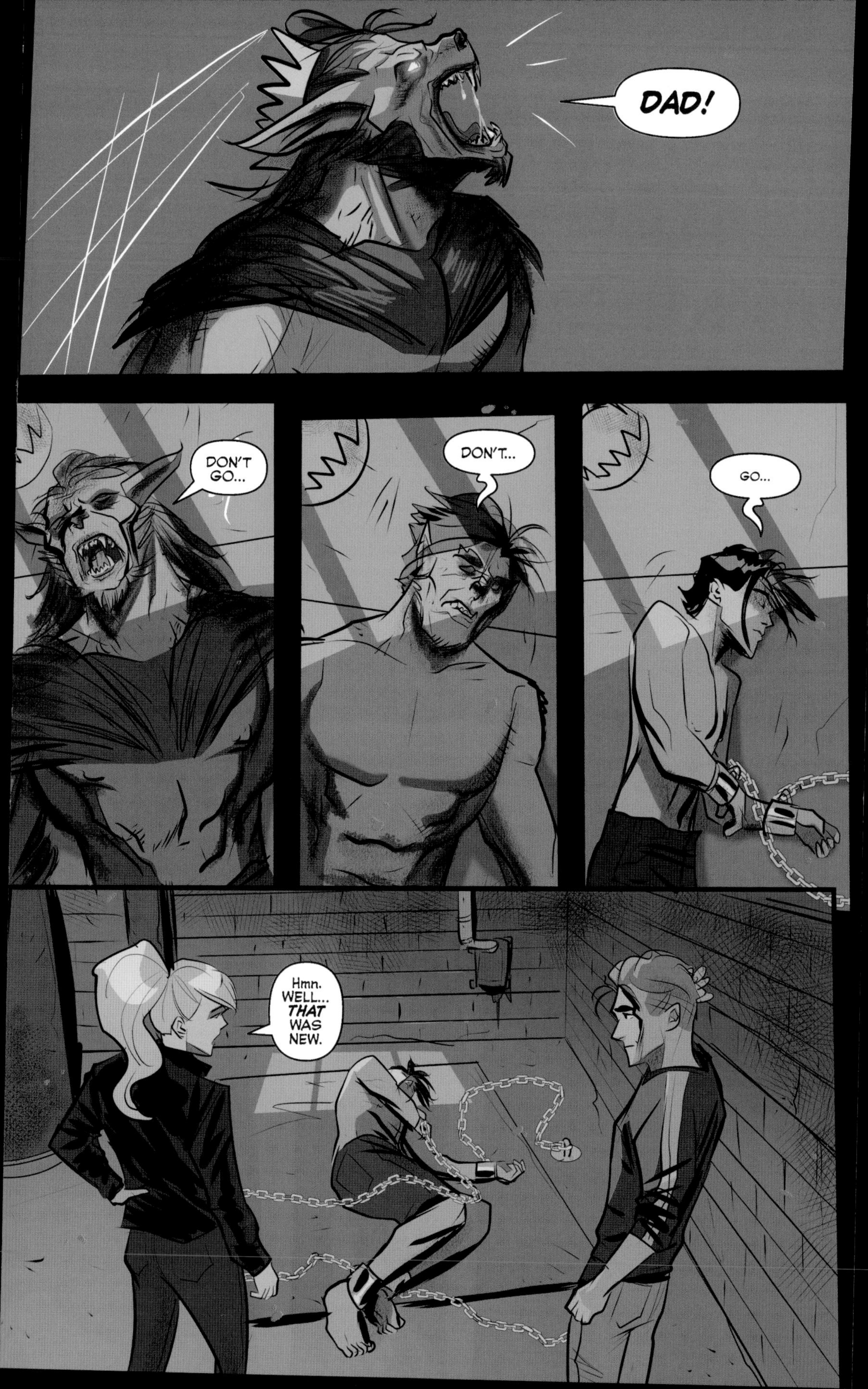
DAD!
DON'T GO...
DON'T...
GO...
Hmn. WELL... *THAT* WAS NEW.

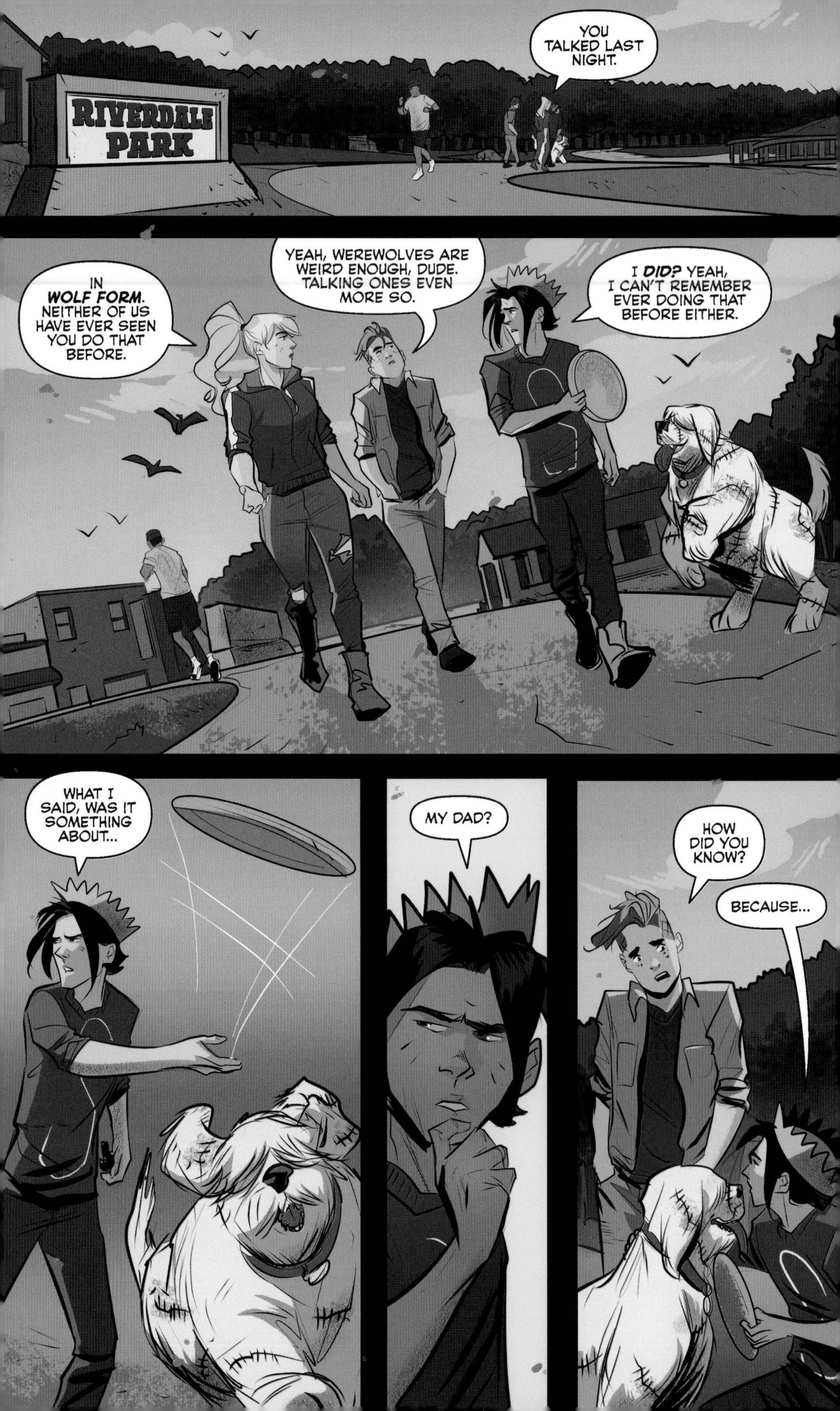
RIVERDALE PARK
YOU TALKED LAST NIGHT.
IN ***WOLF FORM***. NEITHER OF US HAVE EVER SEEN YOU DO THAT BEFORE.
YEAH, WEREWOLVES ARE WEIRD ENOUGH, DUDE. TALKING ONES EVEN MORE SO.
I ***DID?*** YEAH, I CAN'T REMEMBER EVER DOING THAT BEFORE EITHER.
WHAT I SAID, WAS IT SOMETHING ABOUT...
MY DAD?
HOW DID YOU KNOW?
BECAUSE...

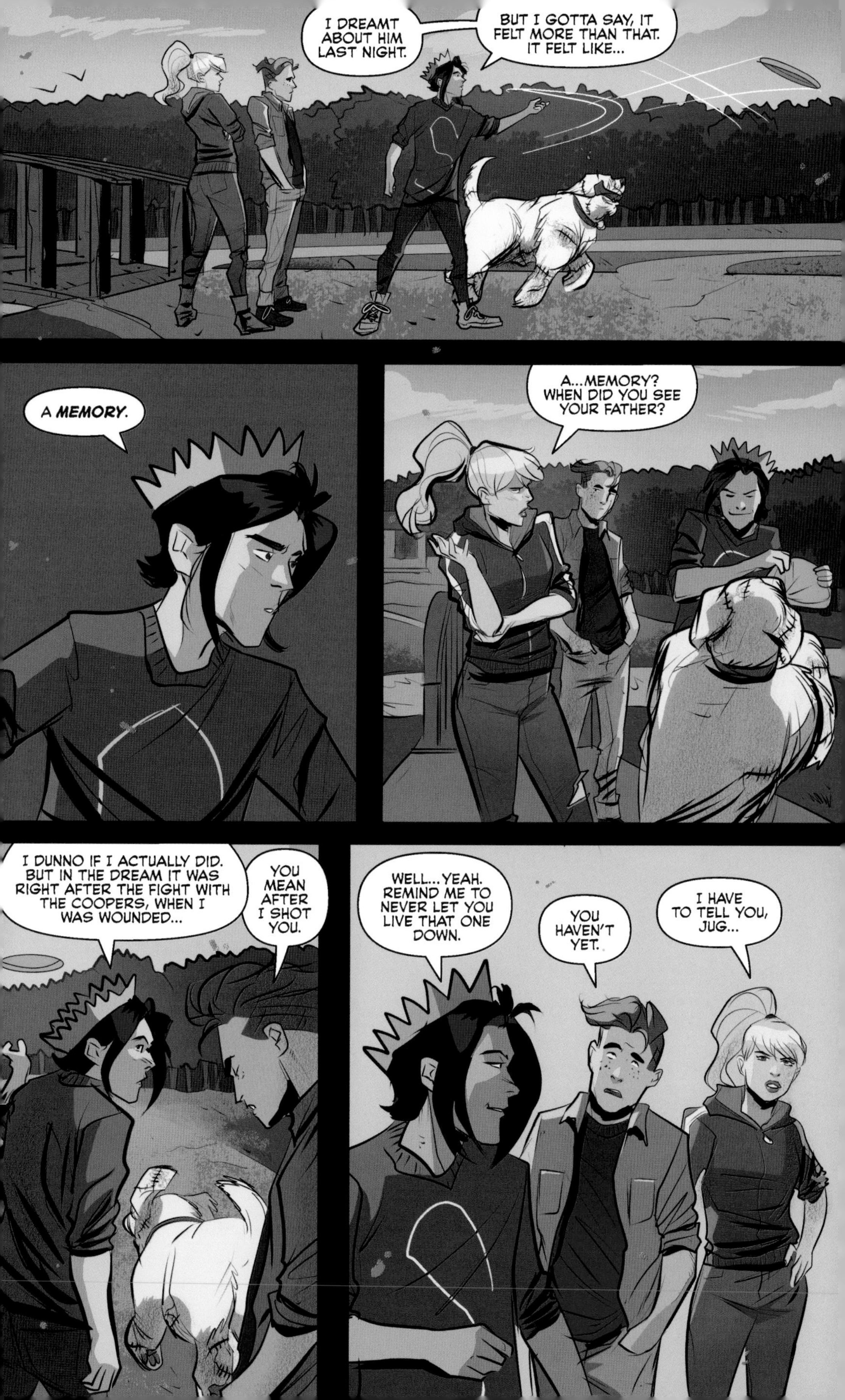
I DREAMT ABOUT HIM LAST NIGHT.
BUT I GOTTA SAY, IT FELT MORE THAN THAT. IT FELT LIKE...
A MEMORY.
A...MEMORY? WHEN DID YOU SEE YOUR FATHER?
I DUNNO IF I ACTUALLY DID. BUT IN THE DREAM IT WAS RIGHT AFTER THE FIGHT WITH THE COOPERS, WHEN I WAS WOUNDED...
YOU MEAN AFTER I SHOT YOU.
WELL...YEAH. REMIND ME TO NEVER LET YOU LIVE THAT ONE DOWN.
YOU HAVEN'T YET.
I HAVE TO TELL YOU, JUG...

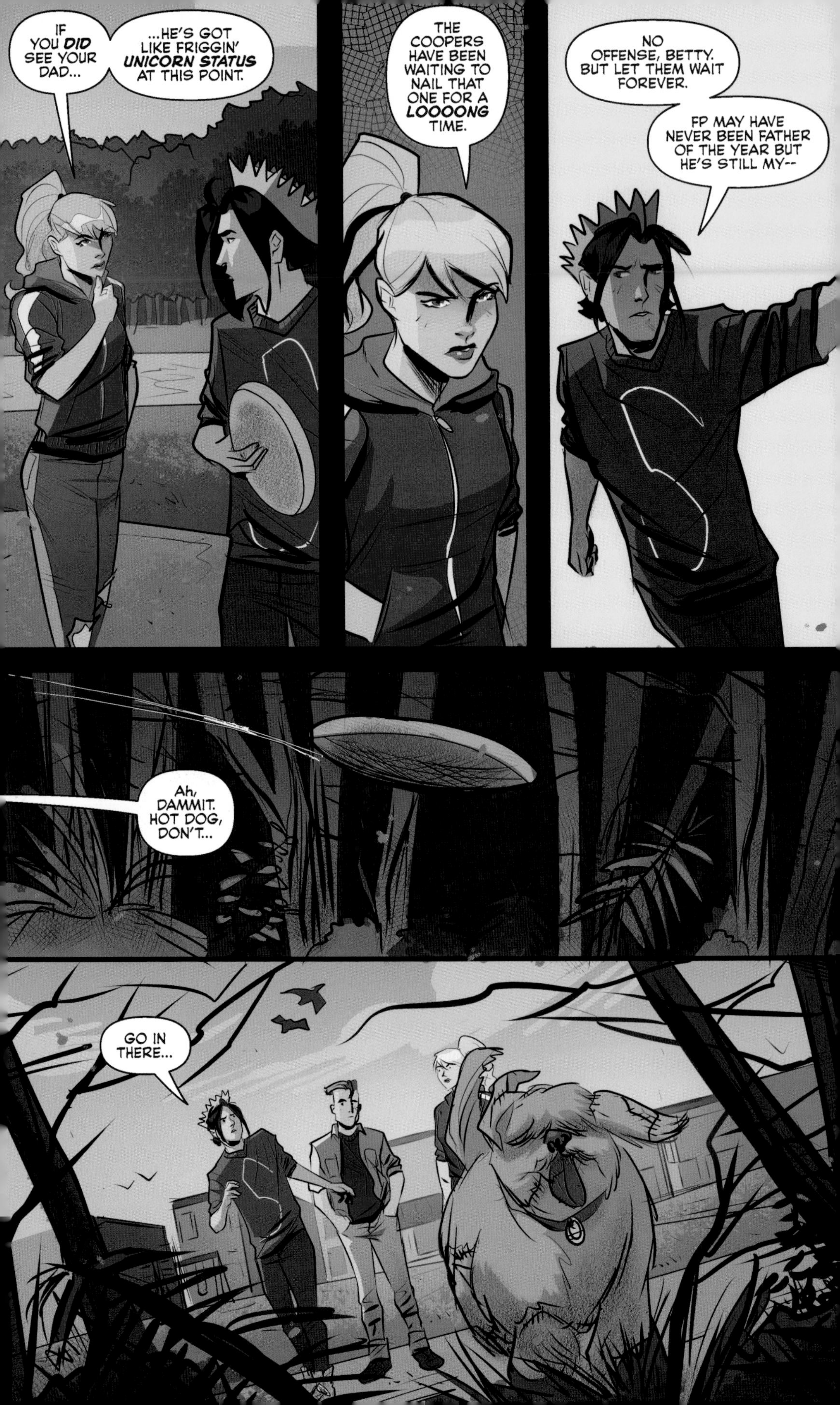
IF YOU DID SEE YOUR DAD...
...HE'S GOT LIKE FRIGGIN' UNICORN STATUS AT THIS POINT.
THE COOPERS HAVE BEEN WAITING TO NAIL THAT ONE FOR A LOOOONG TIME.
NO OFFENSE, BETTY. BUT LET THEM WAIT FOREVER.
FP MAY HAVE NEVER BEEN FATHER OF THE YEAR BUT HE'S STILL MY--
Ah, DAMMIT. HOT DOG, DON'T...
GO IN THERE...

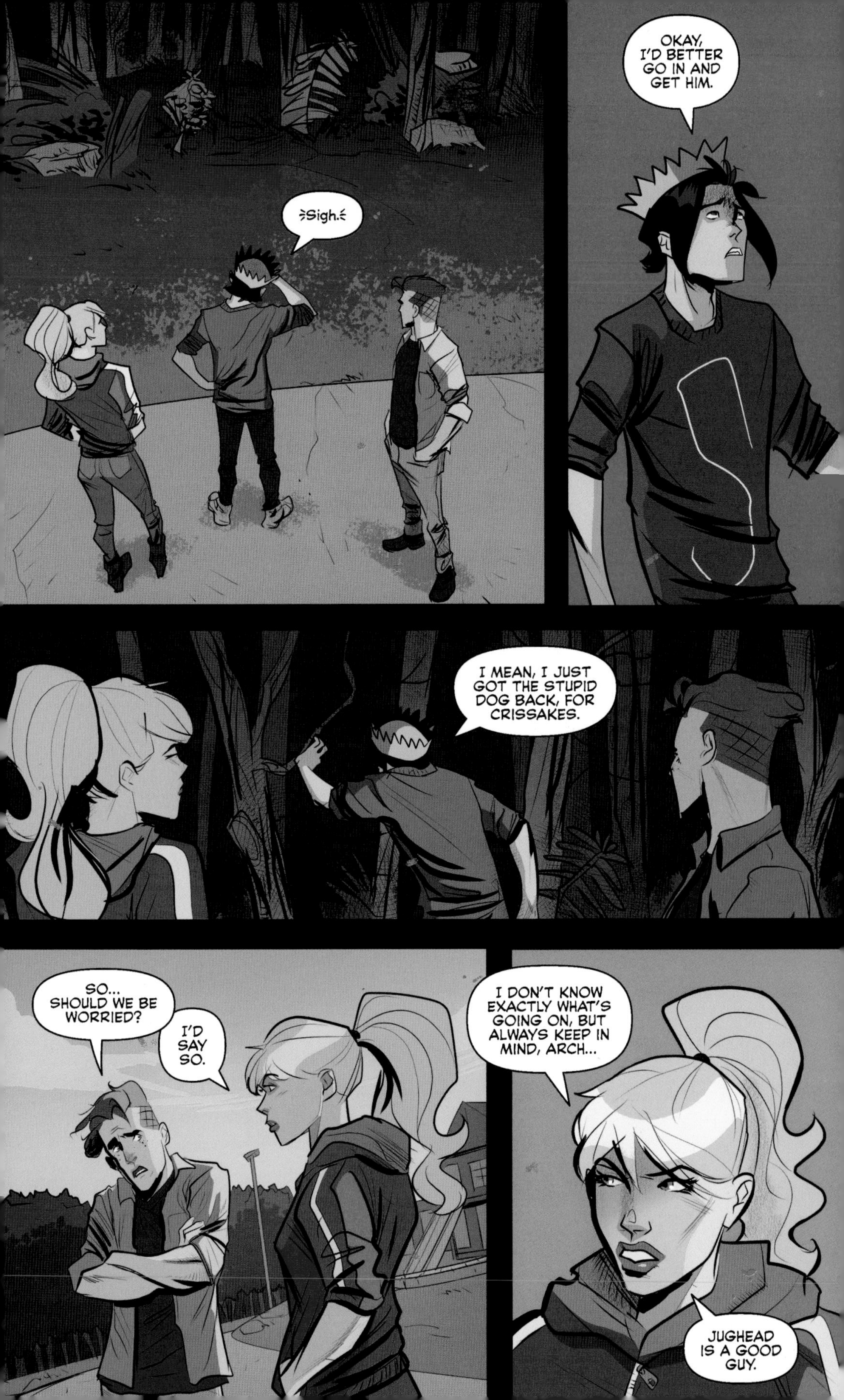

Sigh.
OKAY, I'D BETTER GO IN AND GET HIM.
I MEAN, I JUST GOT THE STUPID DOG BACK, FOR CRISSAKES.
SO... SHOULD WE BE WORRIED?
I'D SAY SO.
I DON'T KNOW EXACTLY WHAT'S GOING ON, BUT ALWAYS KEEP IN MIND, ARCH...
JUGHEAD IS A GOOD GUY.

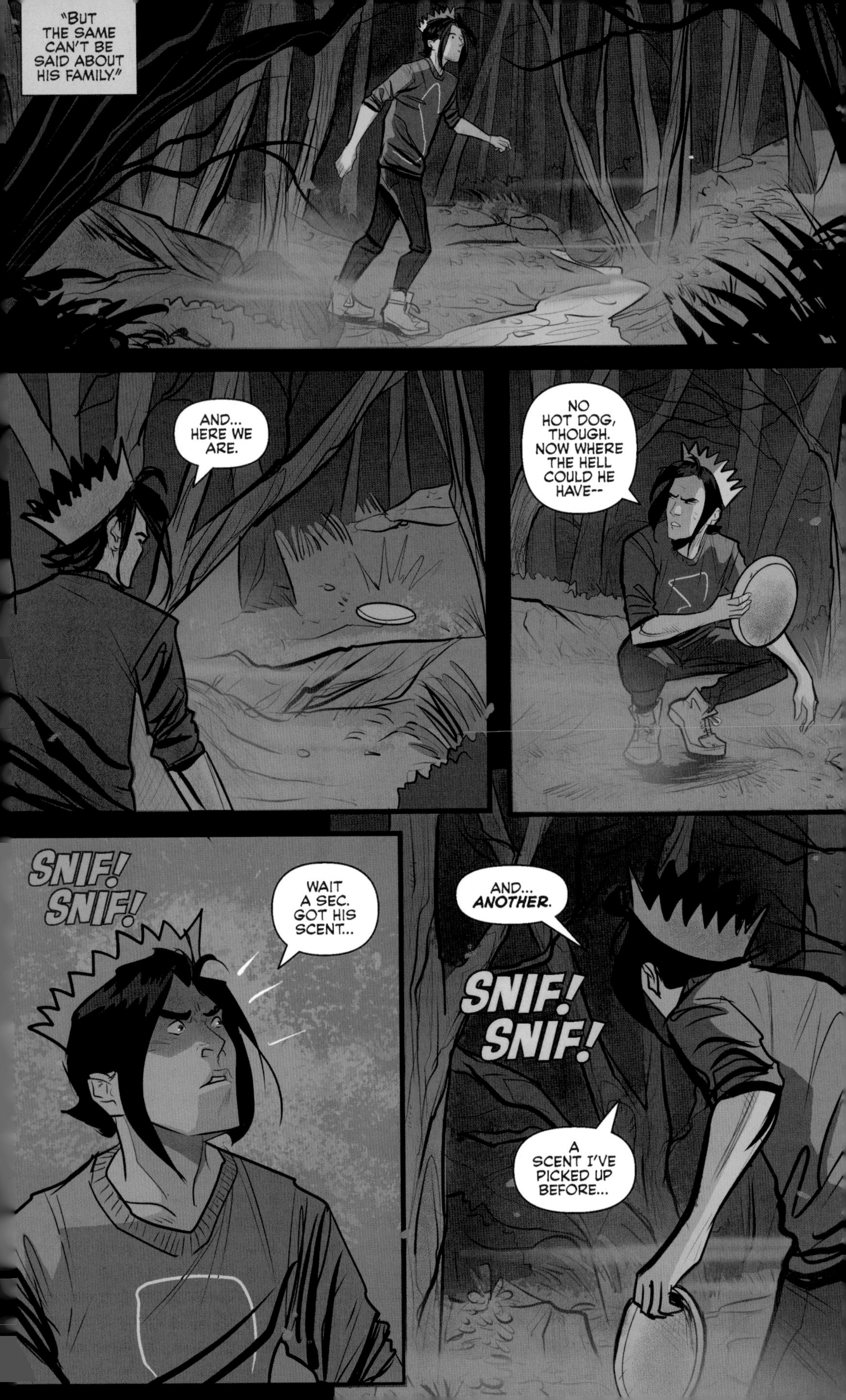
"BUT THE SAME CAN'T BE SAID ABOUT HIS FAMILY."
AND... HERE WE ARE.
NO HOT DOG, THOUGH. NOW WHERE THE HELL COULD HE HAVE--
SNIF! SNIF!
WAIT A SEC. GOT HIS SCENT...
AND... ANOTHER.
SNIF! SNIF!
A SCENT I'VE PICKED UP BEFORE...

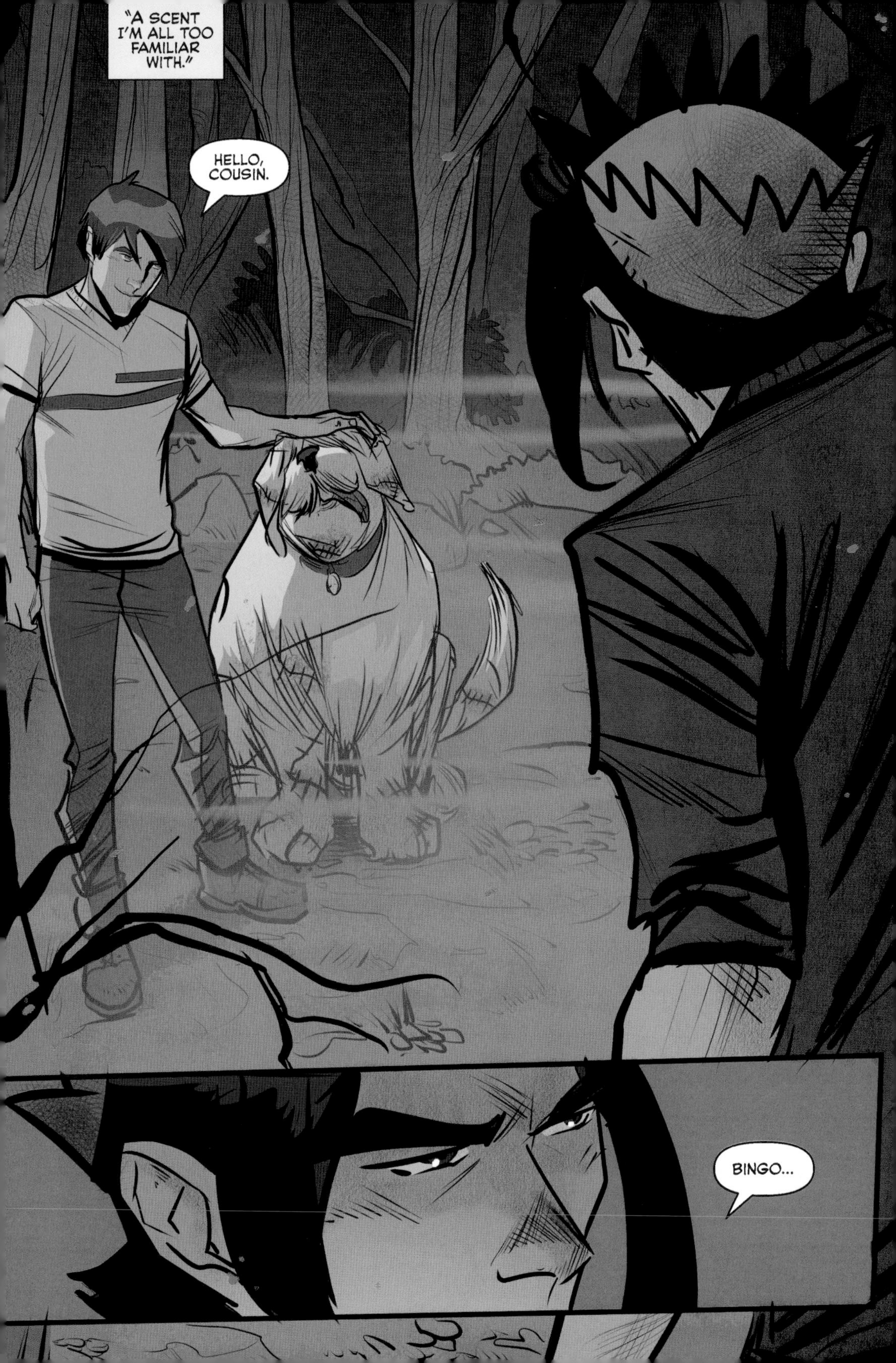
"A SCENT I'M ALL TOO FAMILIAR WITH."
HELLO, COUSIN.
BINGO...

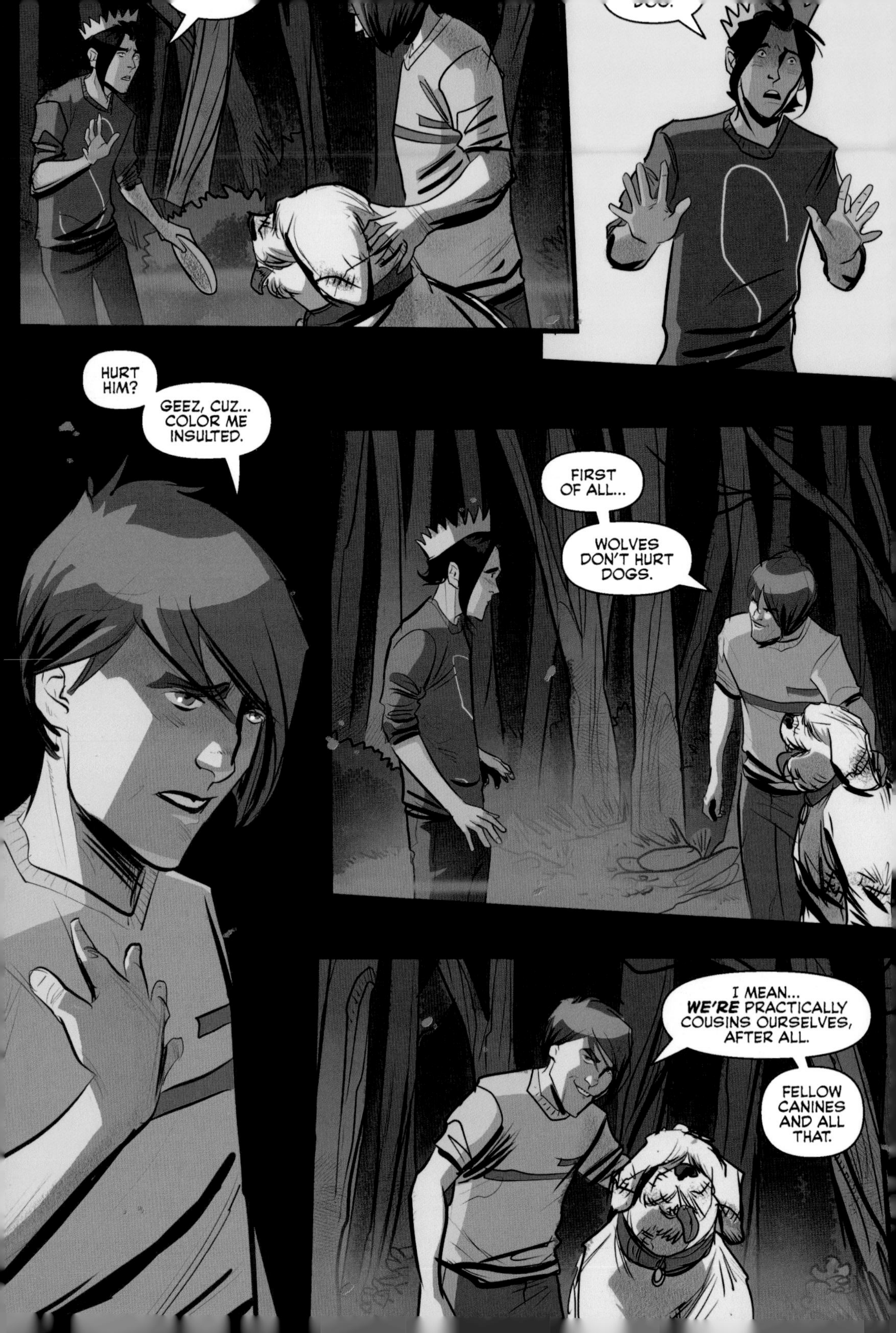
HURT HIM?
GEEZ, CUZ... COLOR ME INSULTED.
FIRST OF ALL...
WOLVES DON'T HURT DOGS.
I MEAN... ***WE'RE*** PRACTICALLY COUSINS OURSELVES, AFTER ALL.
FELLOW CANINES AND ALL THAT.

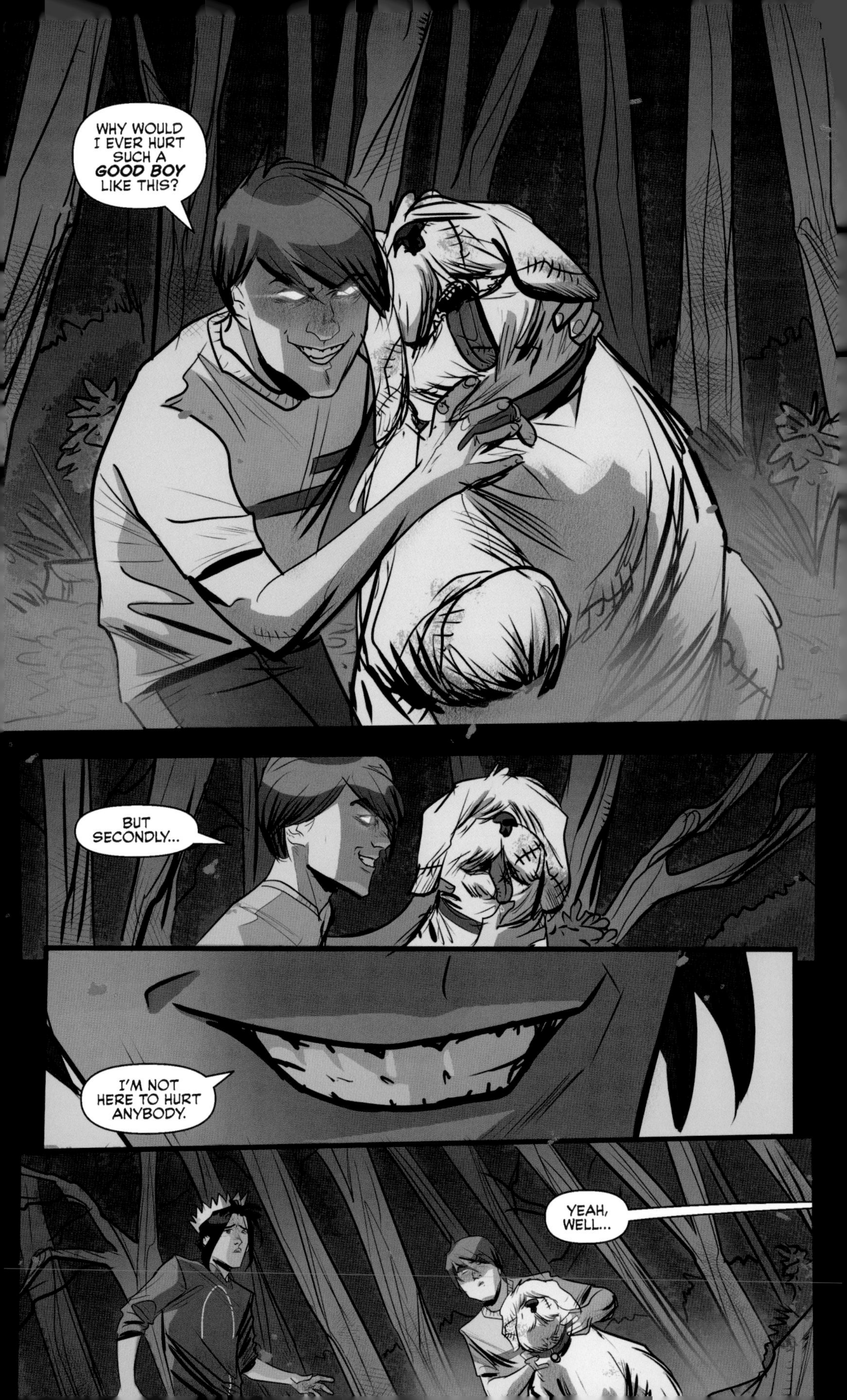
WHY WOULD I EVER HURT SUCH A **GOOD BOY** LIKE THIS?
BUT SECONDLY...
I'M NOT HERE TO HURT ANYBODY.
YEAH, WELL...

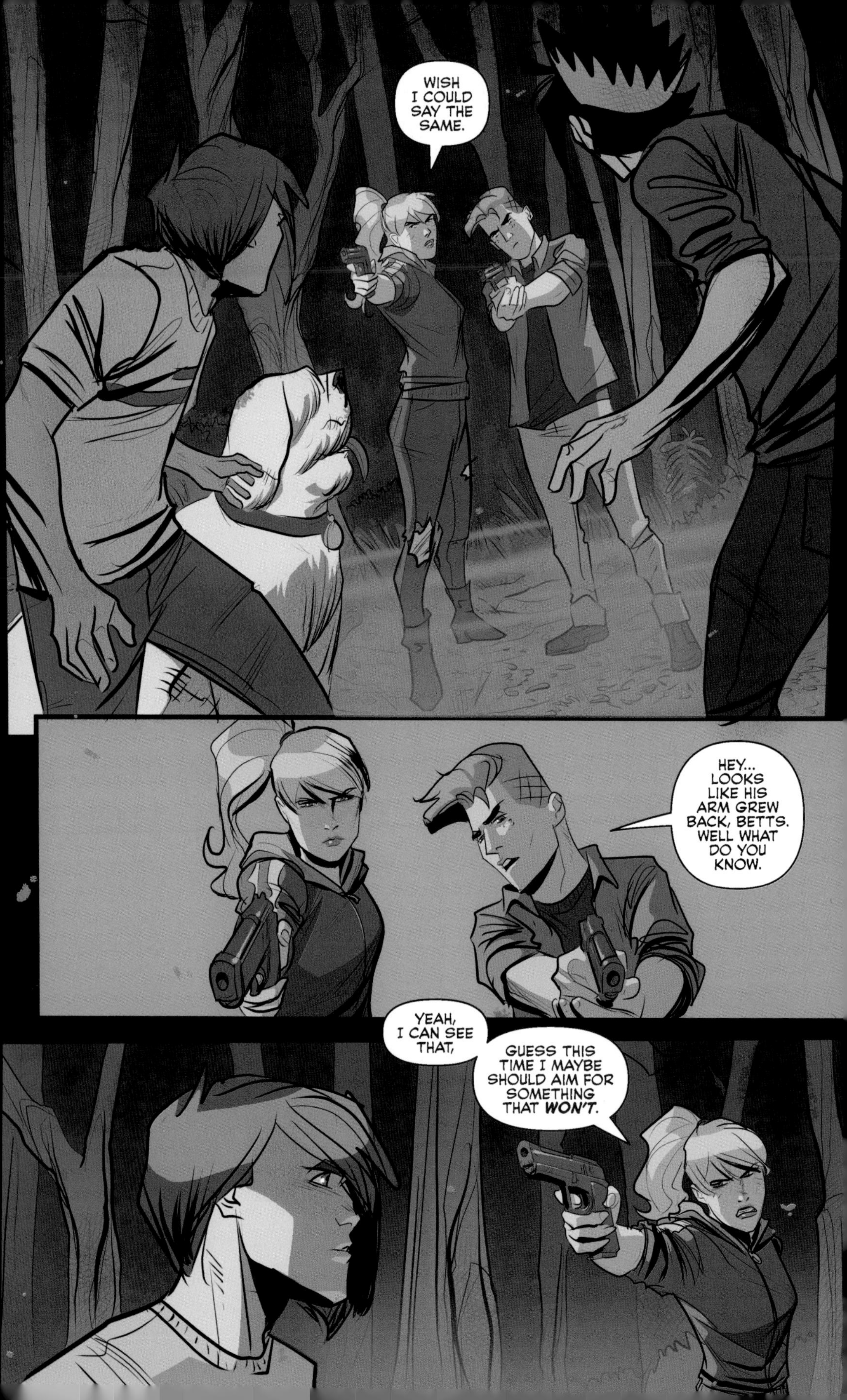
WISH I COULD SAY THE SAME.
HEY... LOOKS LIKE HIS ARM GREW BACK, BETTS. WELL WHAT DO YOU KNOW.
YEAH, I CAN SEE THAT,
GUESS THIS TIME I MAYBE SHOULD AIM FOR SOMETHING THAT *WON'T*.

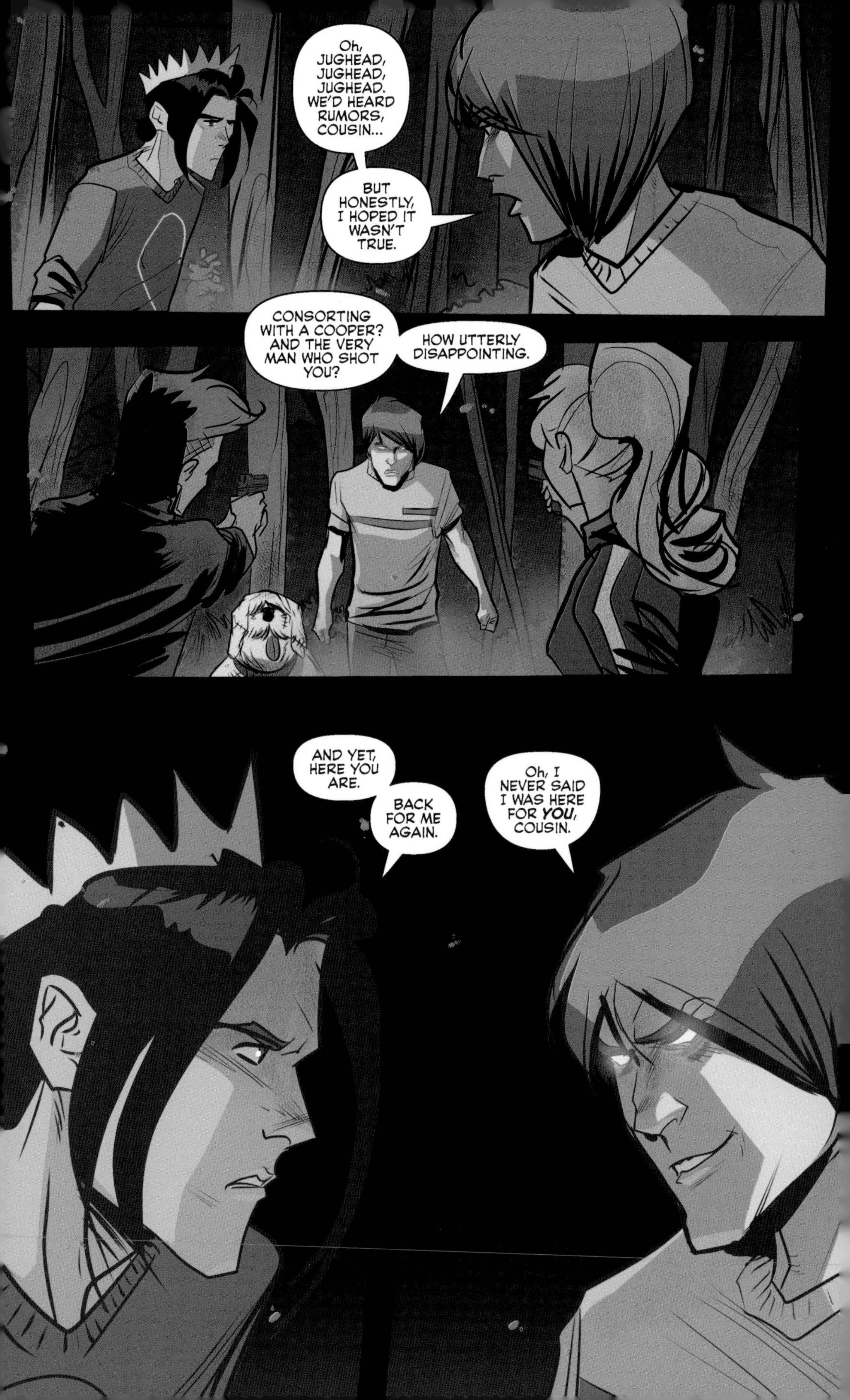
Oh, JUGHEAD, JUGHEAD, JUGHEAD. WE'D HEARD RUMORS, COUSIN...
BUT HONESTLY, I HOPED IT WASN'T TRUE.
CONSORTING WITH A COOPER? AND THE VERY MAN WHO SHOT YOU?
HOW UTTERLY DISAPPOINTING.
AND YET, HERE YOU ARE.
BACK FOR ME AGAIN.
Oh, I NEVER SAID I WAS HERE FOR ***YOU***, COUSIN.

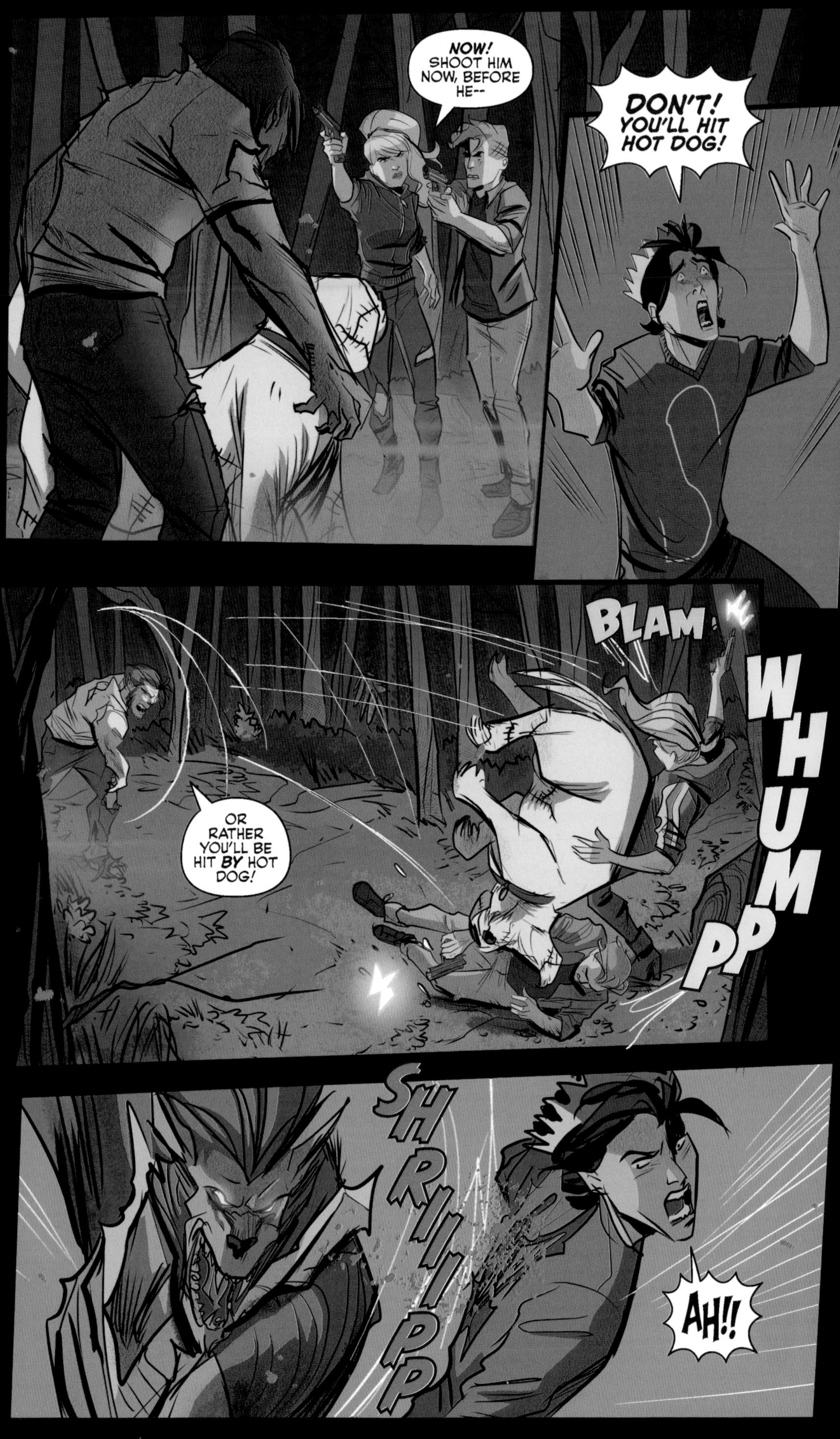
NOW! SHOOT HIM NOW, BEFORE HE--
DON'T! YOU'LL HIT HOT DOG!
BLAM
WHUMPP
OR RATHER YOU'LL BE HIT BY HOT DOG!
SHRIIIPP
AH!!

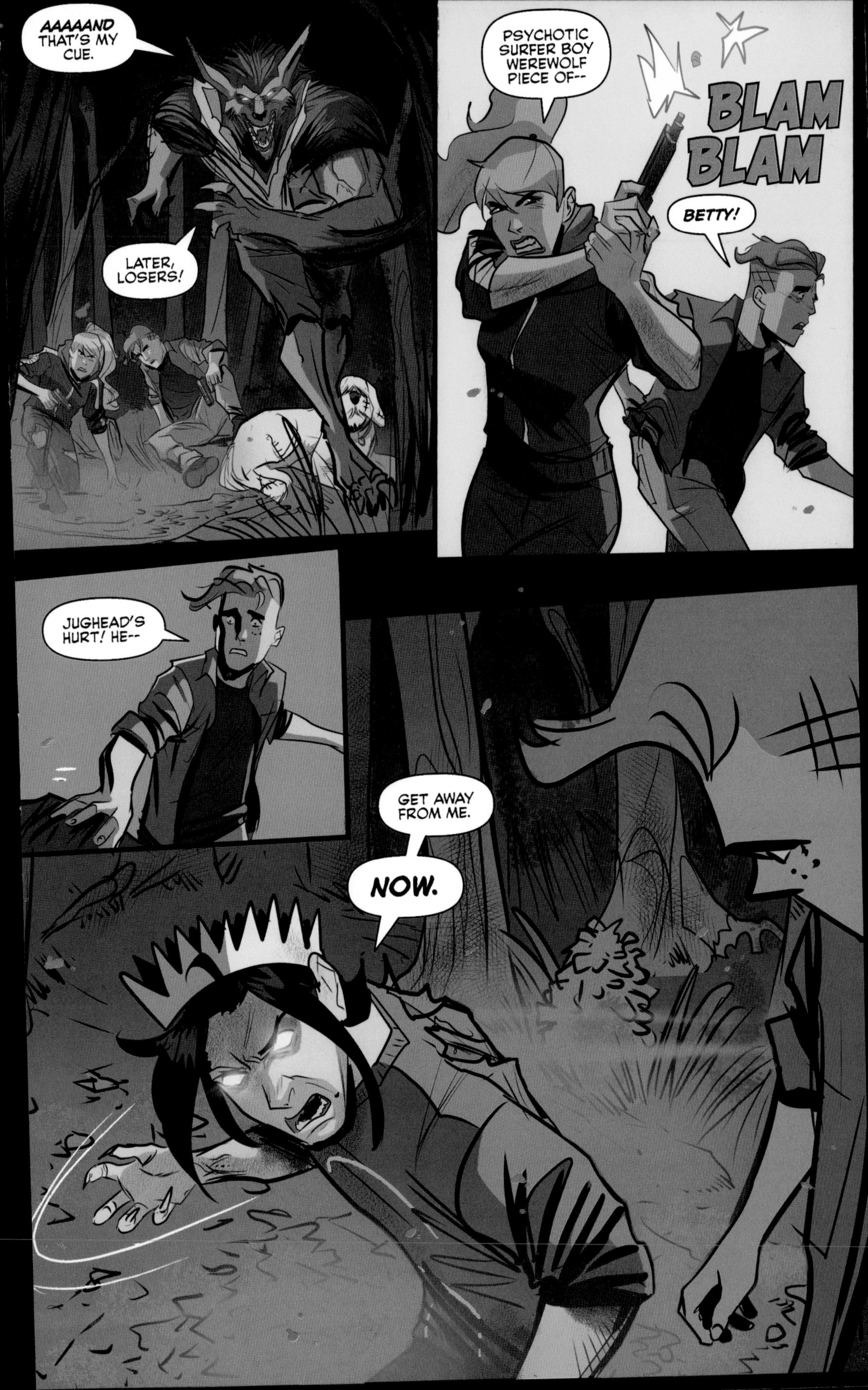
AAAAAND THAT'S MY CUE.
LATER, LOSERS!
PSYCHOTIC SURFER BOY WEREWOLF PIECE OF--
BLAM BLAM
BETTY!
JUGHEAD'S HURT! HE--
GET AWAY FROM ME.
NOW.

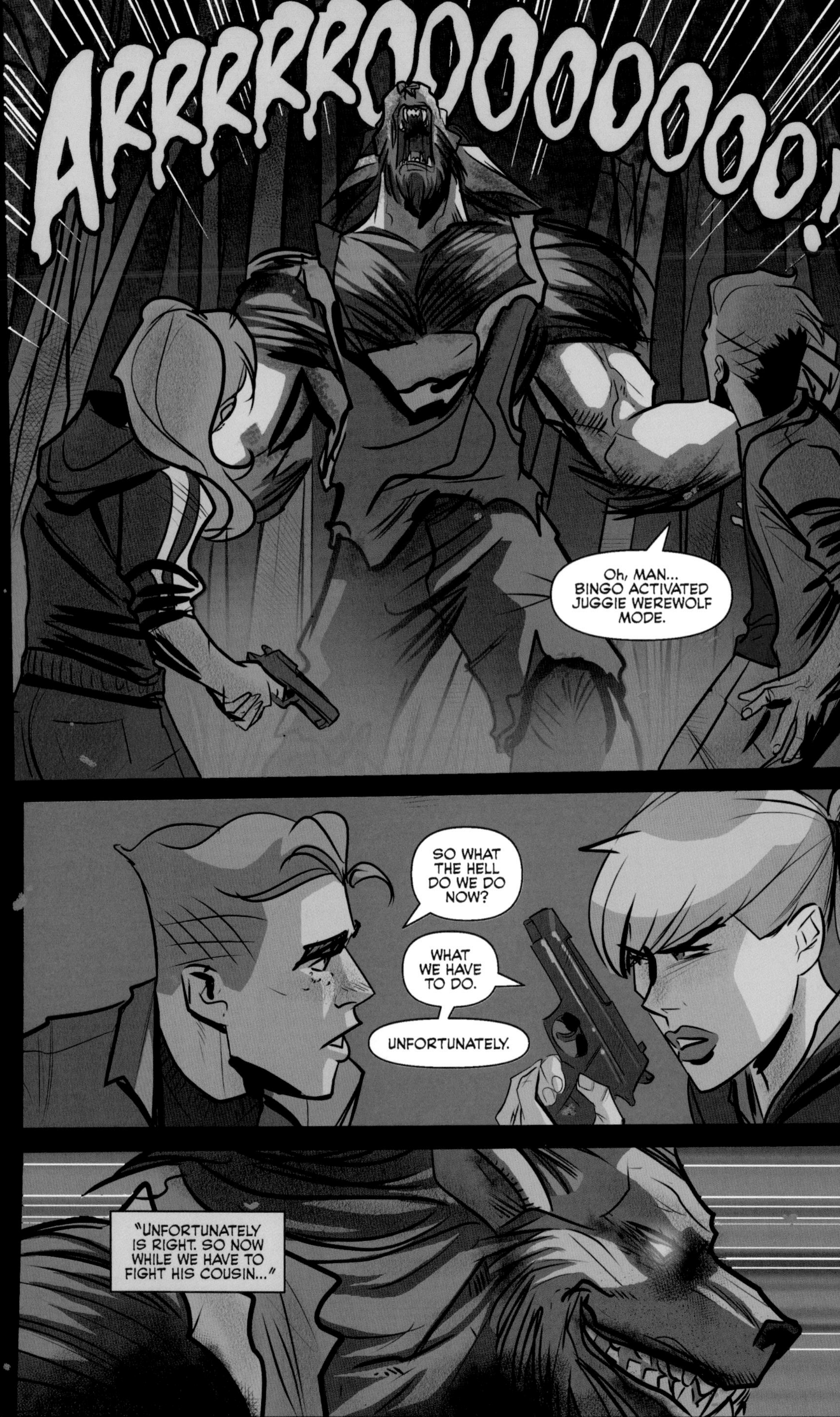
ARRRROOOOOOOO!
Oh, MAN... BINGO ACTIVATED JUGGIE WEREWOLF MODE.
SO WHAT THE HELL DO WE DO NOW?
WHAT WE HAVE TO DO.
UNFORTUNATELY.
"UNFORTUNATELY IS RIGHT. SO NOW WHILE WE HAVE TO FIGHT HIS COUSIN..."

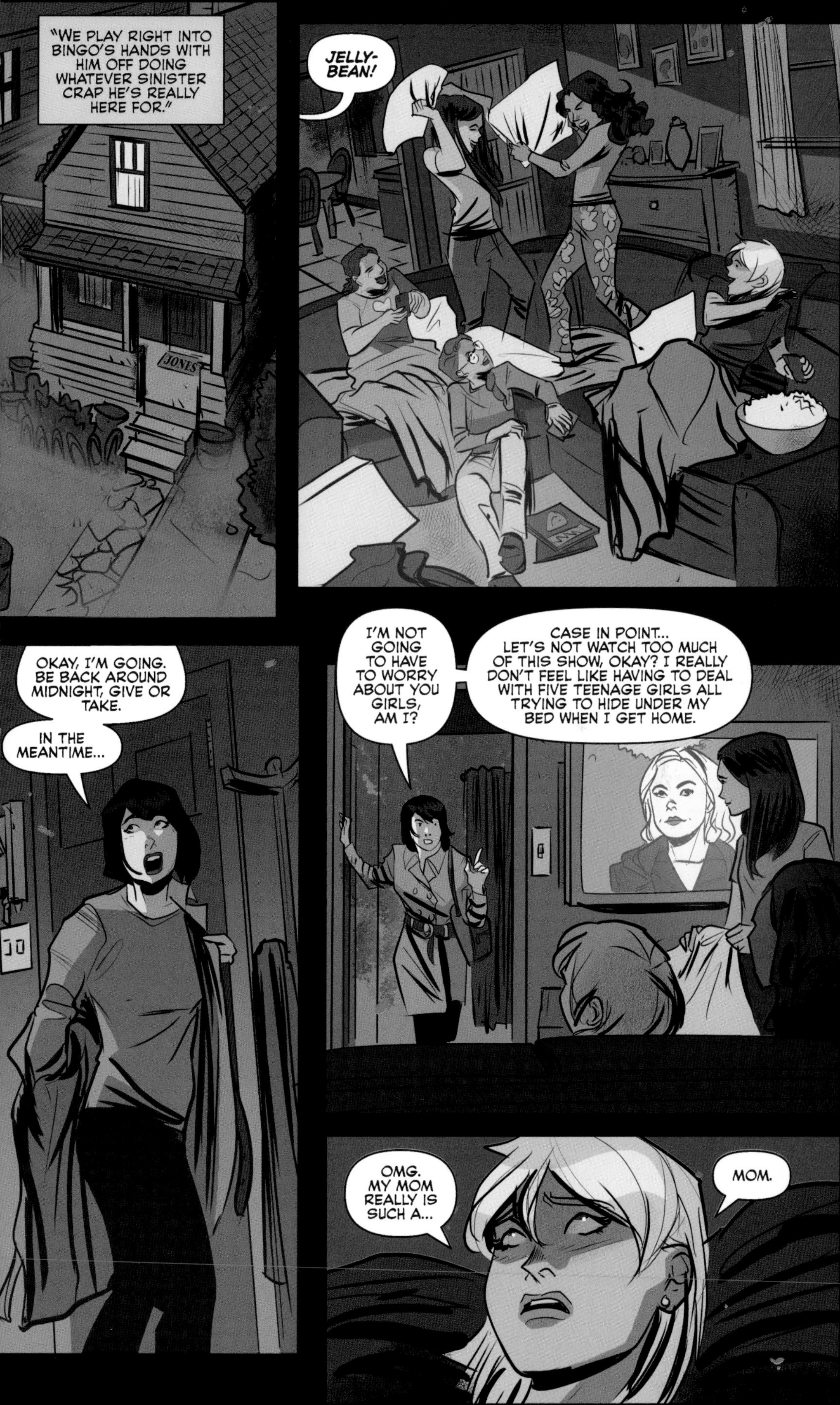

"WE PLAY RIGHT INTO BINGO'S HANDS WITH HIM OFF DOING WHATEVER SINISTER CRAP HE'S REALLY HERE FOR."
JONES
JELLY-BEAN!
OKAY, I'M GOING. BE BACK AROUND MIDNIGHT, GIVE OR TAKE.
IN THE MEANTIME...
I'M NOT GOING TO HAVE TO WORRY ABOUT YOU GIRLS, AM I?
CASE IN POINT... LET'S NOT WATCH TOO MUCH OF THIS SHOW, OKAY? I REALLY DON'T FEEL LIKE HAVING TO DEAL WITH FIVE TEENAGE GIRLS ALL TRYING TO HIDE UNDER MY BED WHEN I GET HOME.
OMG. MY MOM REALLY IS SUCH A...
MOM.

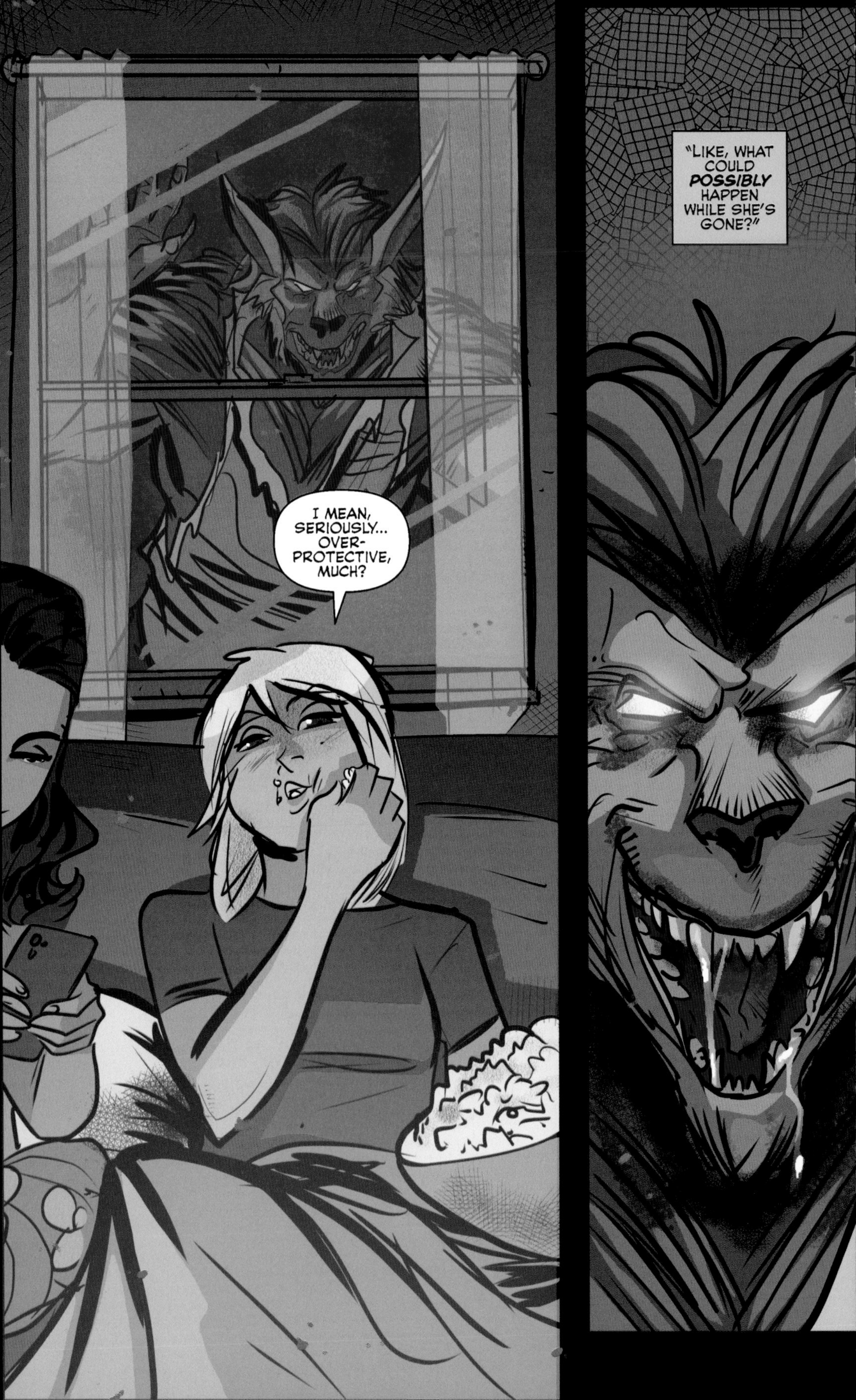
I MEAN, SERIOUSLY... OVER-PROTECTIVE, MUCH?
"LIKE, WHAT COULD POSSIBLY HAPPEN WHILE SHE'S GONE?"

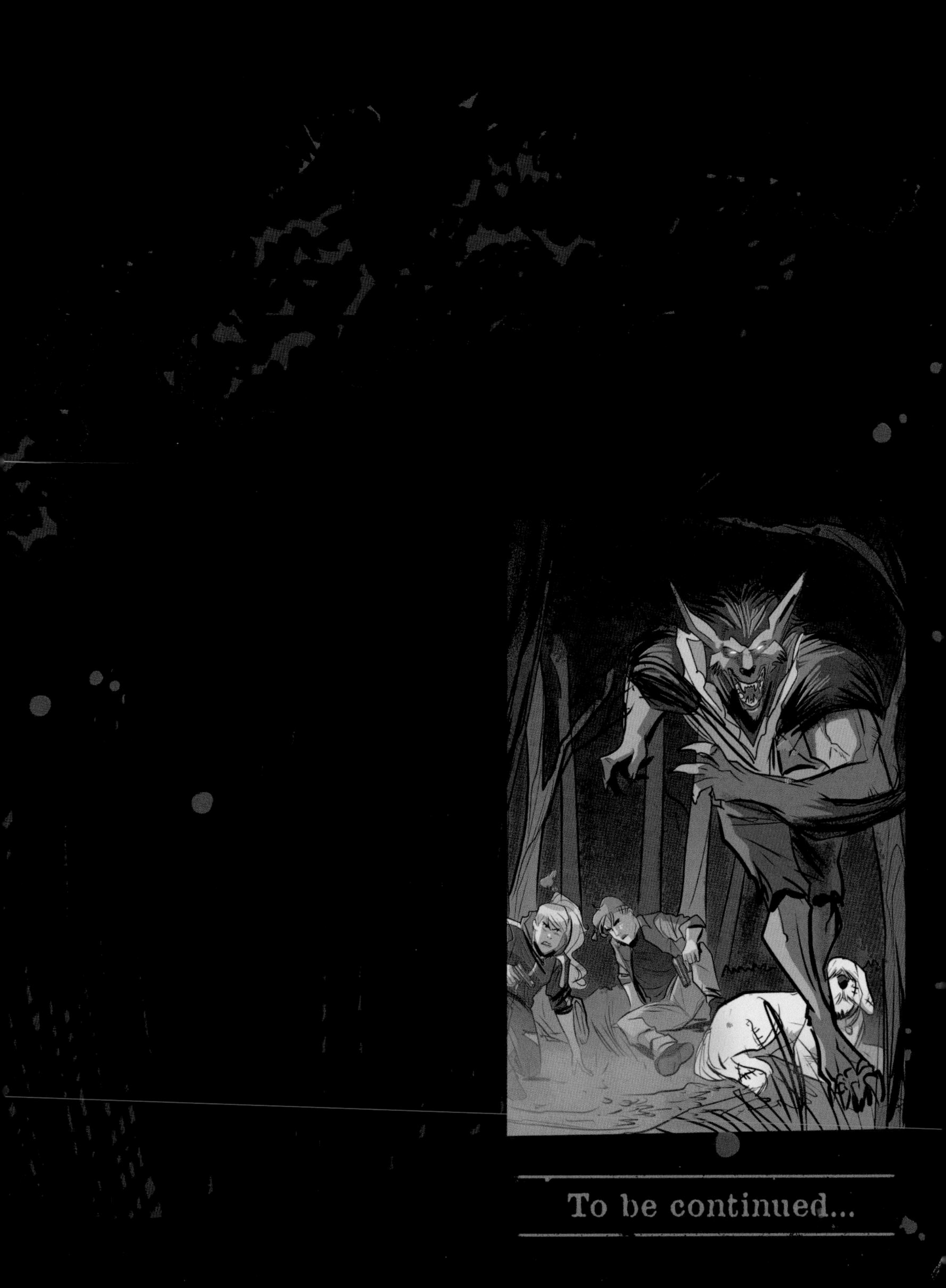
To be continued...

ISSUE THIRTEEN

BINGO WAS HIS NAME, OH NO: PART 2

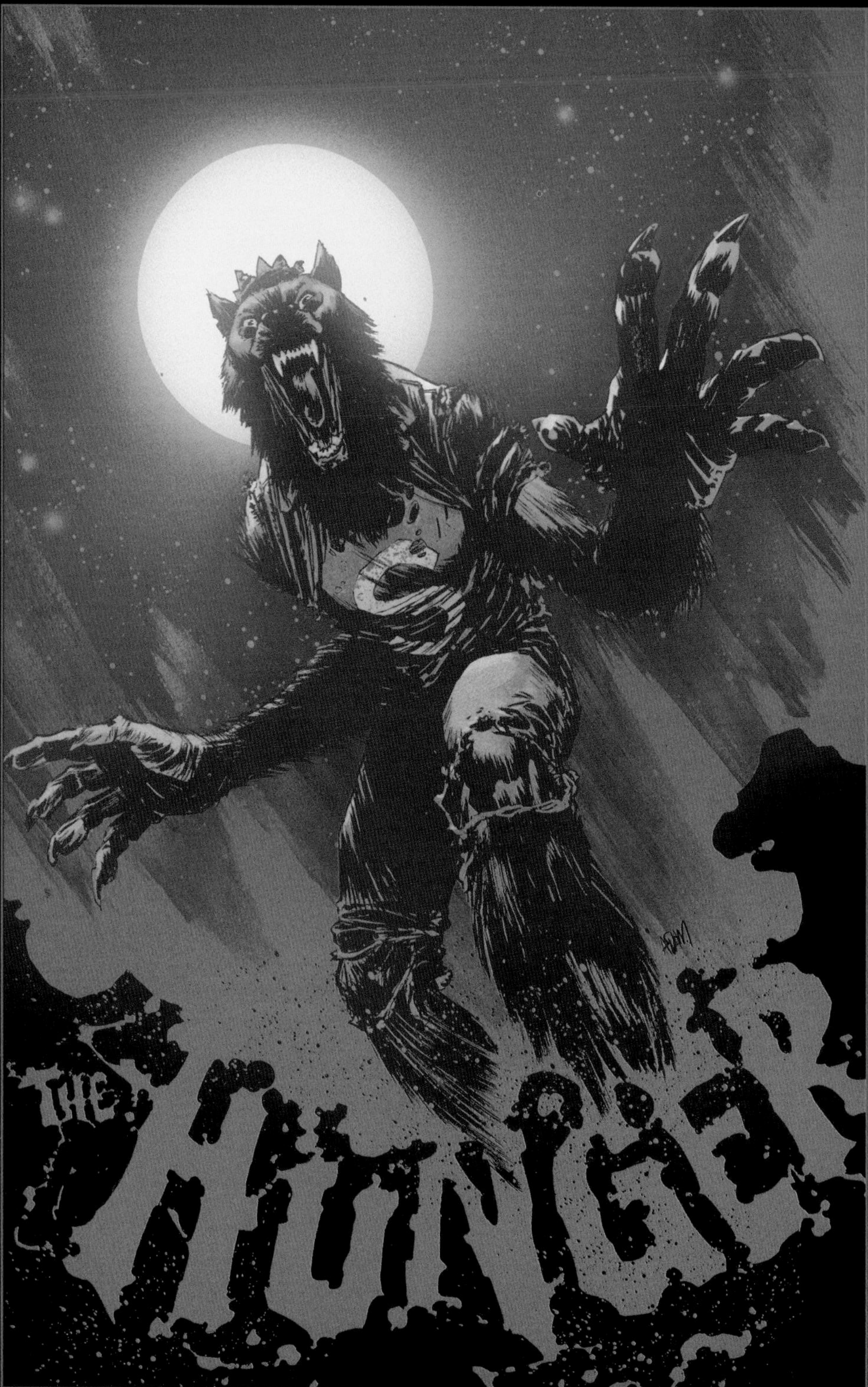
THE
HUNGER

COVER ART Adam Gorham

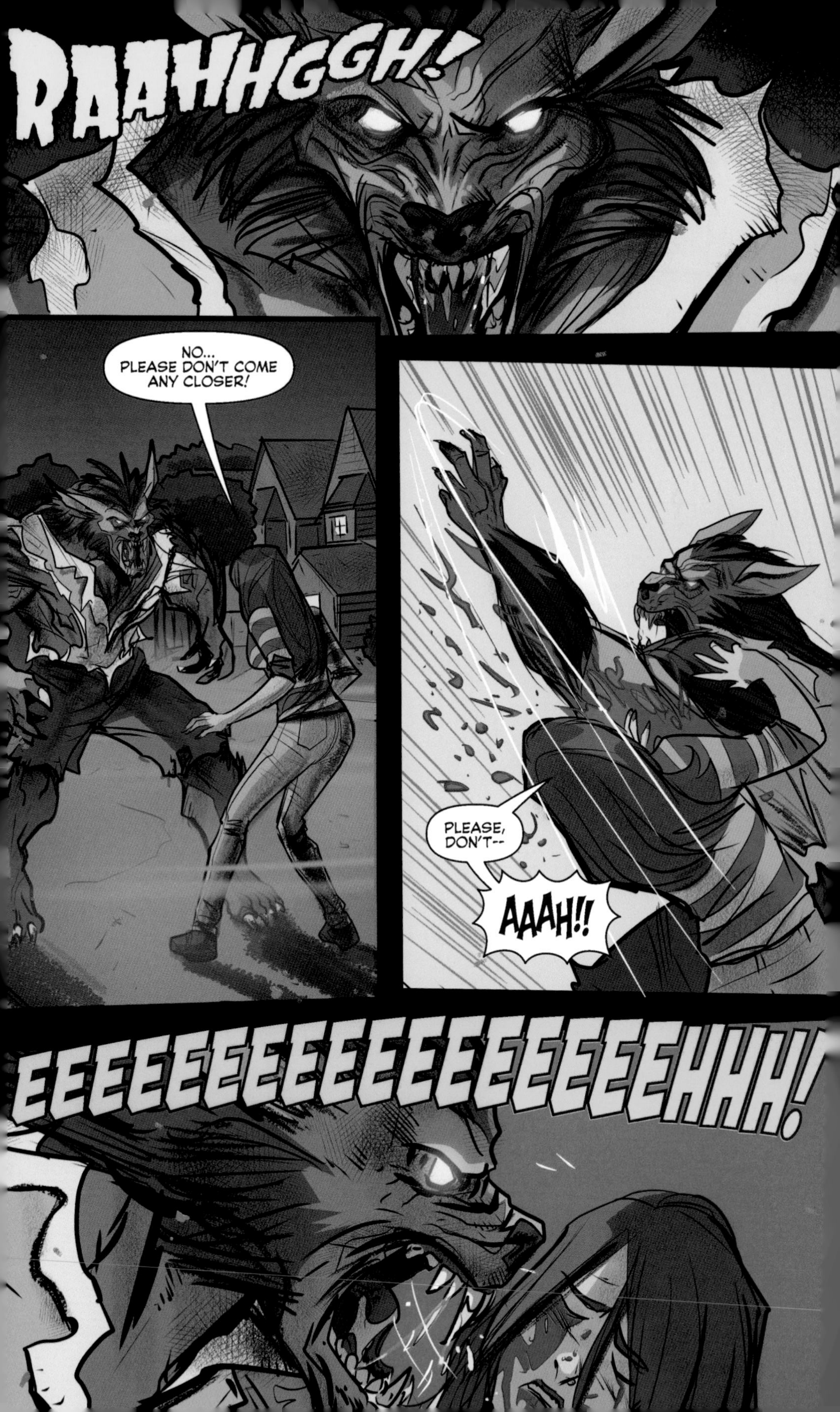
RAAHHGGGH!
NO... PLEASE DON'T COME ANY CLOSER!
PLEASE, DON'T--
AAAH!!
EEEEEEEEEEEEEEEEEEEEEHHH!

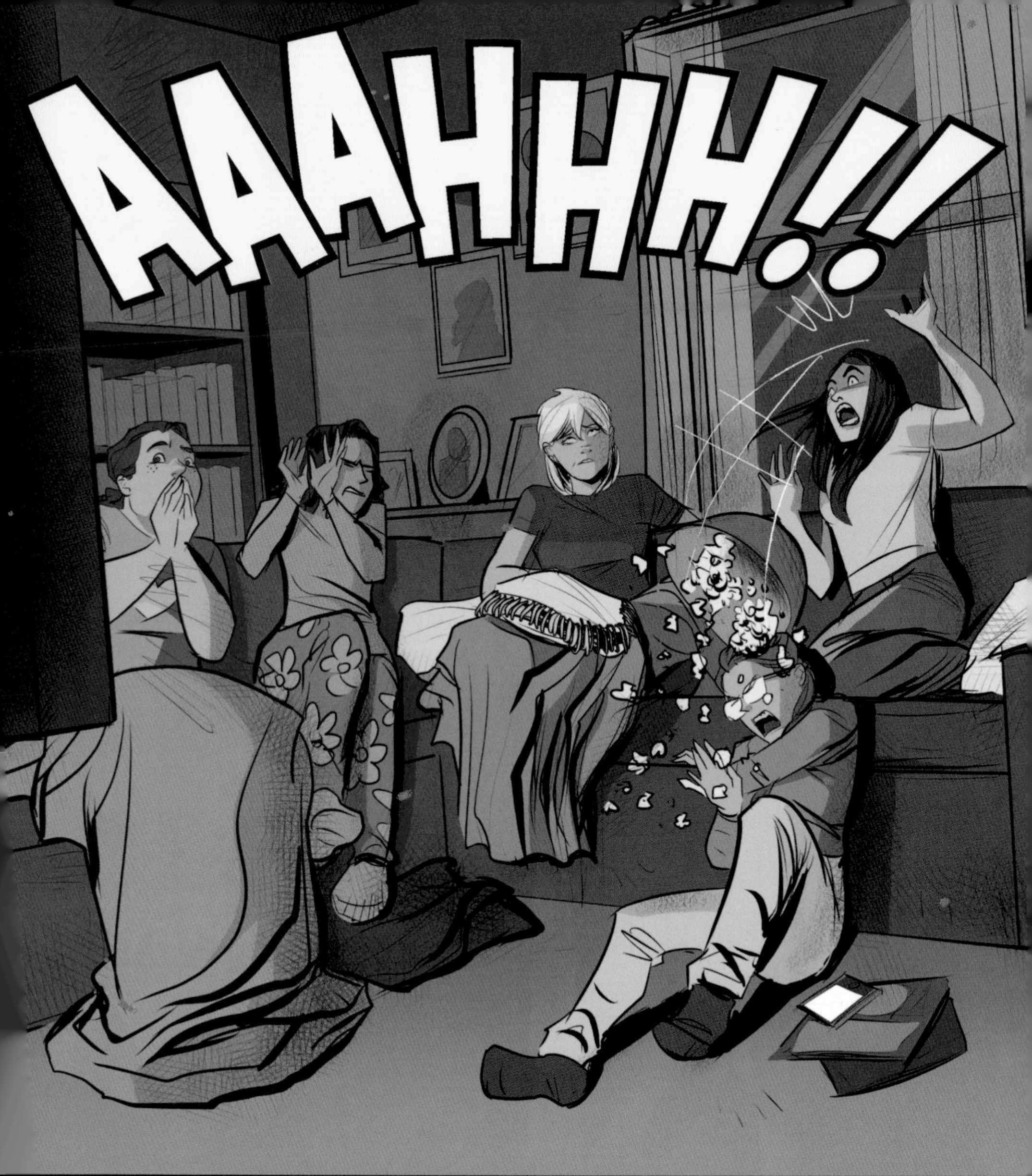
AAAHHH!!

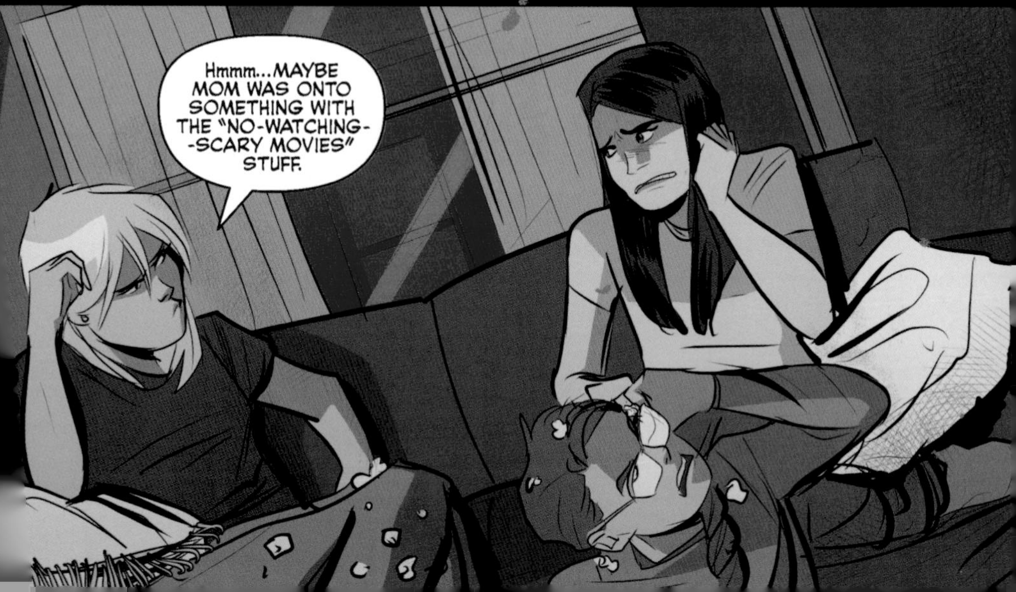
Hmmm...MAYBE MOM WAS ONTO SOMETHING WITH THE "NO-WATCHING-SCARY MOVIES" STUFF.

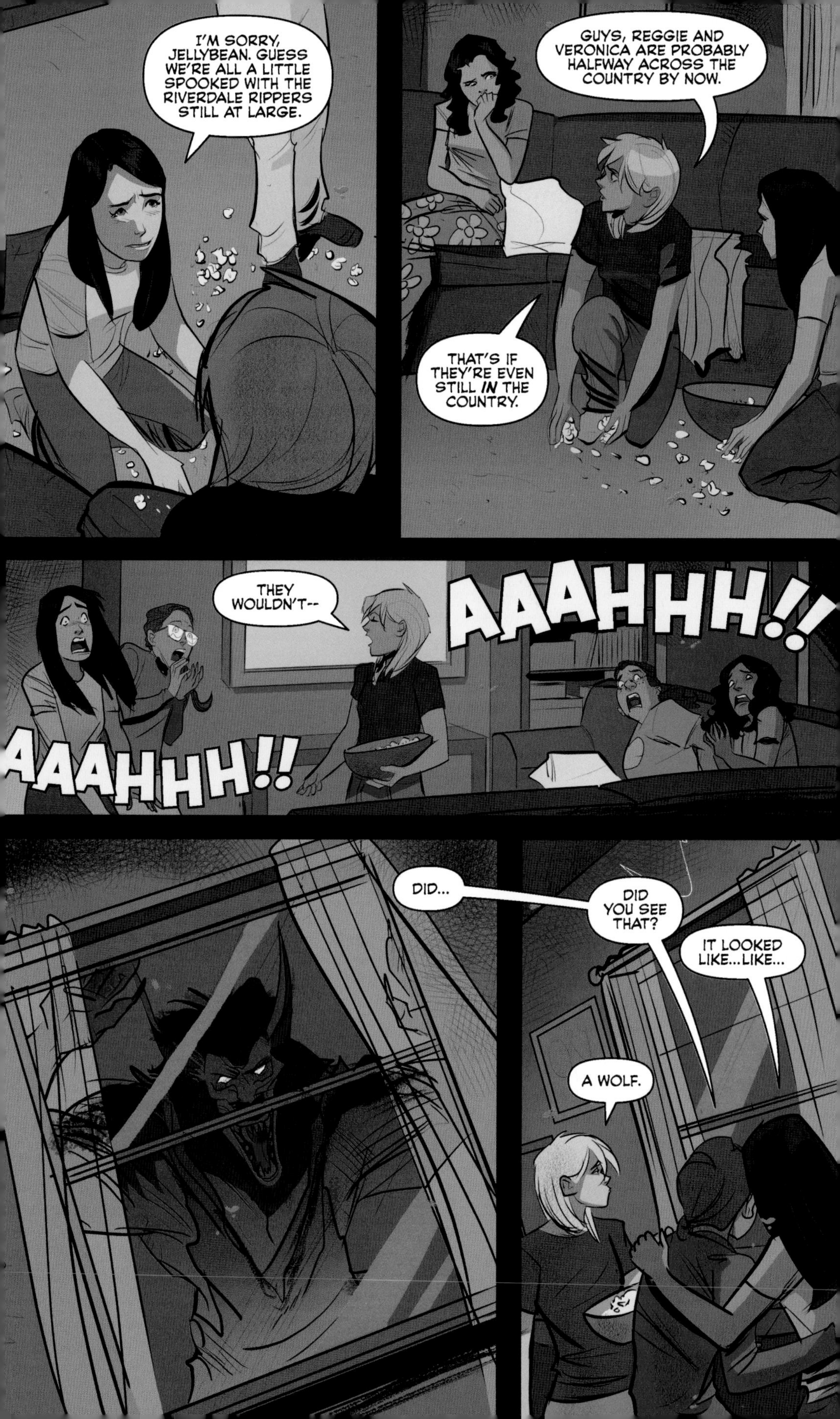
I'M SORRY, JELLYBEAN. GUESS WE'RE ALL A LITTLE SPOOKED WITH THE RIVERDALE RIPPERS STILL AT LARGE.
GUYS, REGGIE AND VERONICA ARE PROBABLY HALFWAY ACROSS THE COUNTRY BY NOW.
THAT'S IF THEY'RE EVEN STILL *IN* THE COUNTRY.
THEY WOULDN'T--
AAAHHH!!
AAAHHH!!
DID...
DID YOU SEE THAT?
IT LOOKED LIKE...LIKE...
A WOLF.

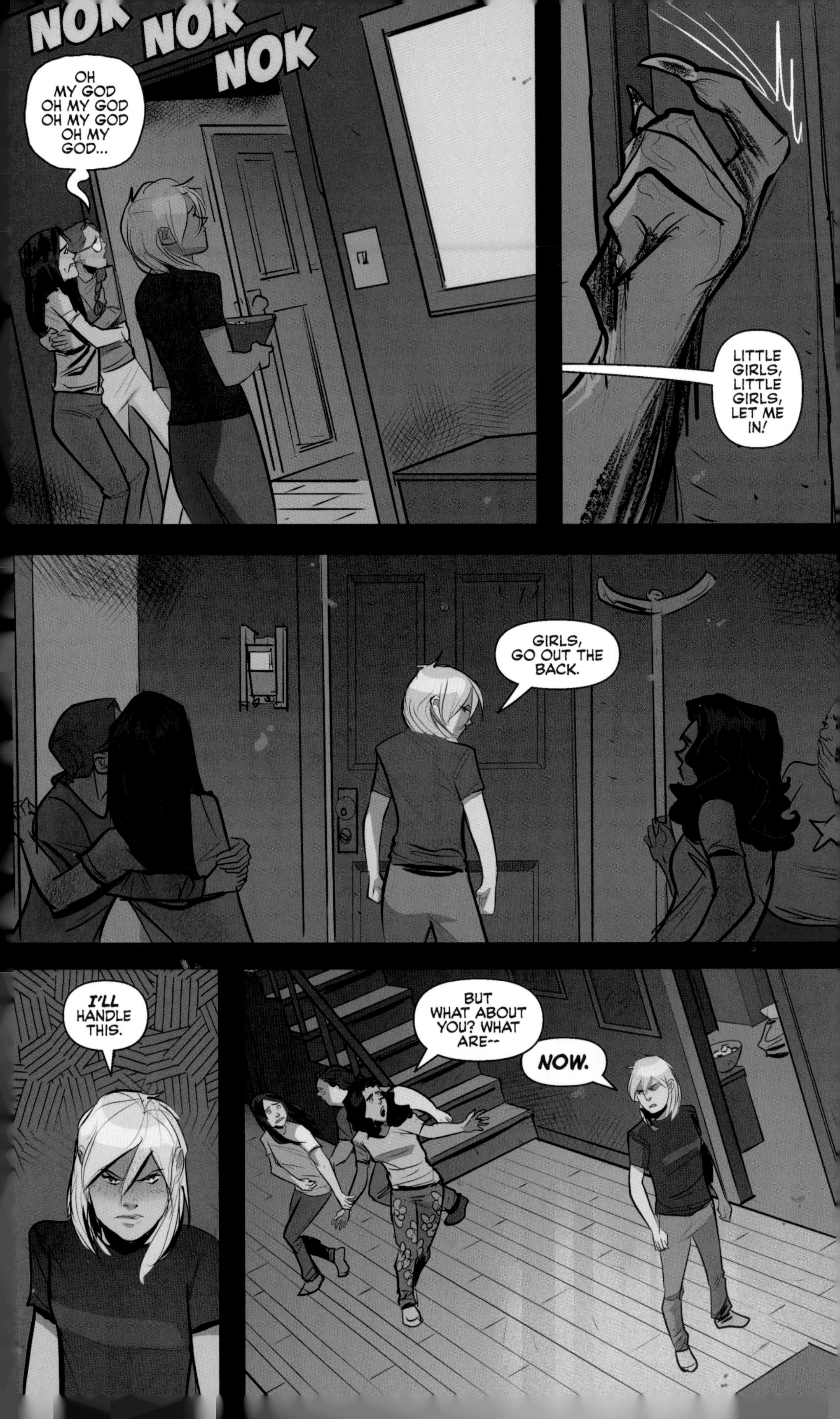
NOK NOK NOK
OH MY GOD OH MY GOD OH MY GOD OH MY GOD...
LITTLE GIRLS, LITTLE GIRLS, LET ME IN!
GIRLS, GO OUT THE BACK.
I'LL HANDLE THIS.
BUT WHAT ABOUT YOU? WHAT ARE--
NOW.

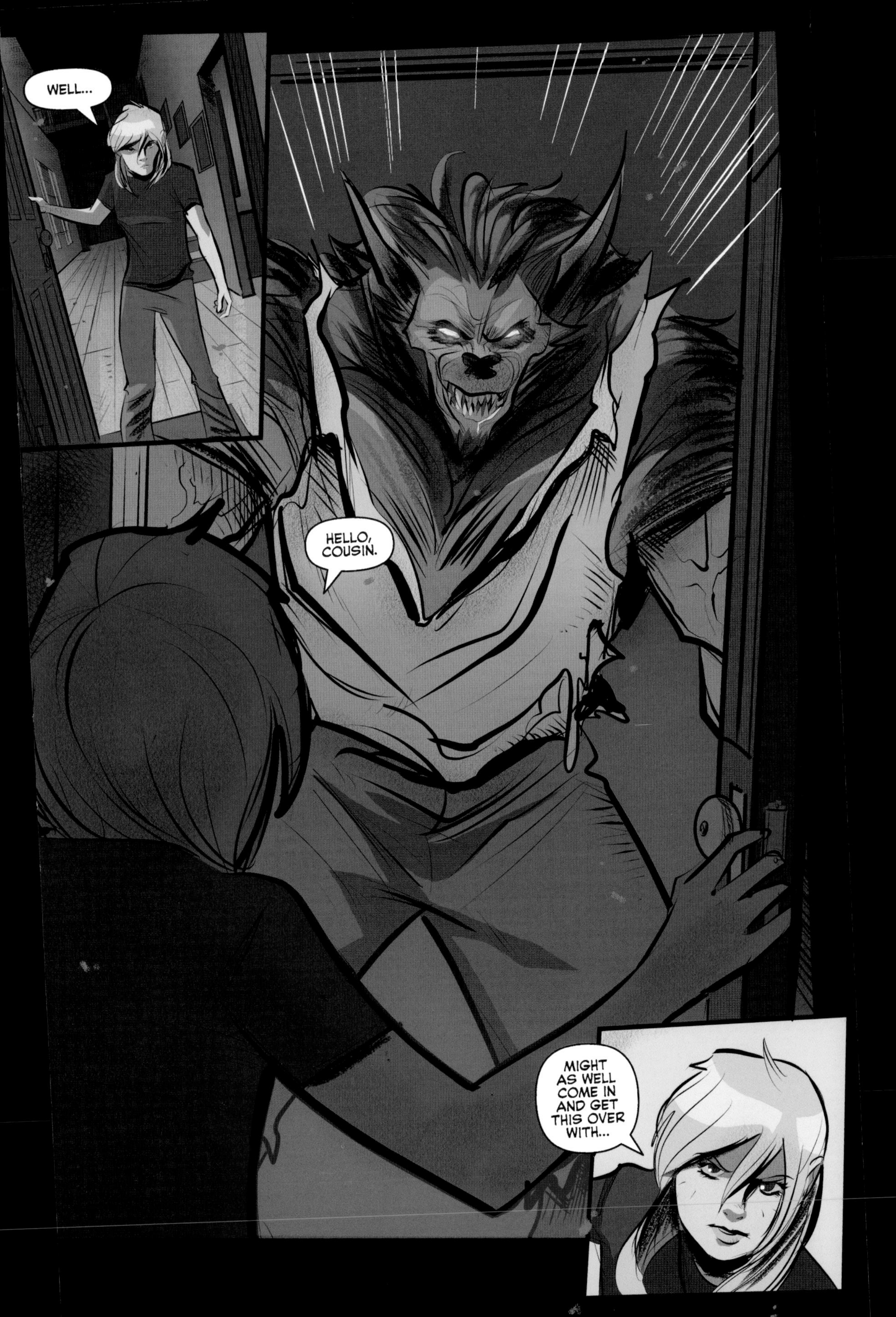
WELL...
HELLO, COUSIN.
MIGHT AS WELL COME IN AND GET THIS OVER WITH...

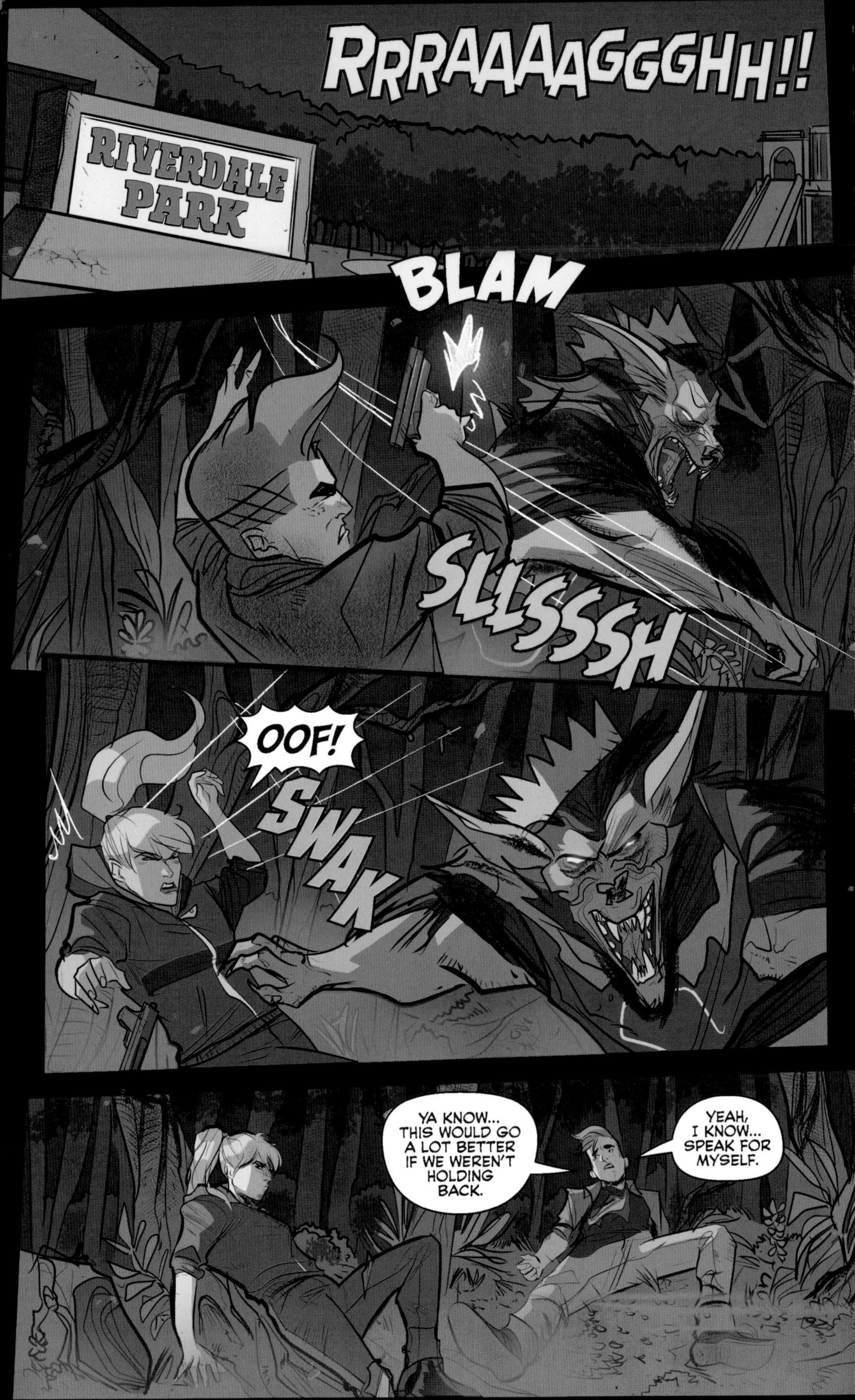
RRRAAAAGGGHH!!
RIVERDALE PARK
BLAM
SLISSSH
OOF!
SWAK
YA KNOW... THIS WOULD GO A LOT BETTER IF WE WEREN'T HOLDING BACK.
YEAH, I KNOW... SPEAK FOR MYSELF.

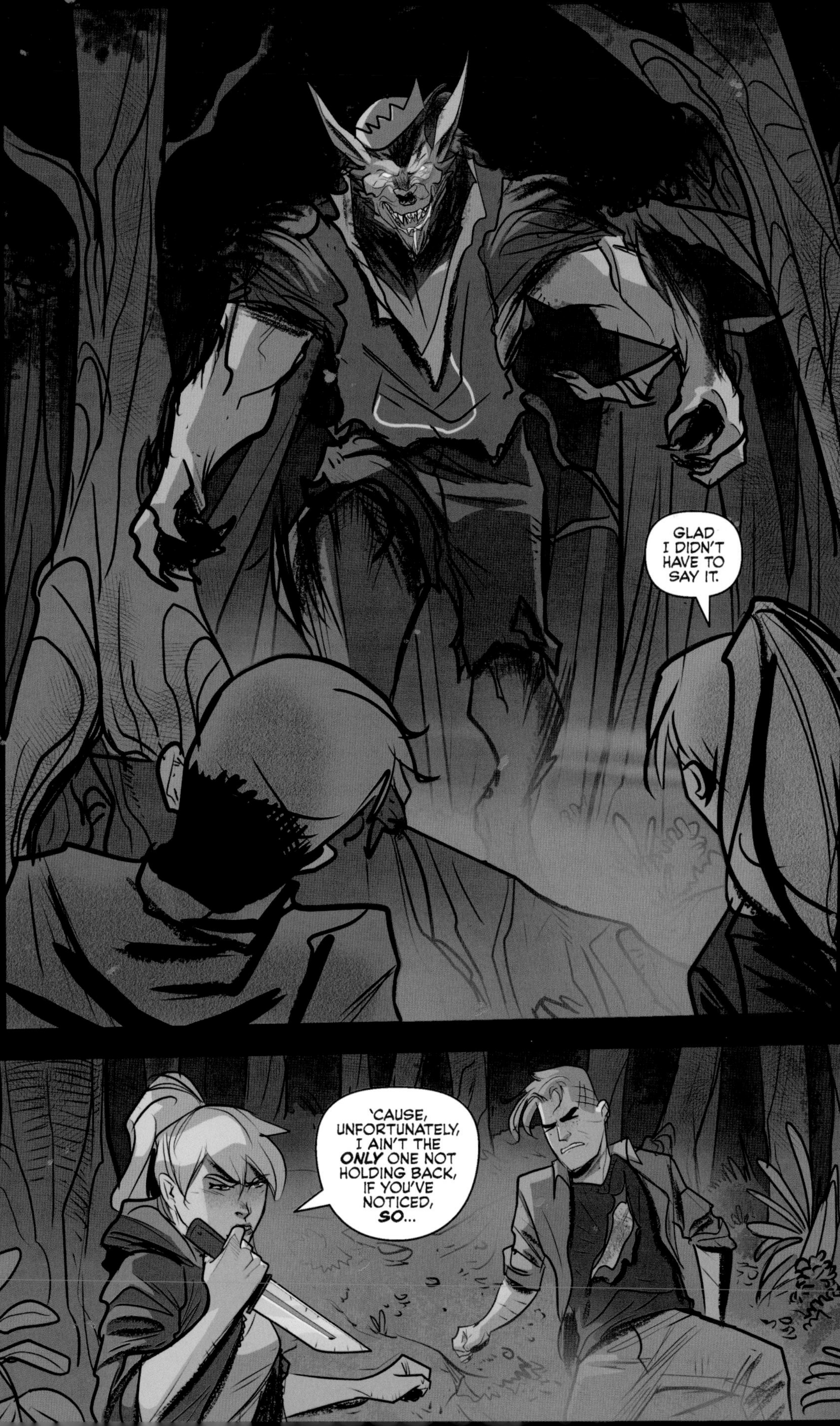
GLAD I DIDN'T HAVE TO SAY IT.
'CAUSE, UNFORTUNATELY, I AIN'T THE ONLY ONE NOT HOLDING BACK, IF YOU'VE NOTICED, SO...

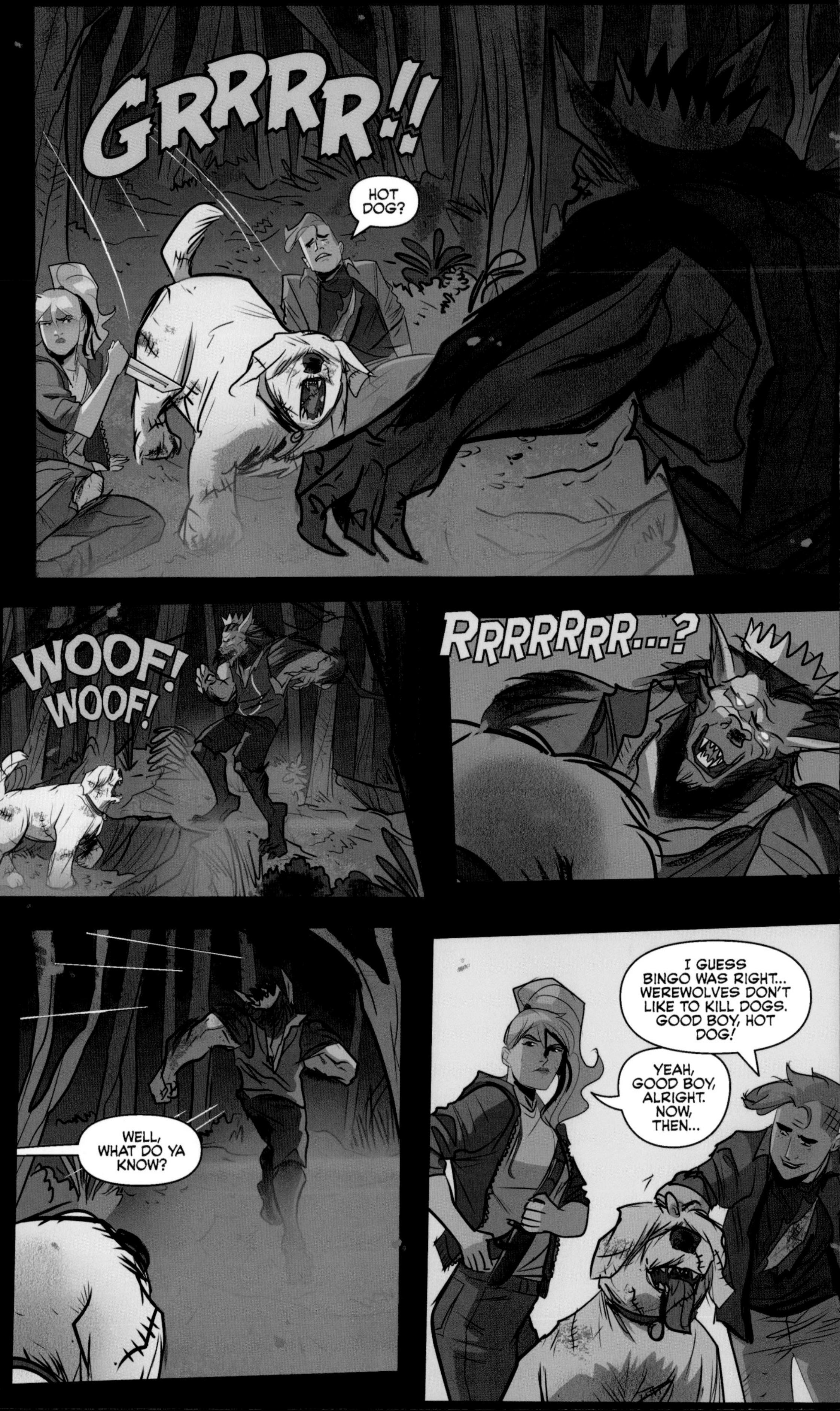
GRRRR!!
HOT DOG?
WOOF! WOOF!
RRRRRRR...?
WELL, WHAT DO YA KNOW?
I GUESS BINGO WAS RIGHT... WEREWOLVES DON'T LIKE TO KILL DOGS. GOOD BOY, HOT DOG!
YEAH, GOOD BOY, ALRIGHT. NOW, THEN...

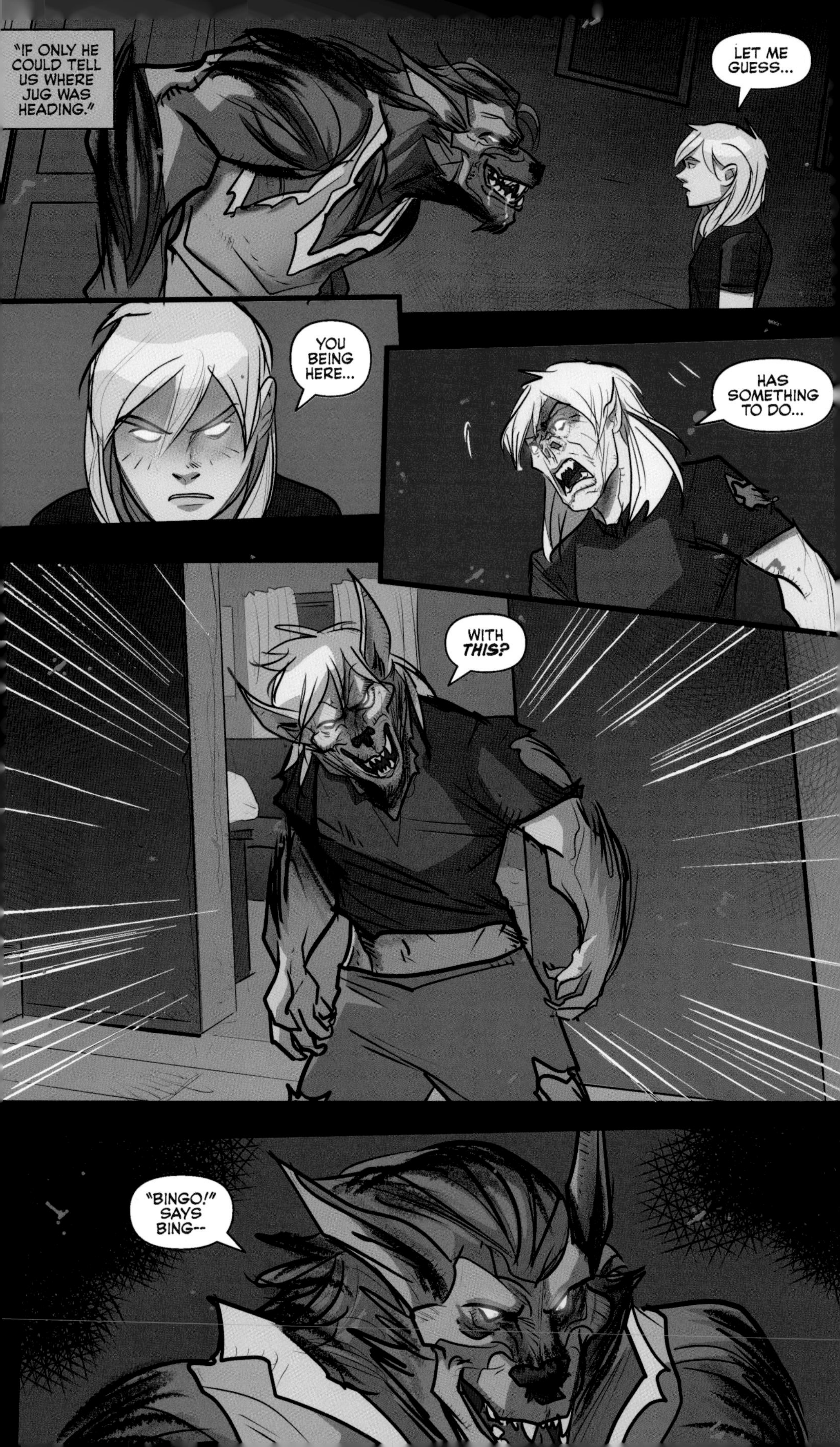
"IF ONLY HE COULD TELL US WHERE JUG WAS HEADING."
LET ME GUESS...
YOU BEING HERE...
HAS SOMETHING TO DO...
WITH *THIS?*
"BINGO!" SAYS BING--

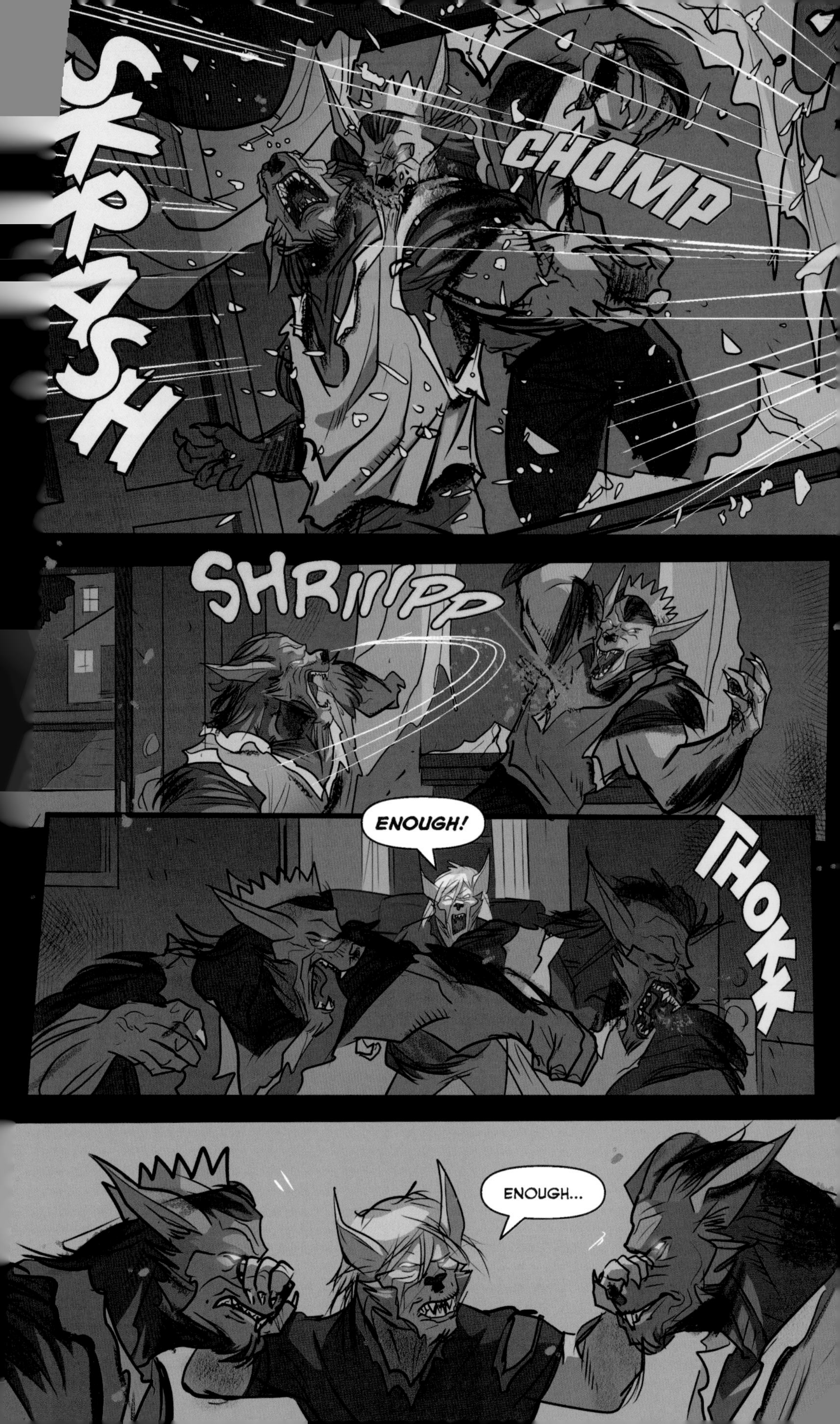
SKRASH
CHOMP
SHRIIIPP
ENOUGH!
THOKK
ENOUGH...

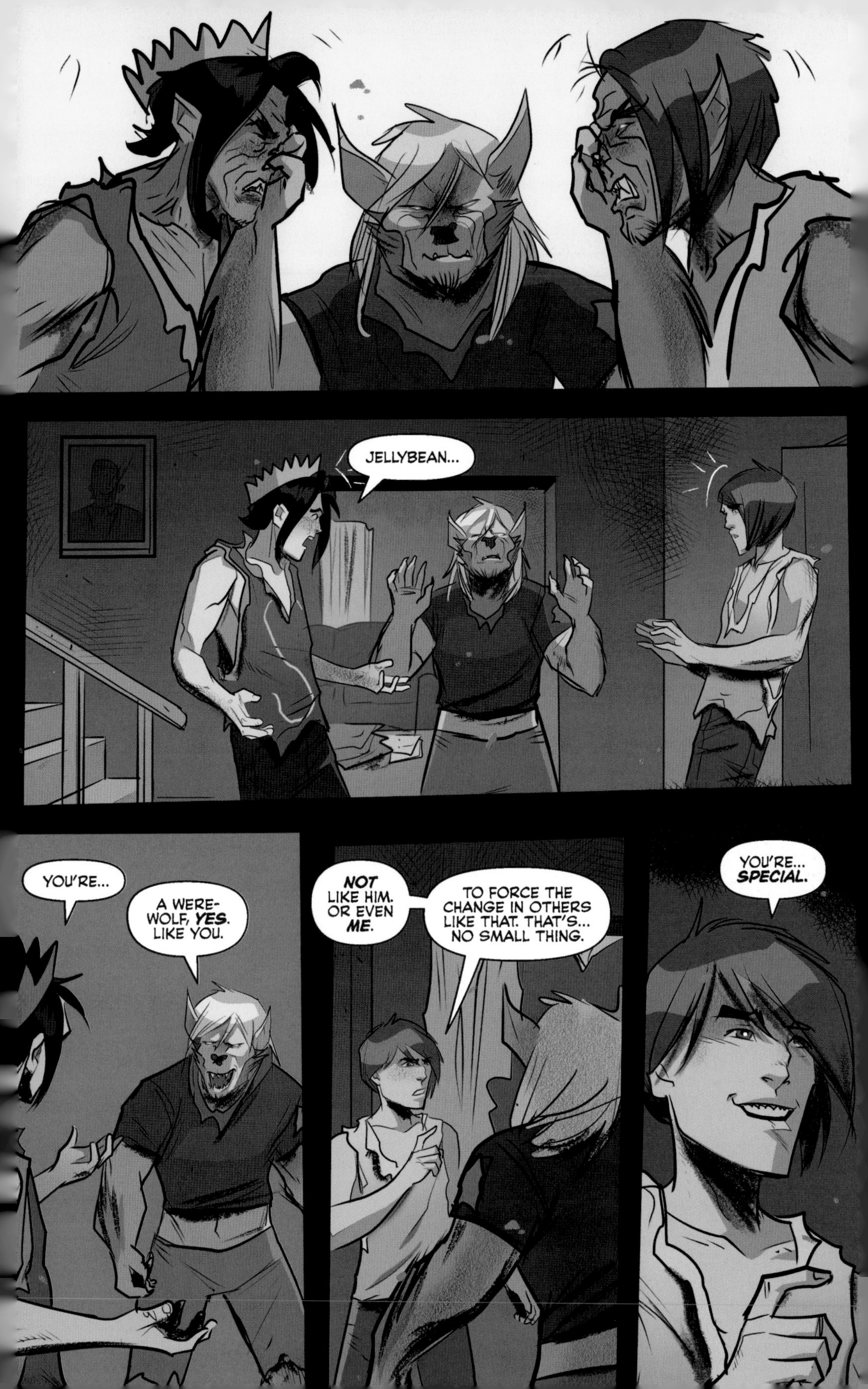
JELLYBEAN...
YOU'RE...
A WERE-WOLF, YES. LIKE YOU.
NOT LIKE HIM. OR EVEN ME.
TO FORCE THE CHANGE IN OTHERS LIKE THAT. THAT'S... NO SMALL THING.
YOU'RE... SPECIAL.

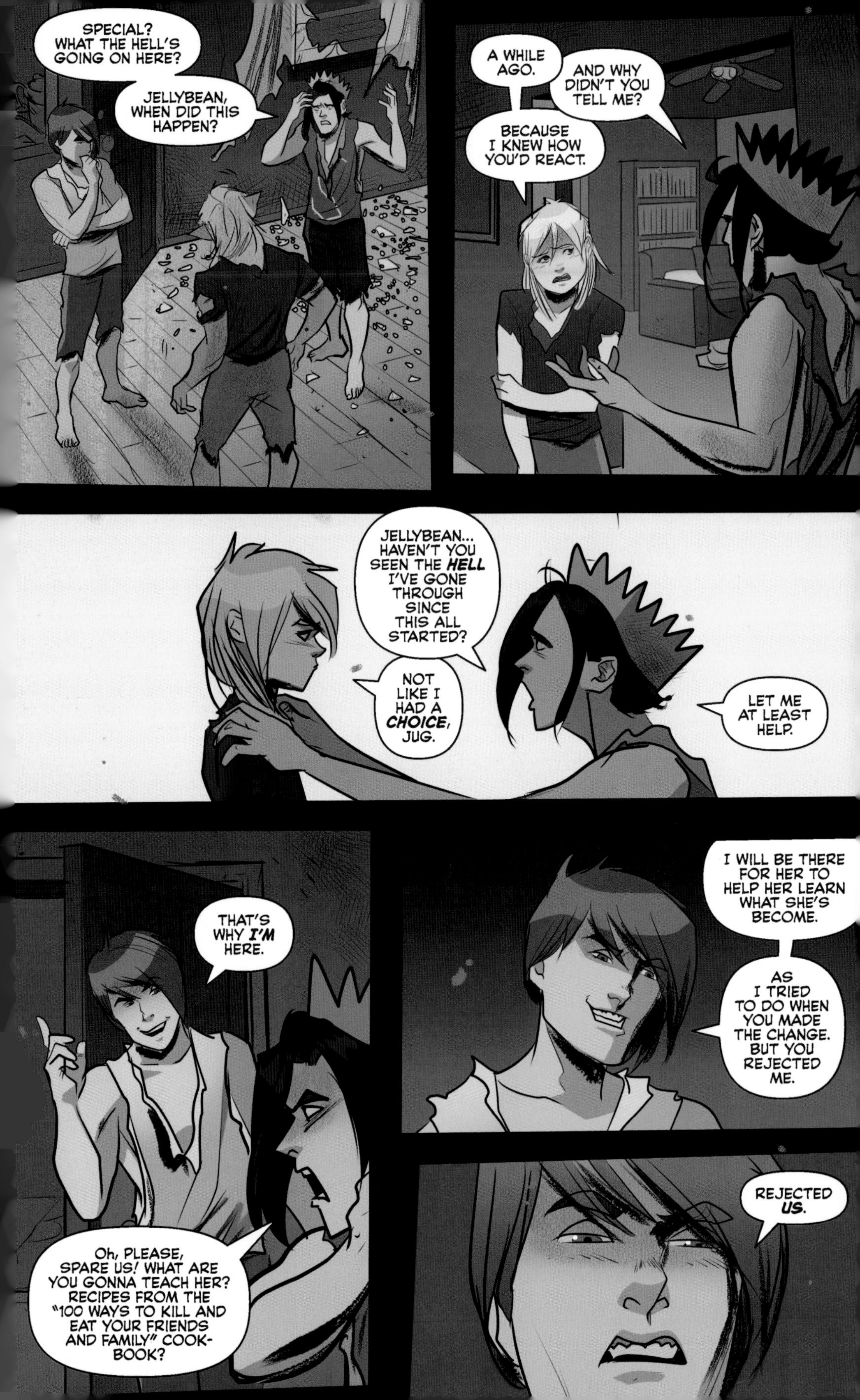
SPECIAL? WHAT THE HELL'S GOING ON HERE?
JELLYBEAN, WHEN DID THIS HAPPEN?
A WHILE AGO.
AND WHY DIDN'T YOU TELL ME?
BECAUSE I KNEW HOW YOU'D REACT.
JELLYBEAN... HAVEN'T YOU SEEN THE HELL I'VE GONE THROUGH SINCE THIS ALL STARTED?
NOT LIKE I HAD A CHOICE, JUG.
LET ME AT LEAST HELP.
THAT'S WHY I'M HERE.
I WILL BE THERE FOR HER TO HELP HER LEARN WHAT SHE'S BECOME.
AS I TRIED TO DO WHEN YOU MADE THE CHANGE. BUT YOU REJECTED ME.
Oh, PLEASE, SPARE US! WHAT ARE YOU GONNA TEACH HER? RECIPES FROM THE "100 WAYS TO KILL AND EAT YOUR FRIENDS AND FAMILY" COOK-BOOK?
REJECTED US.

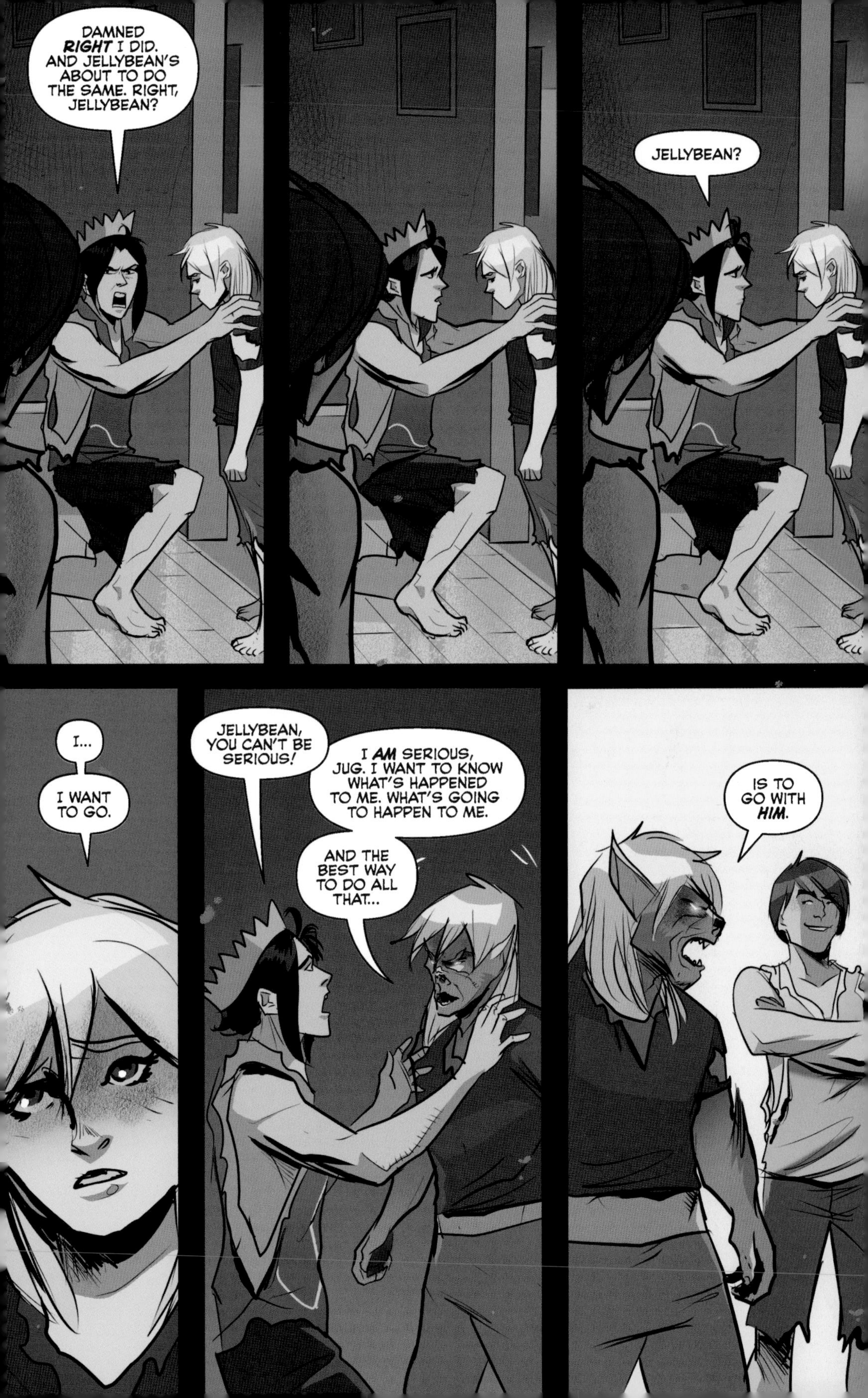
DAMNED *RIGHT* I DID. AND JELLYBEAN'S ABOUT TO DO THE SAME. RIGHT, JELLYBEAN?
JELLYBEAN?
I...
I WANT TO GO.
JELLYBEAN, YOU CAN'T BE SERIOUS!
I *AM* SERIOUS, JUG. I WANT TO KNOW WHAT'S HAPPENED TO ME. WHAT'S GOING TO HAPPEN TO ME.
AND THE BEST WAY TO DO ALL THAT...
IS TO GO WITH *HIM*.

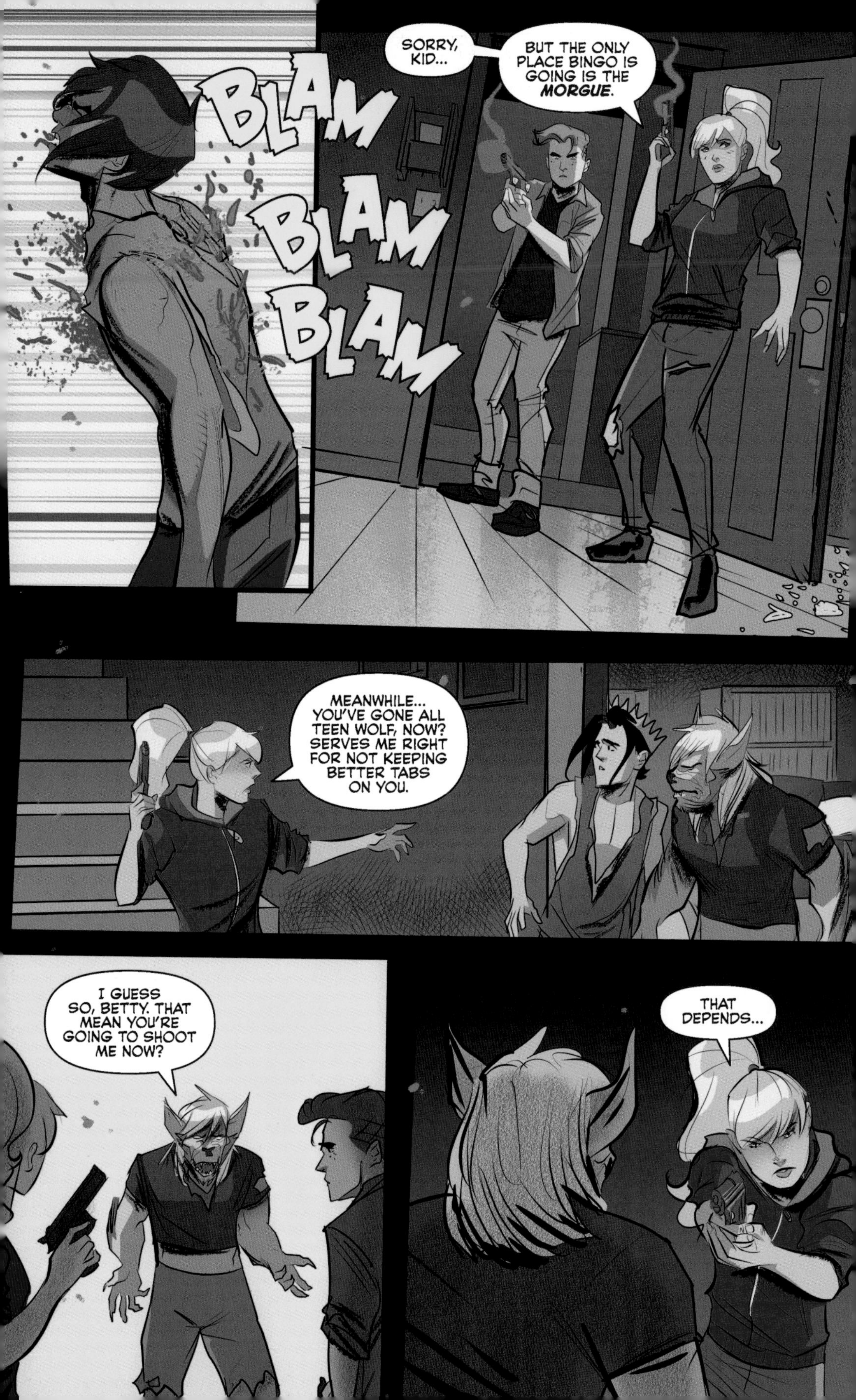
BLAM
BLAM
BLAM
SORRY, KID...
BUT THE ONLY PLACE BINGO IS GOING IS THE MORGUE.
MEANWHILE... YOU'VE GONE ALL TEEN WOLF, NOW? SERVES ME RIGHT FOR NOT KEEPING BETTER TABS ON YOU.
I GUESS SO, BETTY. THAT MEAN YOU'RE GOING TO SHOOT ME NOW?
THAT DEPENDS...

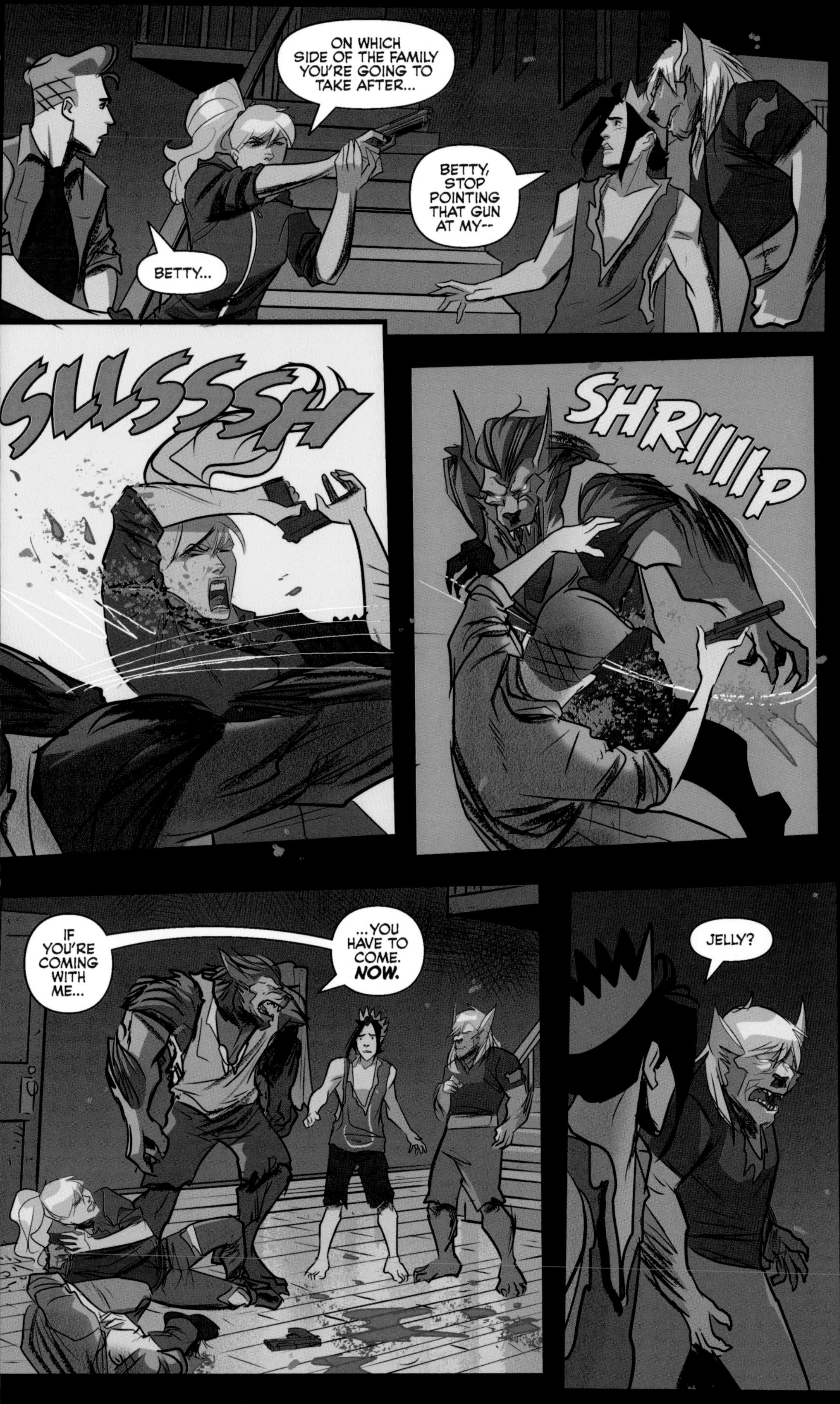
ON WHICH SIDE OF THE FAMILY YOU'RE GOING TO TAKE AFTER...
BETTY...
BETTY, STOP POINTING THAT GUN AT MY--
SLLSSSH
SHRIIIIP
IF YOU'RE COMING WITH ME...
...YOU HAVE TO COME. **NOW.**
JELLY?

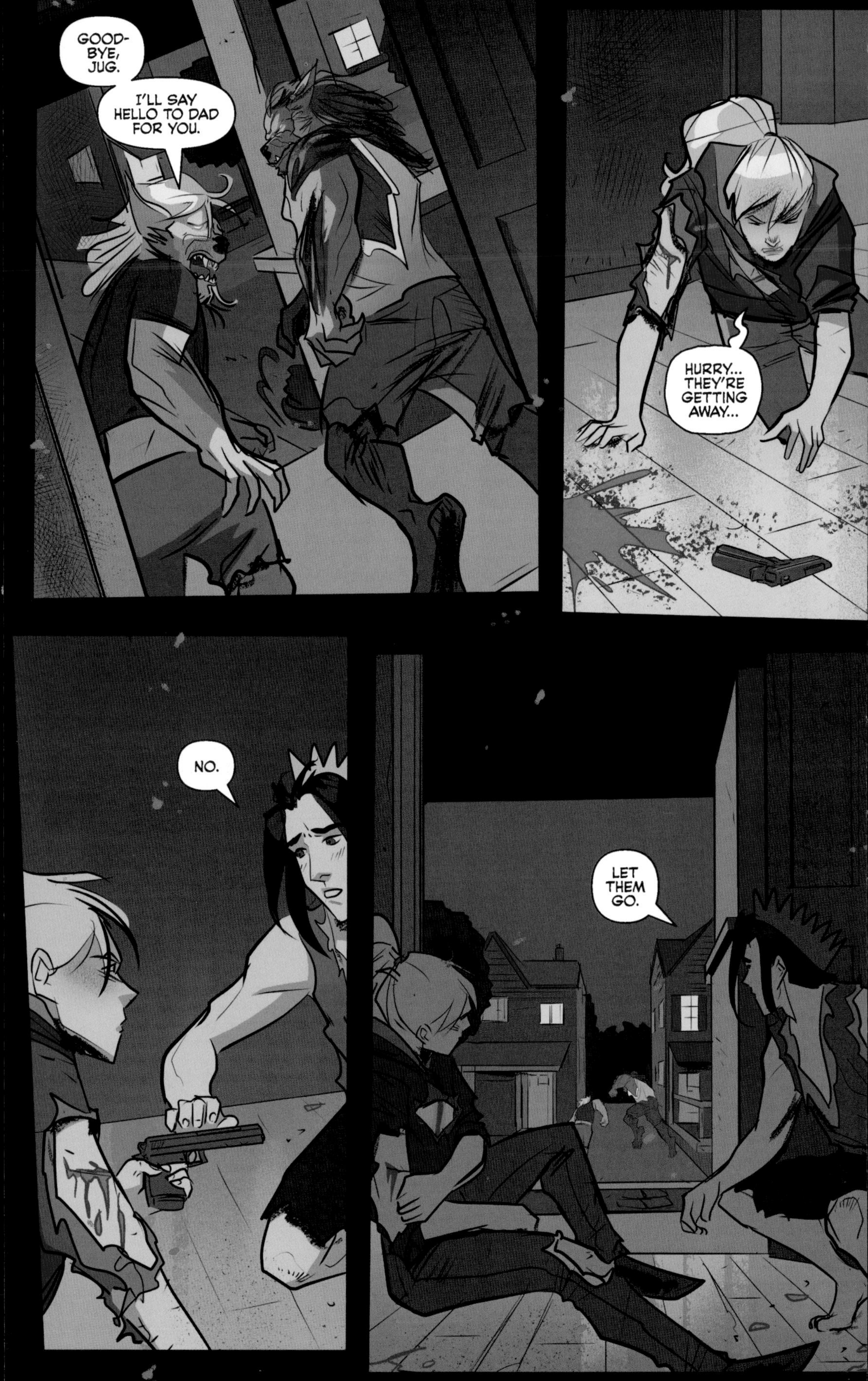
GOOD-BYE, JUG.
I'LL SAY HELLO TO DAD FOR YOU.
HURRY... THEY'RE GETTING AWAY...
NO.
LET THEM GO.

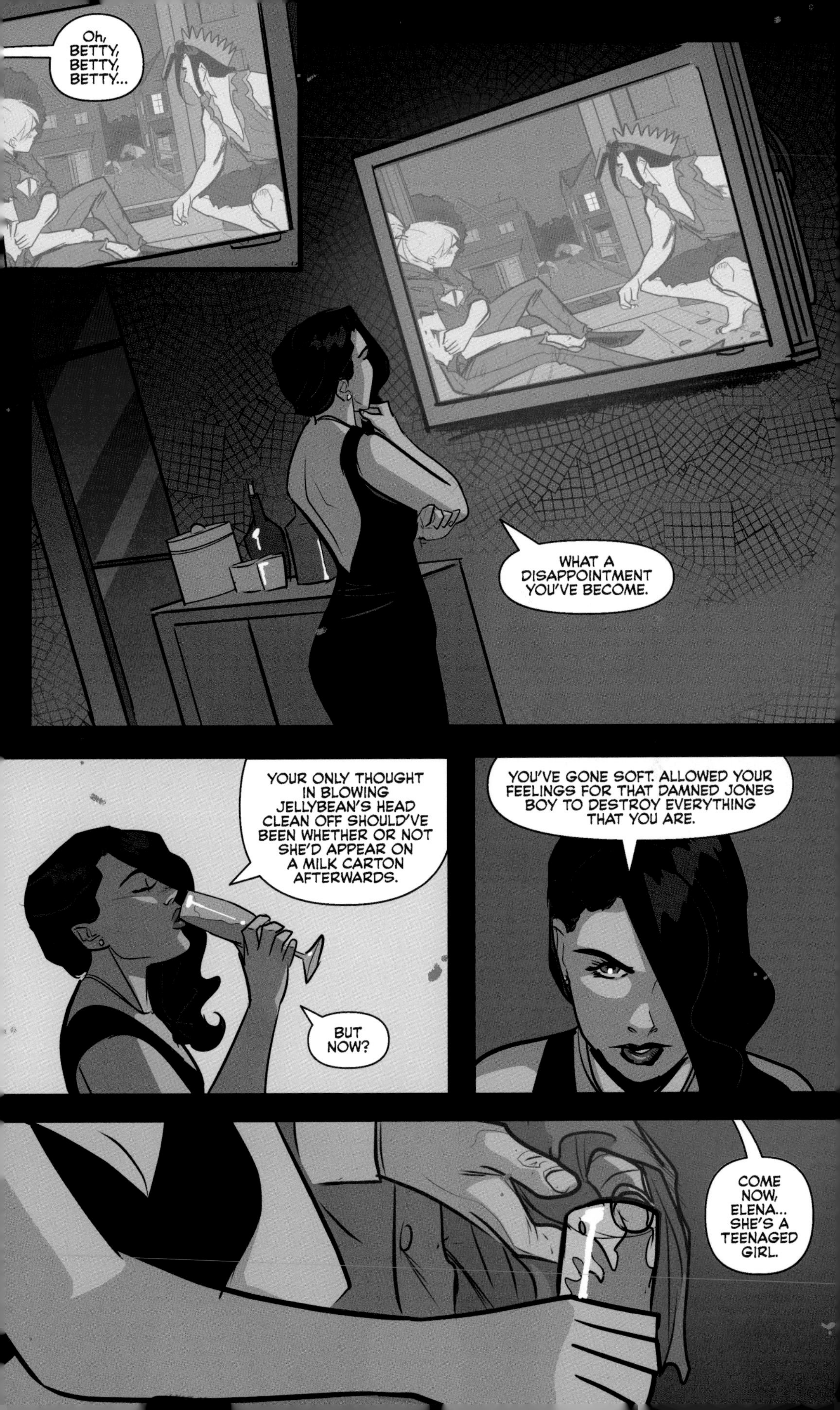
Oh, BETTY, BETTY, BETTY...
WHAT A DISAPPOINTMENT YOU'VE BECOME.
YOUR ONLY THOUGHT IN BLOWING JELLYBEAN'S HEAD CLEAN OFF SHOULD'VE BEEN WHETHER OR NOT SHE'D APPEAR ON A MILK CARTON AFTERWARDS.
BUT NOW?
YOU'VE GONE SOFT. ALLOWED YOUR FEELINGS FOR THAT DAMNED JONES BOY TO DESTROY EVERYTHING THAT YOU ARE.
COME NOW, ELENA... SHE'S A TEENAGED GIRL.

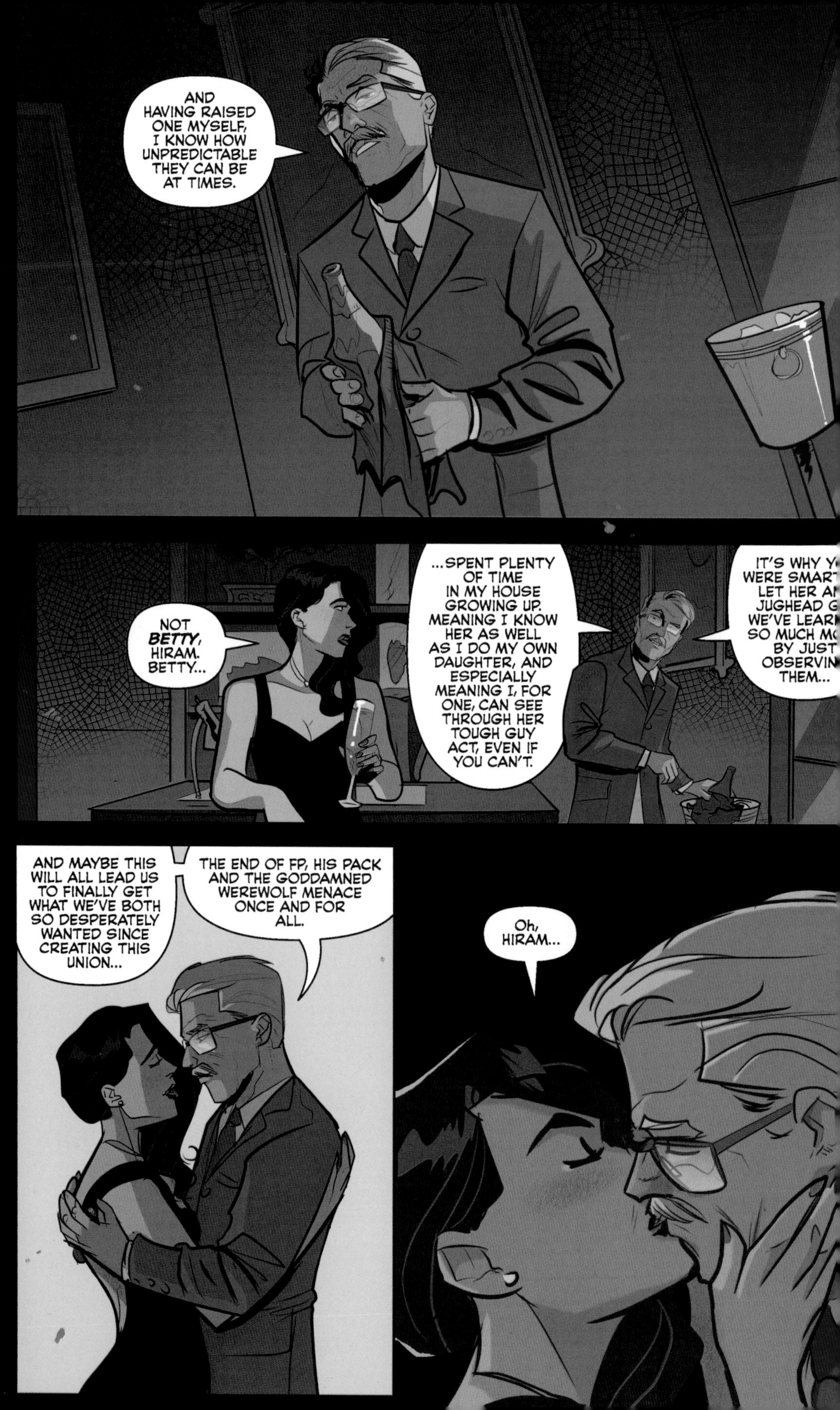
AND HAVING RAISED ONE MYSELF, I KNOW HOW UNPREDICTABLE THEY CAN BE AT TIMES.
NOT *BETTY*, HIRAM. BETTY...
...SPENT PLENTY OF TIME IN MY HOUSE GROWING UP. MEANING I KNOW HER AS WELL AS I DO MY OWN DAUGHTER, AND ESPECIALLY MEANING I, FOR ONE, CAN SEE THROUGH HER TOUGH GUY ACT, EVEN IF YOU CAN'T.
IT'S WHY Y WERE SMAR LET HER A JUGHEAD WE'VE LEAR SO MUCH M BY JUST OBSERVIN THEM...
AND MAYBE THIS WILL ALL LEAD US TO FINALLY GET WHAT WE'VE BOTH SO DESPERATELY WANTED SINCE CREATING THIS UNION...
THE END OF FP, HIS PACK AND THE GODDAMNED WEREWOLF MENACE ONCE AND FOR ALL.
Oh, HIRAM...

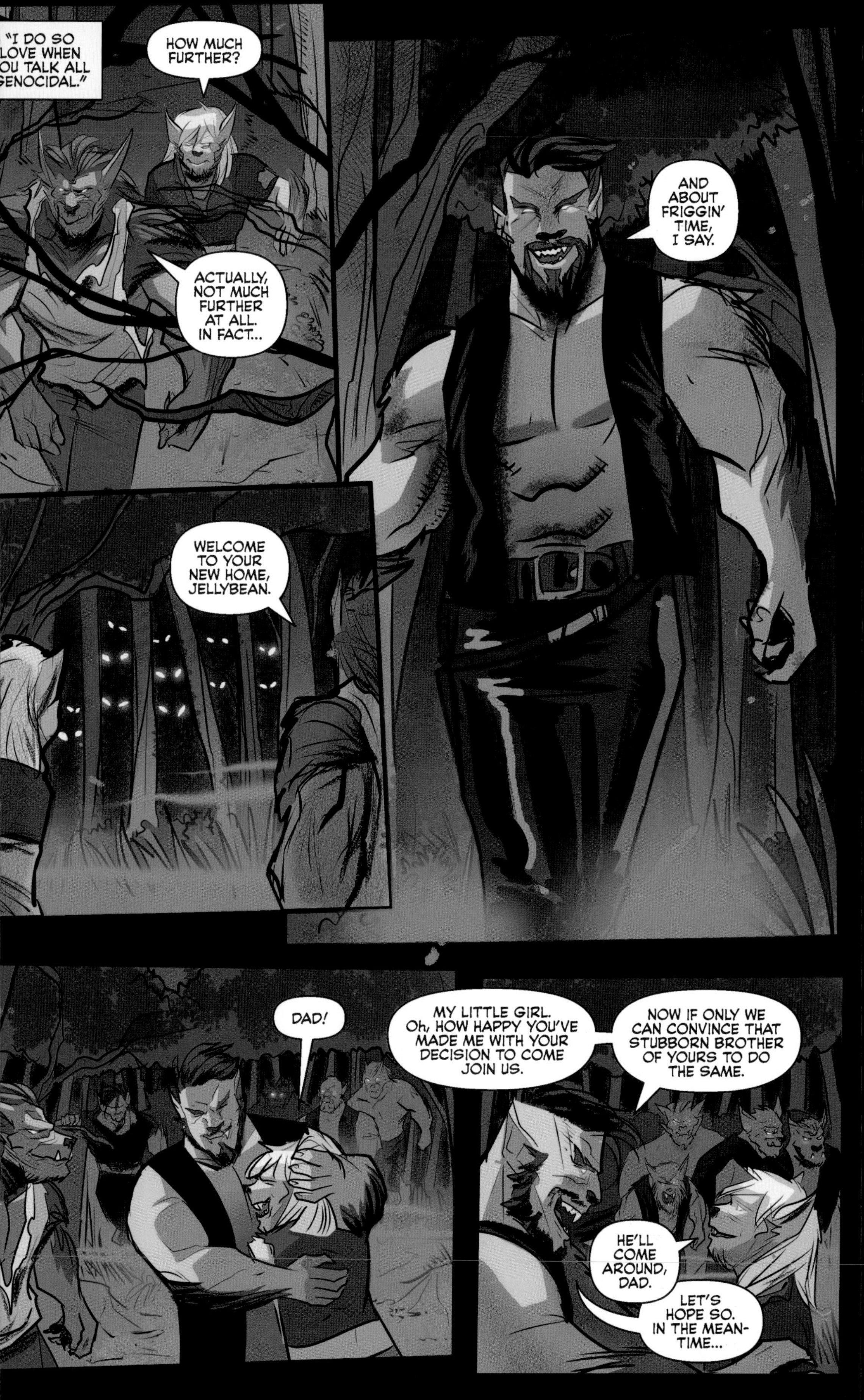
"I DO SO
LOVE WHEN
YOU TALK ALL
GENOCIDAL."
HOW MUCH FURTHER?
ACTUALLY, NOT MUCH FURTHER AT ALL. IN FACT...
AND ABOUT FRIGGIN' TIME, I SAY.
WELCOME TO YOUR NEW HOME, JELLYBEAN.
DAD!
MY LITTLE GIRL. Oh, HOW HAPPY YOU'VE MADE ME WITH YOUR DECISION TO COME JOIN US.
NOW IF ONLY WE CAN CONVINCE THAT STUBBORN BROTHER OF YOURS TO DO THE SAME.
HE'LL COME AROUND, DAD.
LET'S HOPE SO. IN THE MEAN-TIME...

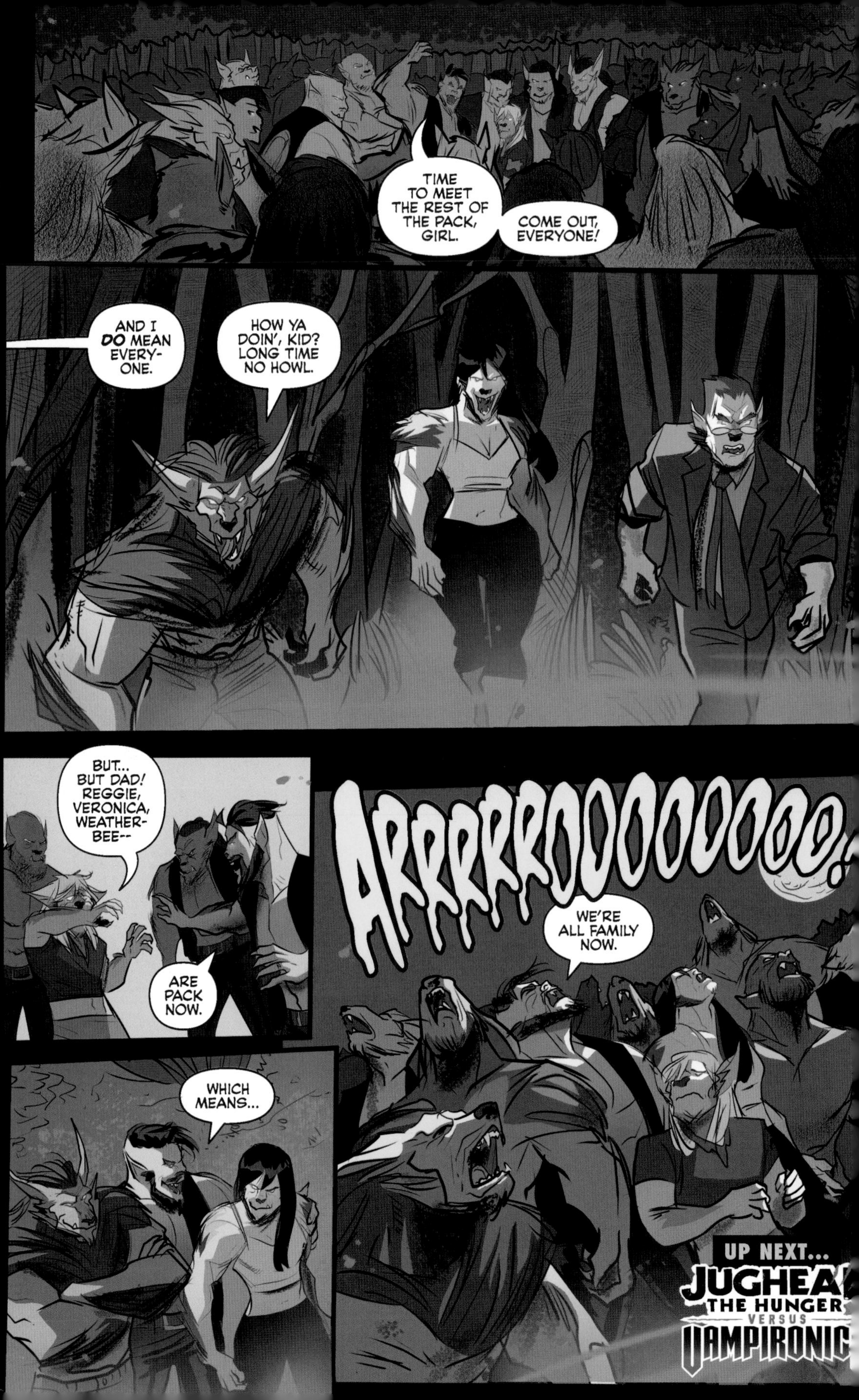
TIME TO MEET THE REST OF THE PACK, GIRL.
COME OUT, EVERYONE!
AND I DO MEAN EVERY-ONE.
HOW YA DOIN', KID? LONG TIME NO HOWL.
BUT... BUT DAD! REGGIE, VERONICA, WEATHER-BEE--
ARE PACK NOW.
WHICH MEANS...
ARRRRROOOOOOOO...!
WE'RE ALL FAMILY NOW.
UP NEXT...
JUGHEAD THE HUNGER VERSUS VAMPIRONIC

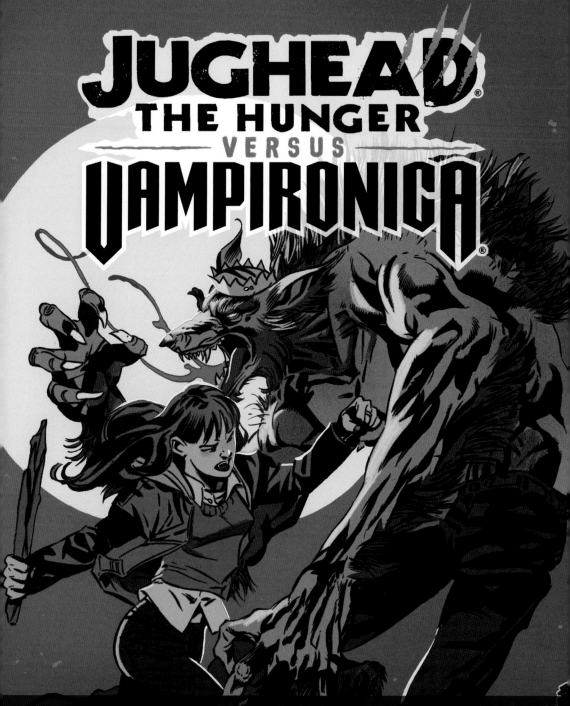

JUGHEAD THE HUNGER VERSUS VAMPIRONICA

n the world of JUGHEAD THE HUNGER, there are no vampires, having been wiped out in their great war with the werewolves. In he VAMPIRONICA universe, the opposite is the case, as it was the ampires who were the victors. So what happens when these two eternal nemies are brought together again? Whatever it is, it can't be good for poor ol' Jug and Vampironica, you can count on that much...

VARIANT COVER GALLERY

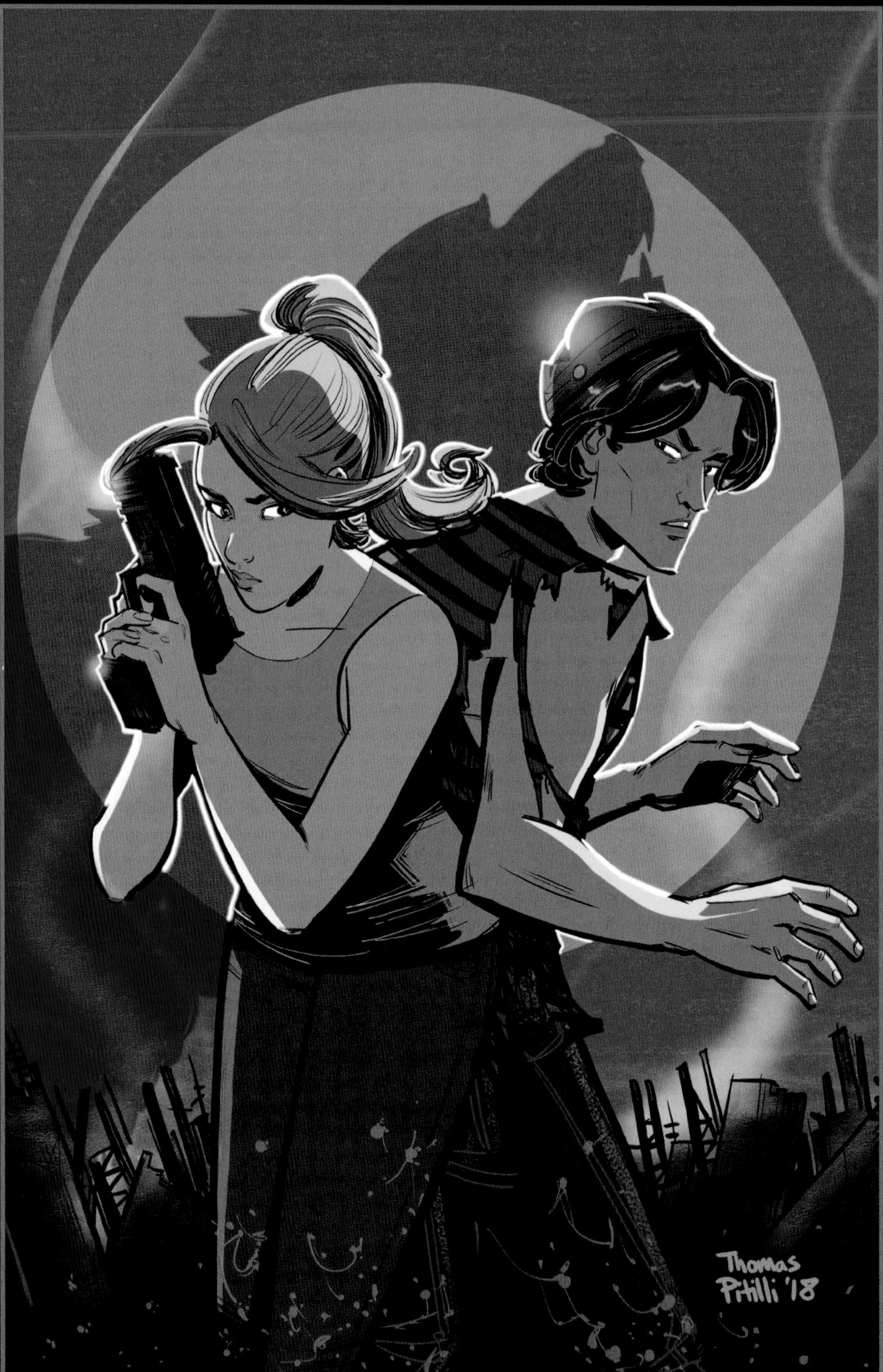
Thomas
Pitilli '18

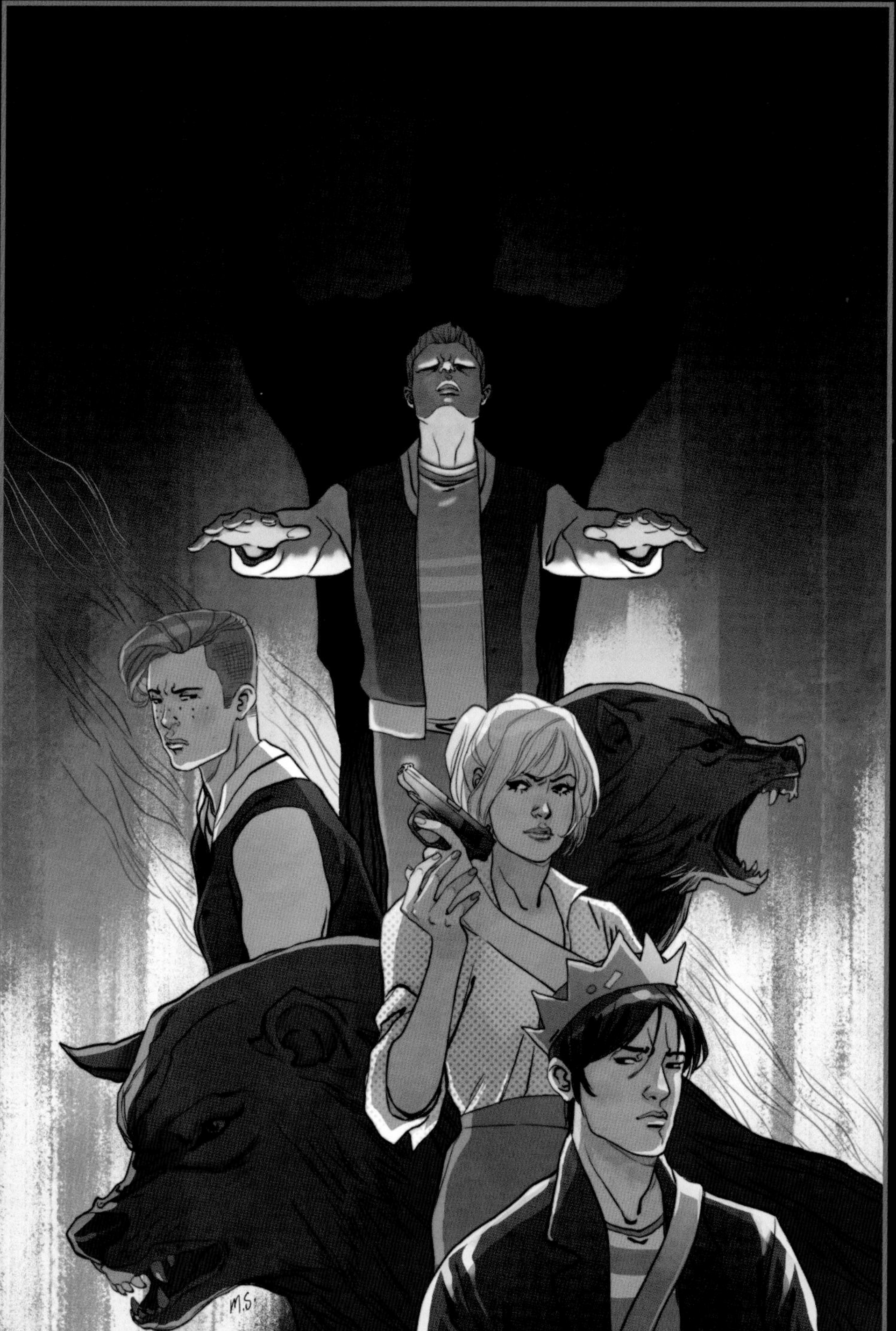

ISSUE NINE - Marguerite Sauvage

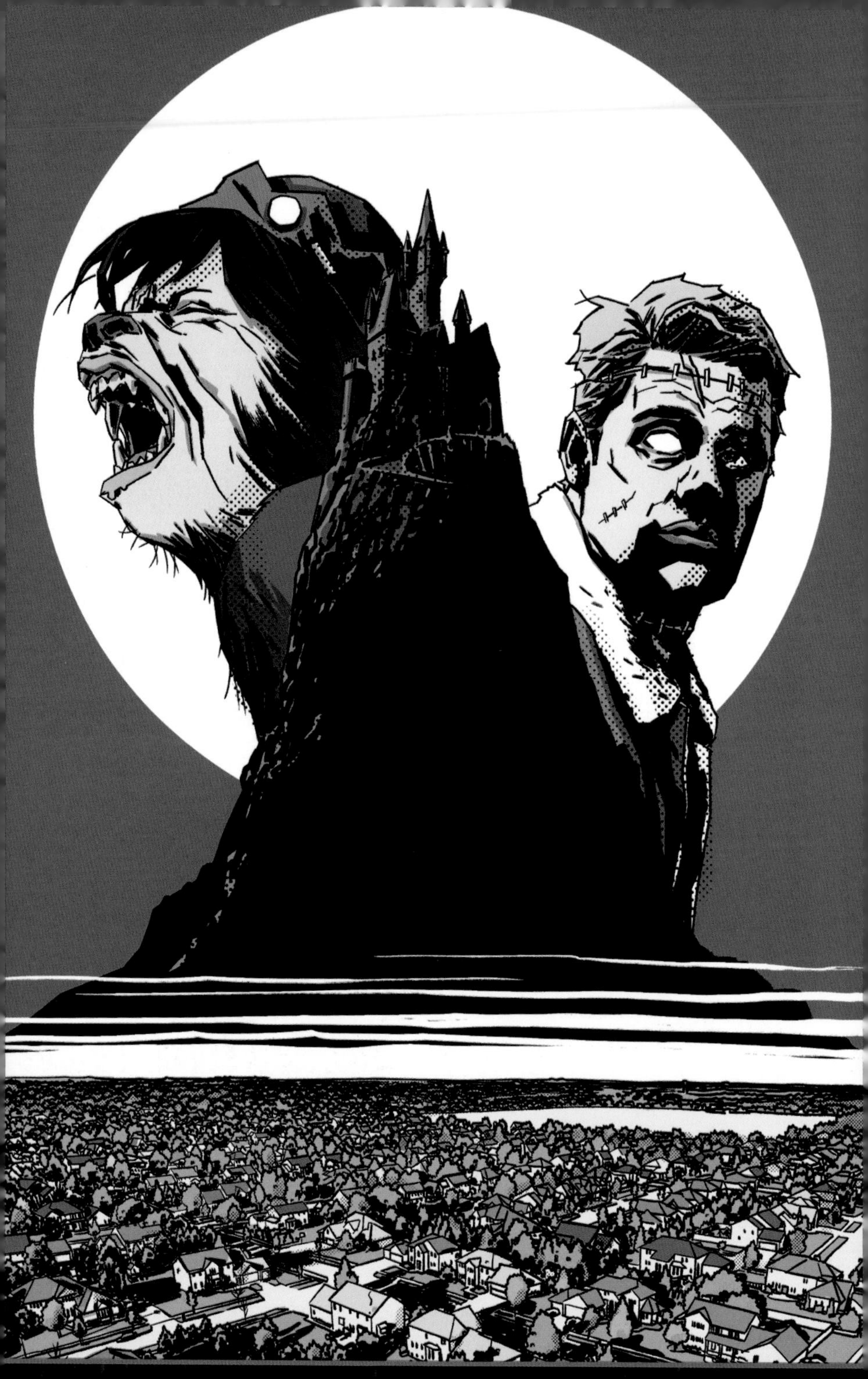

ISSUE TEN - Matthew Dow Smith

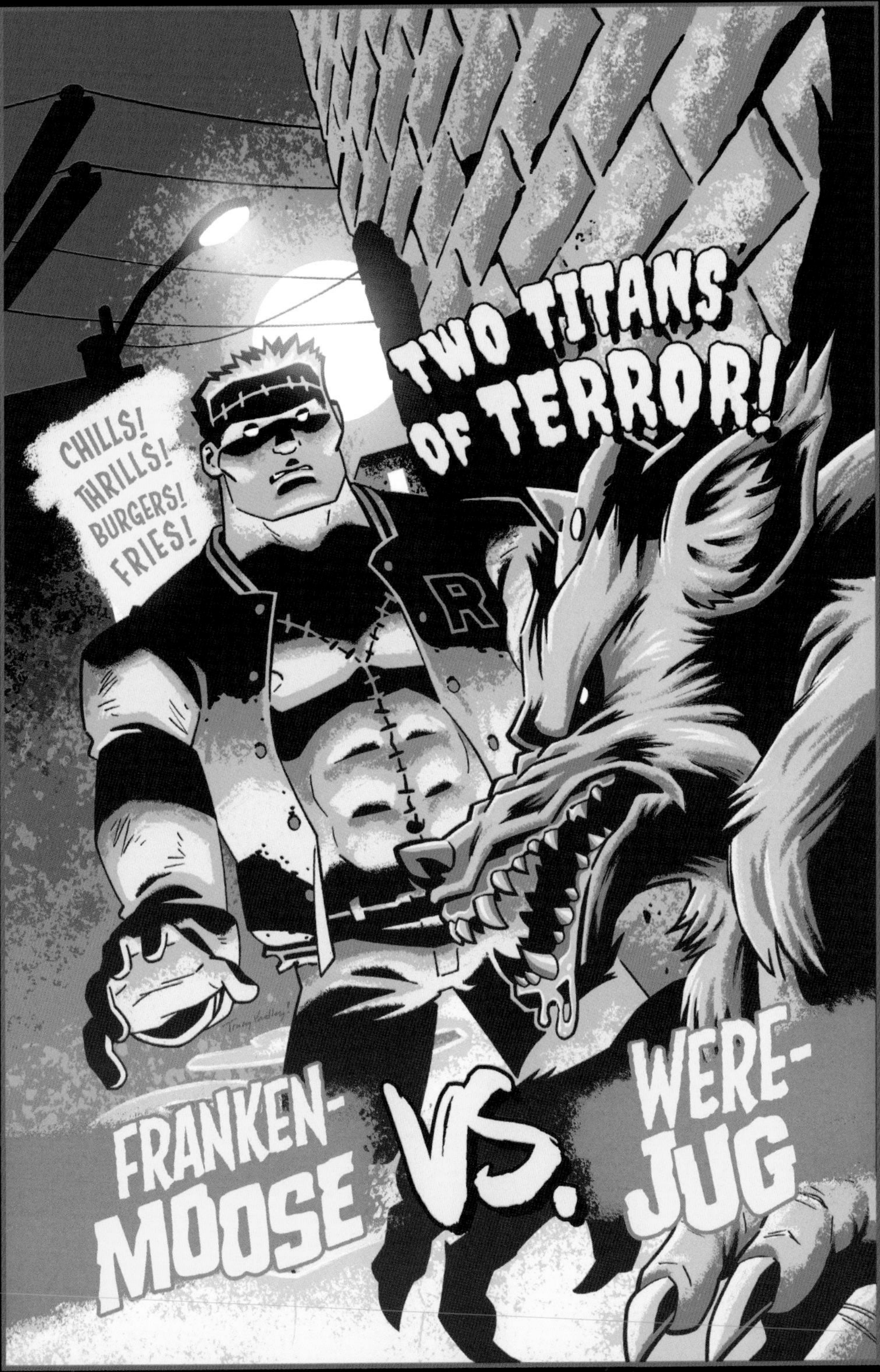
TWO TITANS OF TERROR!
CHILL$! THRILL$! BURGER$! FRIE$!
FRANKEN-MOOSE VS. WERE-JUG

ISSUE TEN - Tracy Yardley

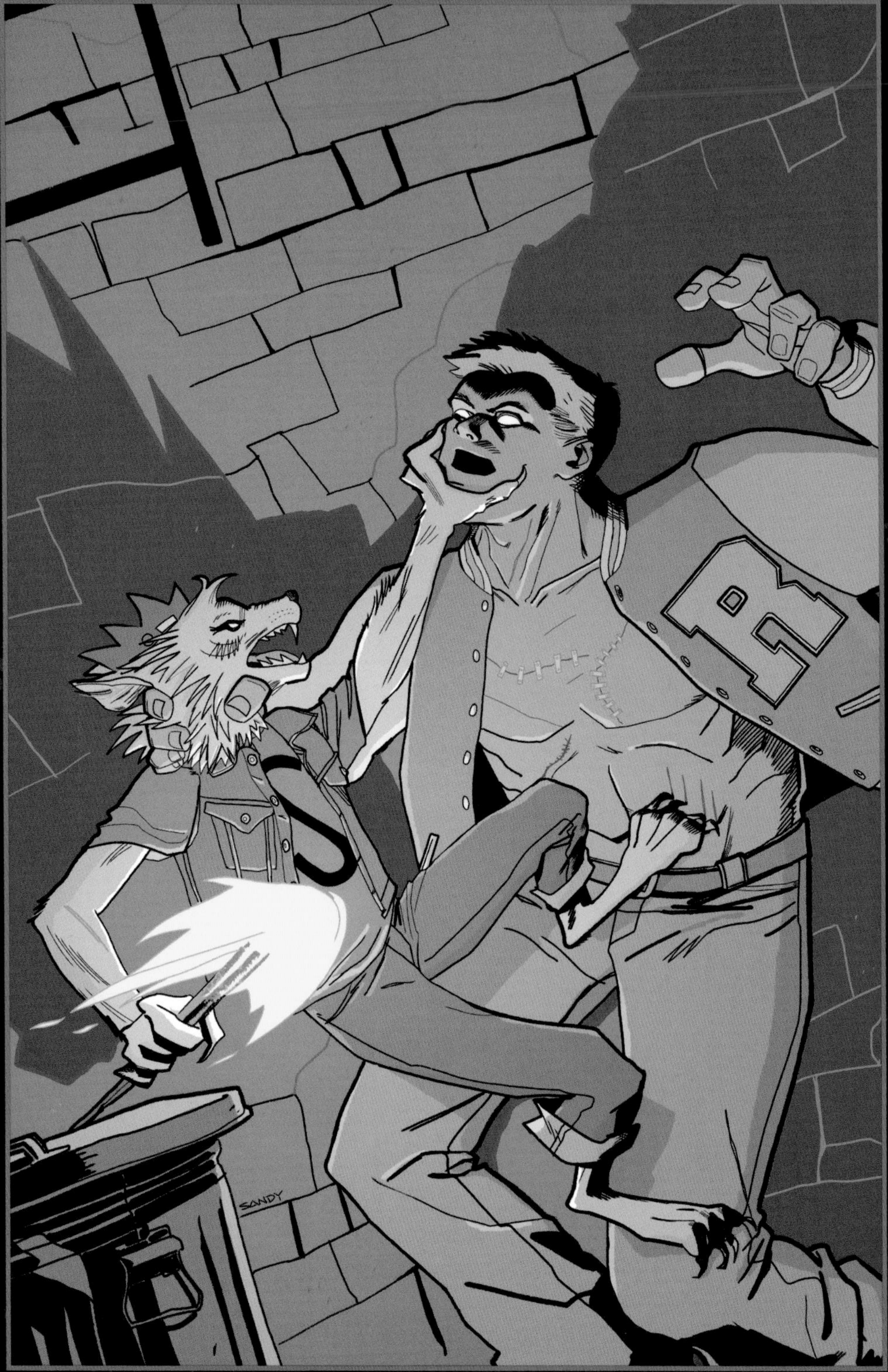
SANDY

ISSUE ELEVEN - Sandy Jarrell

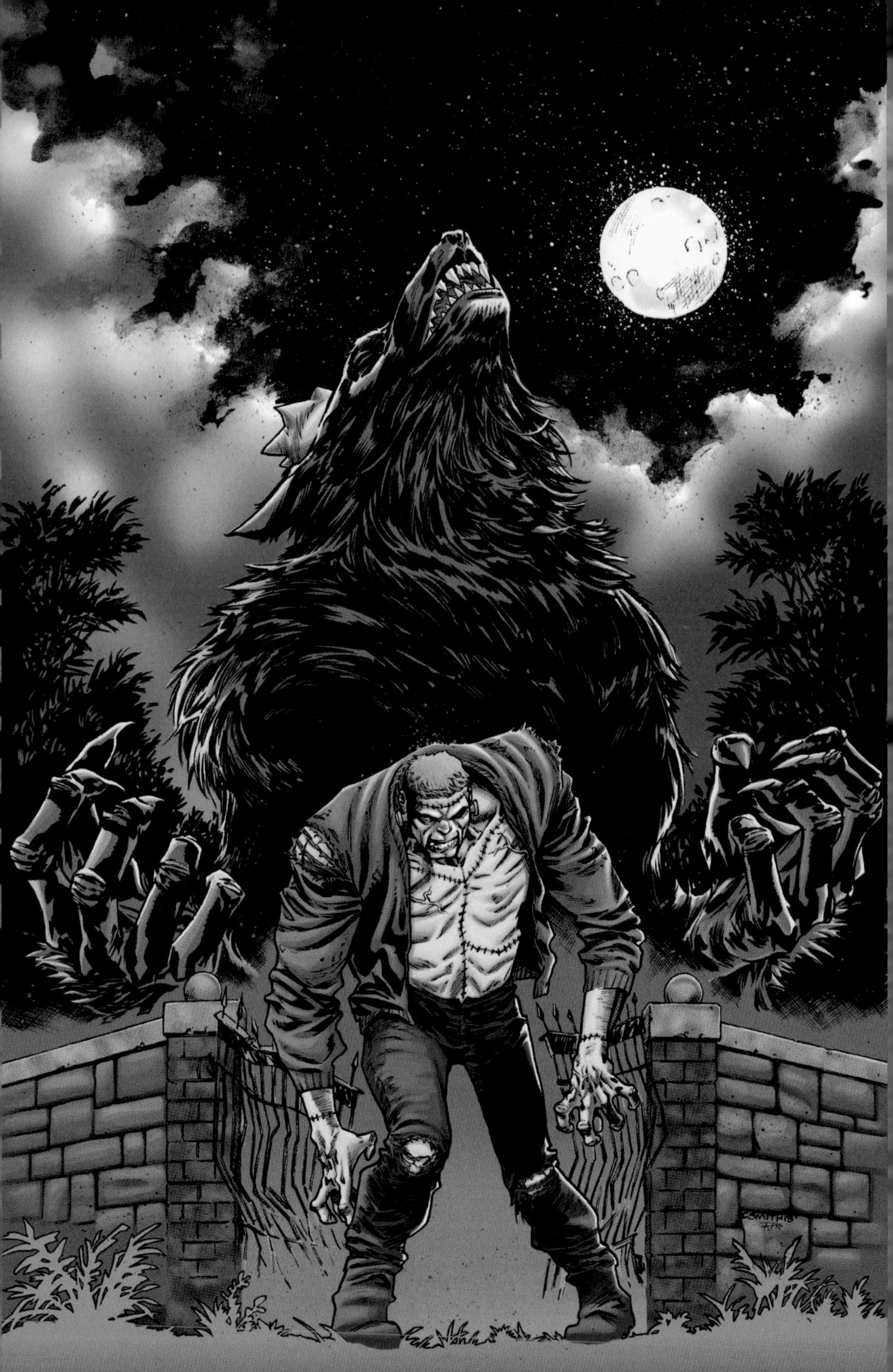

ISSU Smith

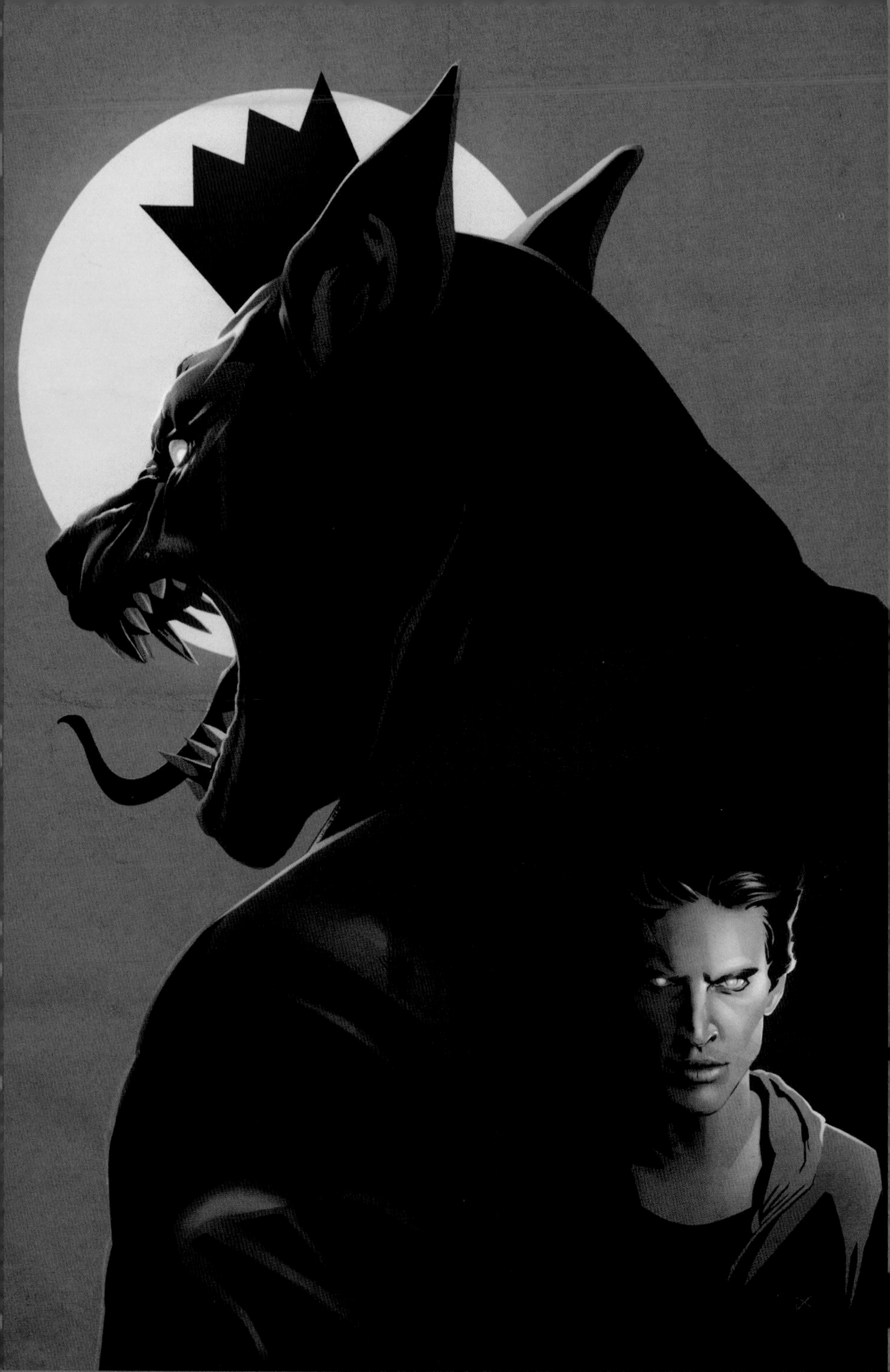

ISSUE TWELVE - Dennis Calero

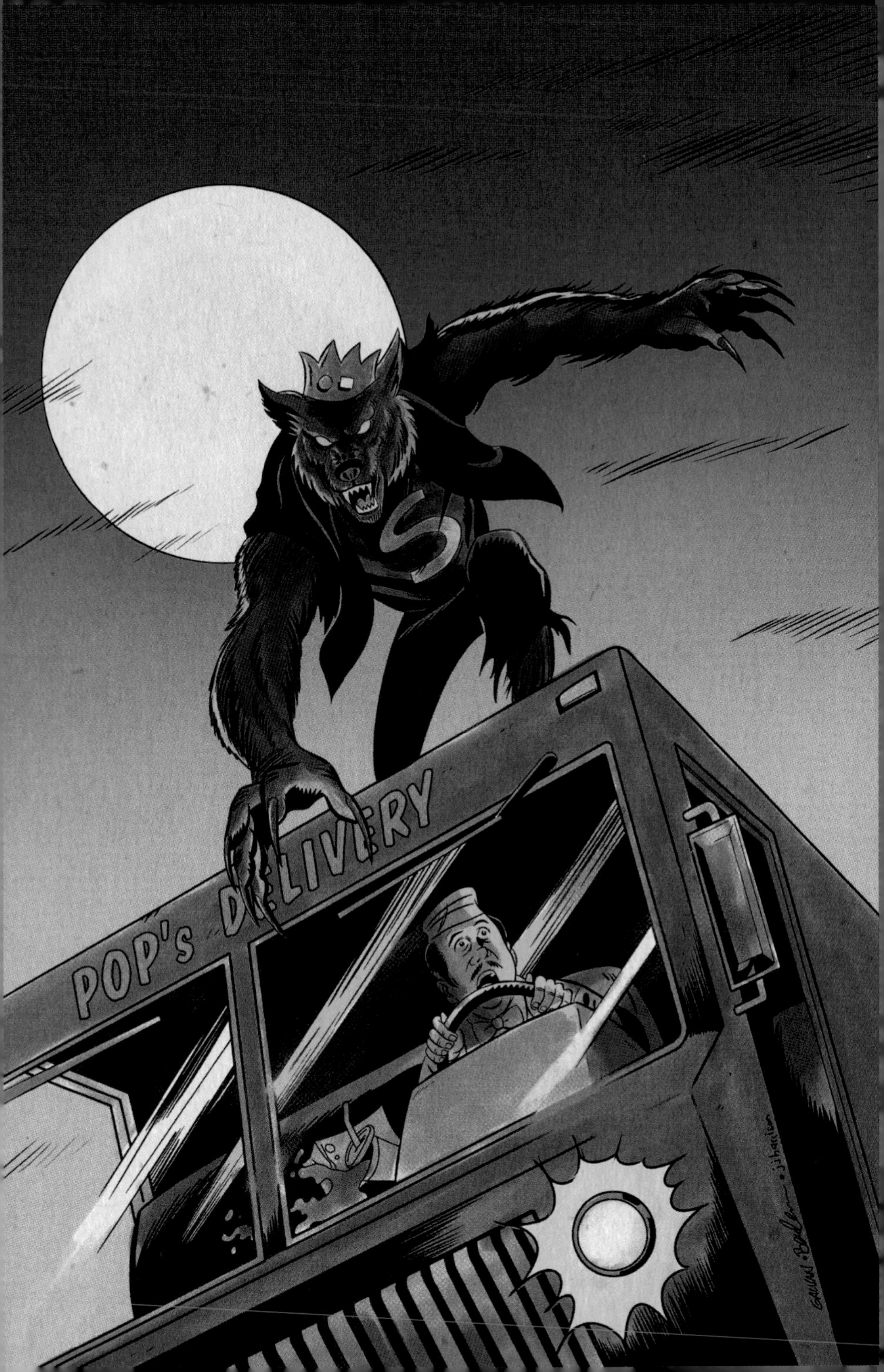
POP's DELIVERY

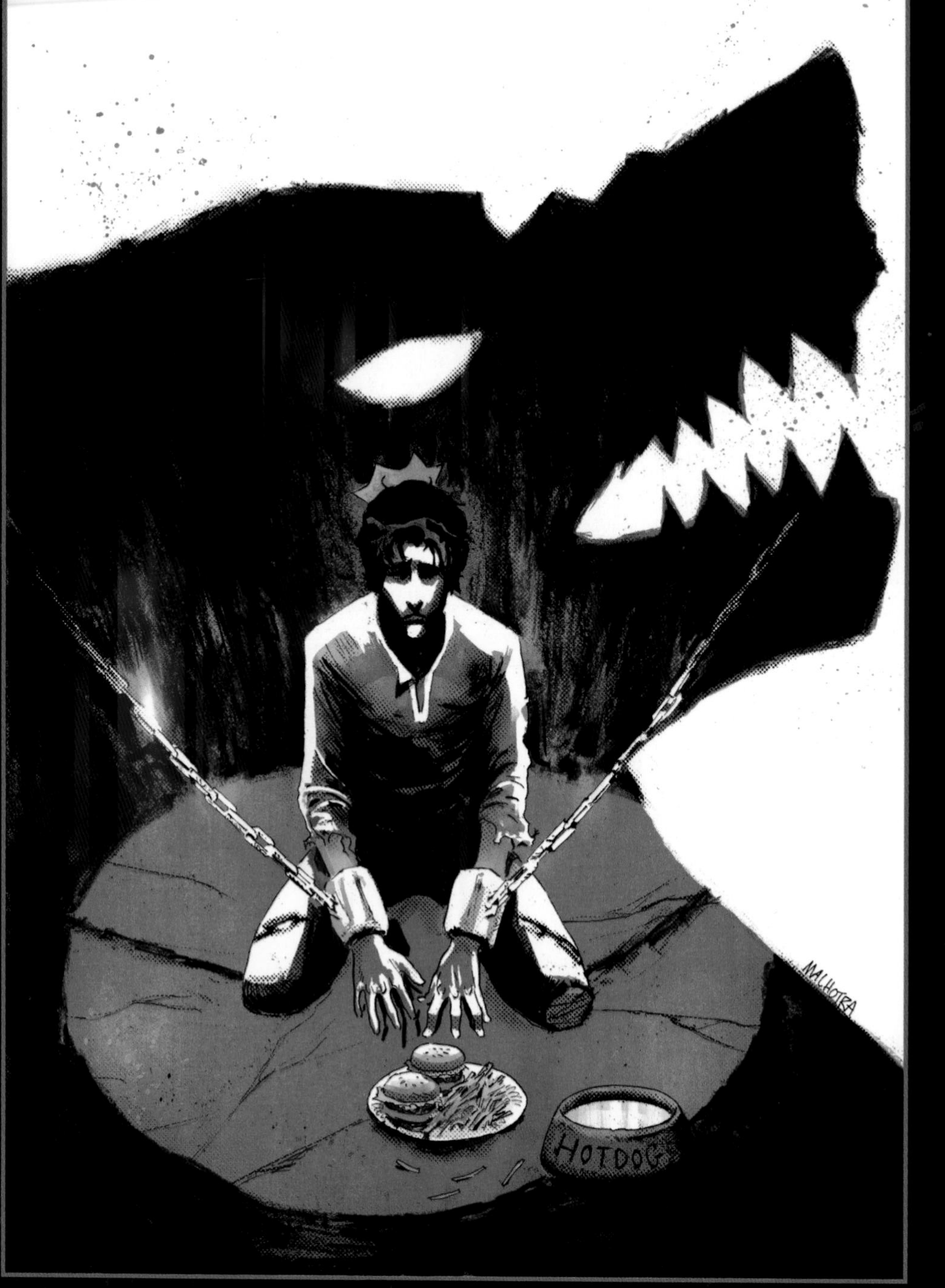
MALHOTRA
HOTDOG

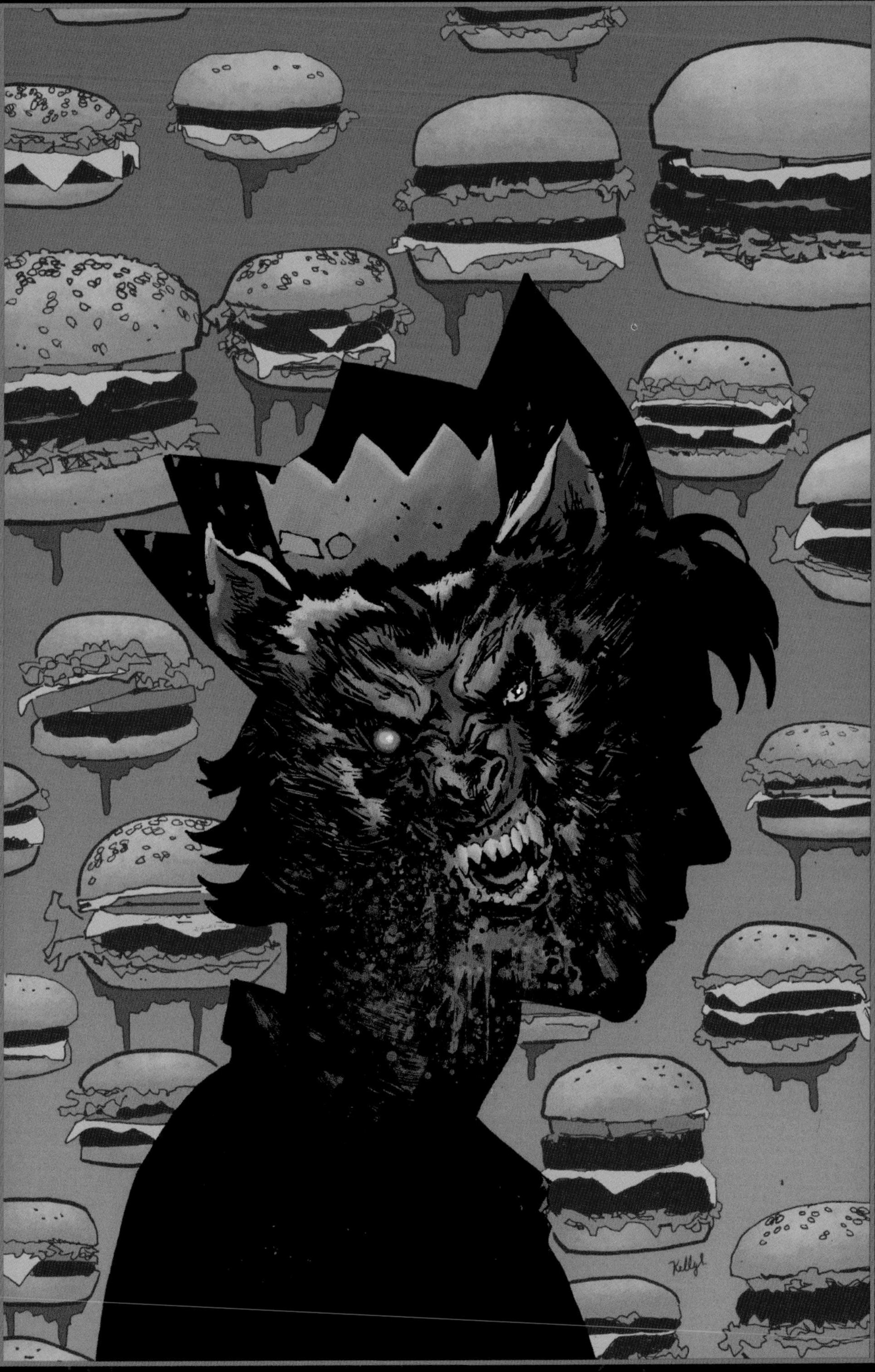

ISSUE THIRTEEN - **Greg Scott**

BONUS STORY

Cheryl and Jason Blossom are a pair of seemingly normal kids in Riverdale. They're wealthy, popular and likeable—but they also harbor a deep, dark secret—one of the Blossom Twins is the Anti-Christ. Both want the title, and no one in Riverdale is safe.

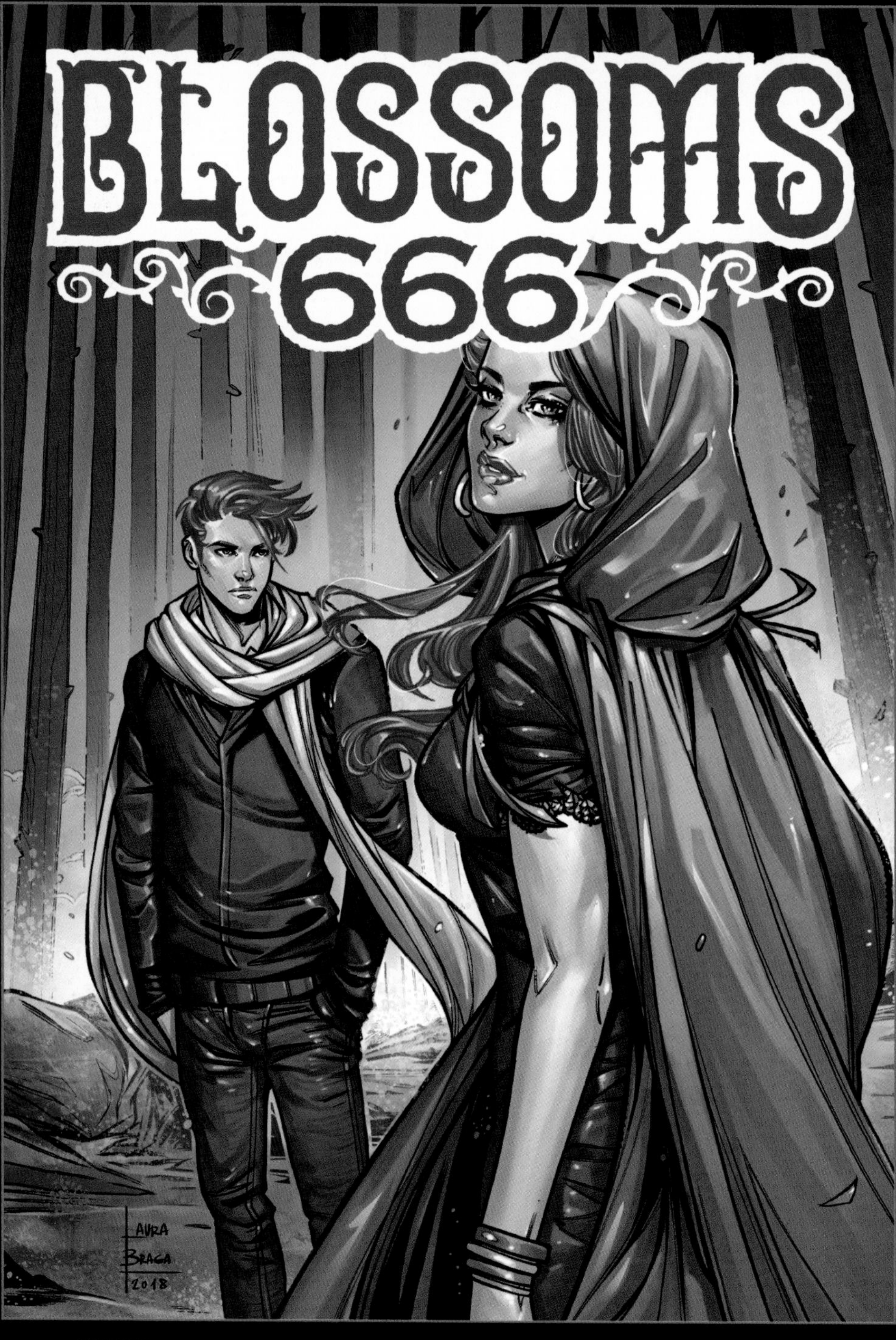
BLOSSOMS
666
LAURA
BRAGA
2018

STORY	ART	COLORS	LETTERS
Cullen Bunn	Laura Braga	Matt Herms	Jack Morelli

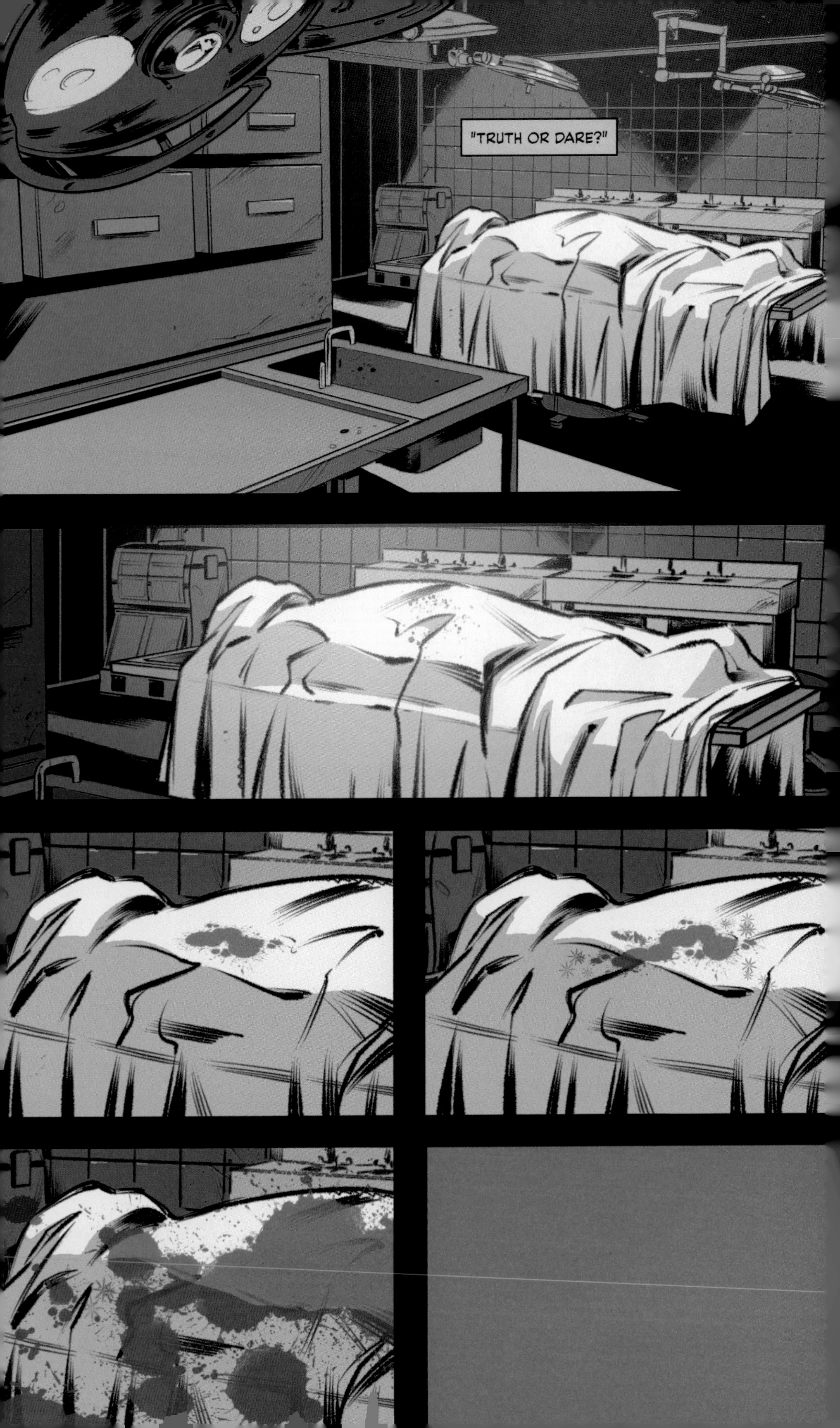
"TRUTH OR DARE?"

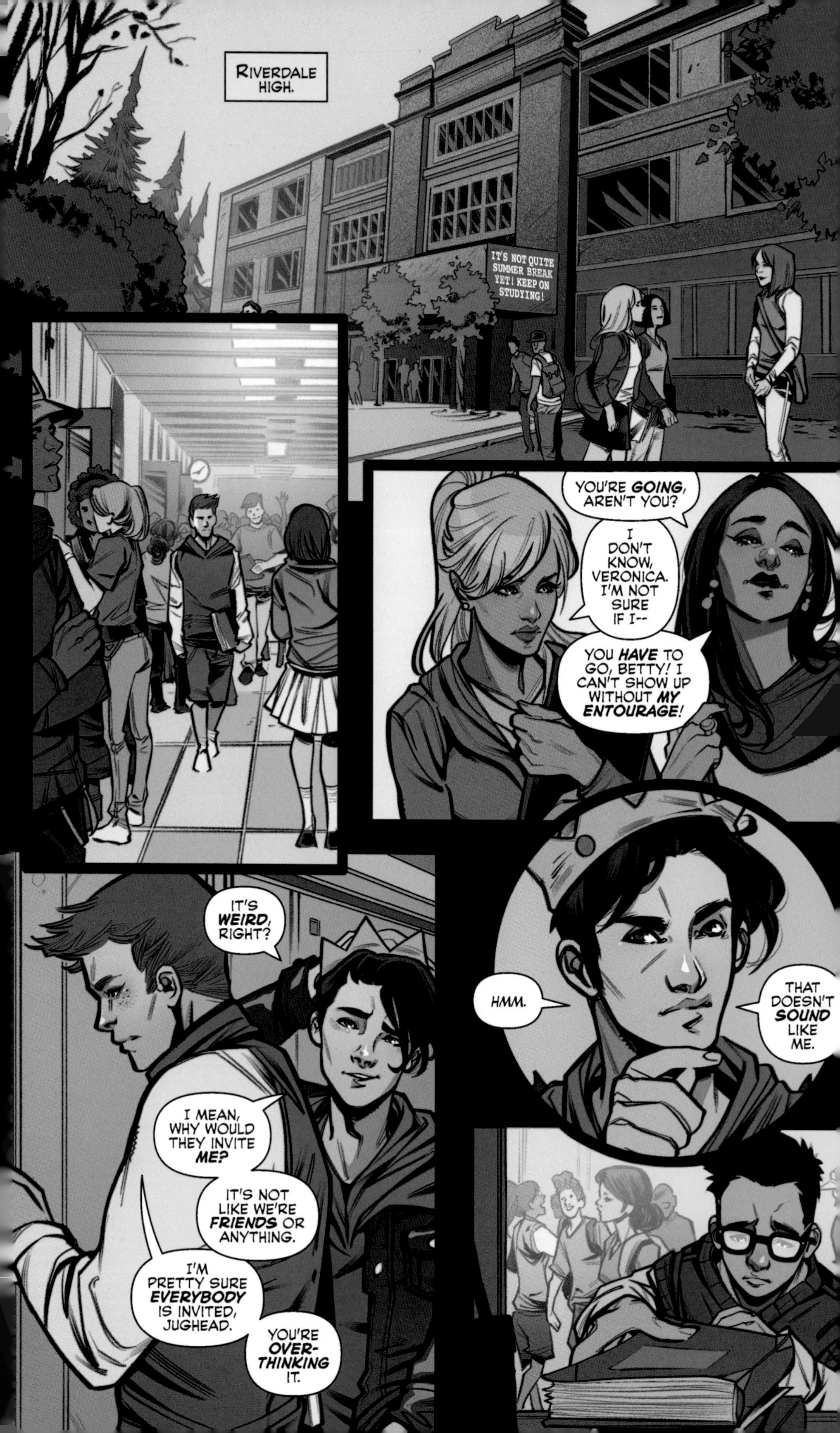
RIVERDALE HIGH.
IT'S NOT QUITE SUMMER BREAK YET! KEEP ON STUDYING!
YOU'RE GOING, AREN'T YOU?
I DON'T KNOW, VERONICA. I'M NOT SURE IF I--
YOU HAVE TO GO, BETTY! I CAN'T SHOW UP WITHOUT MY ENTOURAGE!
IT'S WEIRD, RIGHT?
I MEAN, WHY WOULD THEY INVITE ME?
IT'S NOT LIKE WE'RE FRIENDS OR ANYTHING.
I'M PRETTY SURE EVERYBODY IS INVITED, JUGHEAD.
YOU'RE OVER-THINKING IT.
HMM.
THAT DOESN'T SOUND LIKE ME.

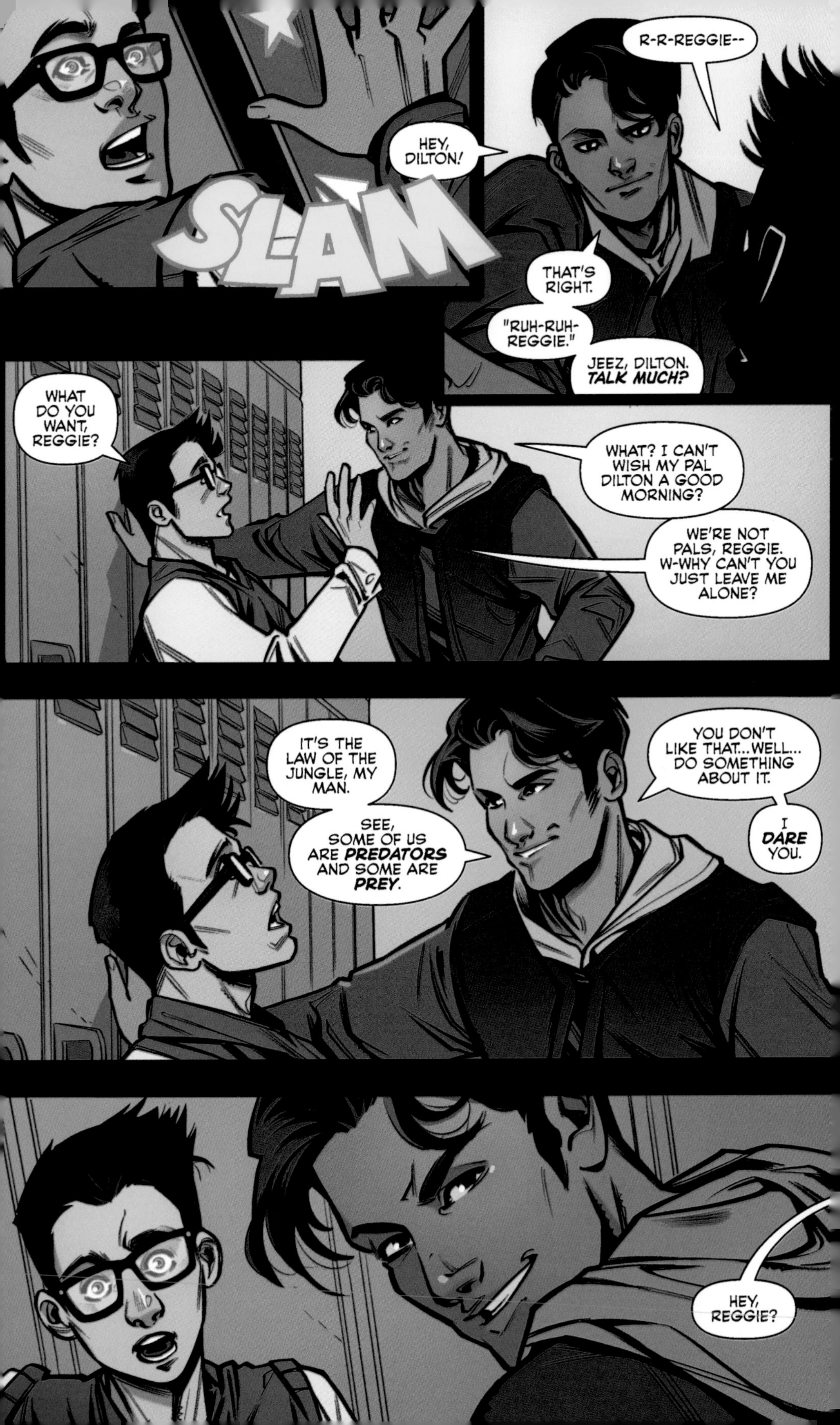

HEY, DILTON!
SLAM
R-R-REGGIE--
THAT'S RIGHT.
"RUH-RUH-REGGIE."
JEEZ, DILTON. TALK MUCH?
WHAT DO YOU WANT, REGGIE?
WHAT? I CAN'T WISH MY PAL DILTON A GOOD MORNING?
WE'RE NOT PALS, REGGIE. W-WHY CAN'T YOU JUST LEAVE ME ALONE?
IT'S THE LAW OF THE JUNGLE, MY MAN.
SEE, SOME OF US ARE PREDATORS AND SOME ARE PREY.
YOU DON'T LIKE THAT...WELL... DO SOMETHING ABOUT IT.
I DARE YOU.
HEY, REGGIE?

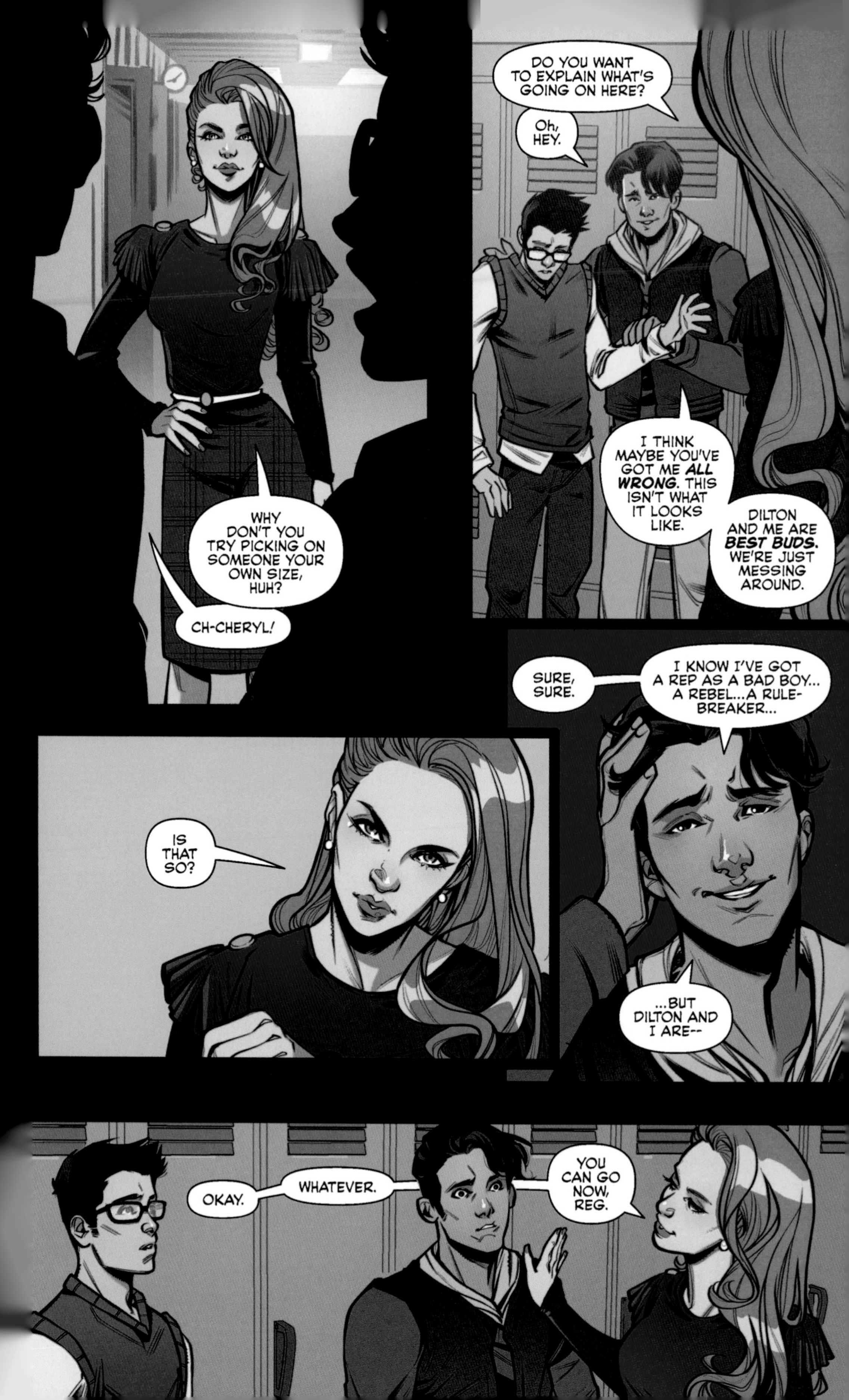
WHY DON'T YOU TRY PICKING ON SOMEONE YOUR OWN SIZE, HUH?
CH-CHERYL!
DO YOU WANT TO EXPLAIN WHAT'S GOING ON HERE?
Oh, HEY.
I THINK MAYBE YOU'VE GOT ME ALL WRONG. THIS ISN'T WHAT IT LOOKS LIKE.
DILTON AND ME ARE BEST BUDS. WE'RE JUST MESSING AROUND.
IS THAT SO?
I KNOW I'VE GOT A REP AS A BAD BOY... A REBEL...A RULE-BREAKER...
SURE, SURE.
...BUT DILTON AND I ARE--
YOU CAN GO NOW, REG.
WHATEVER.
OKAY.

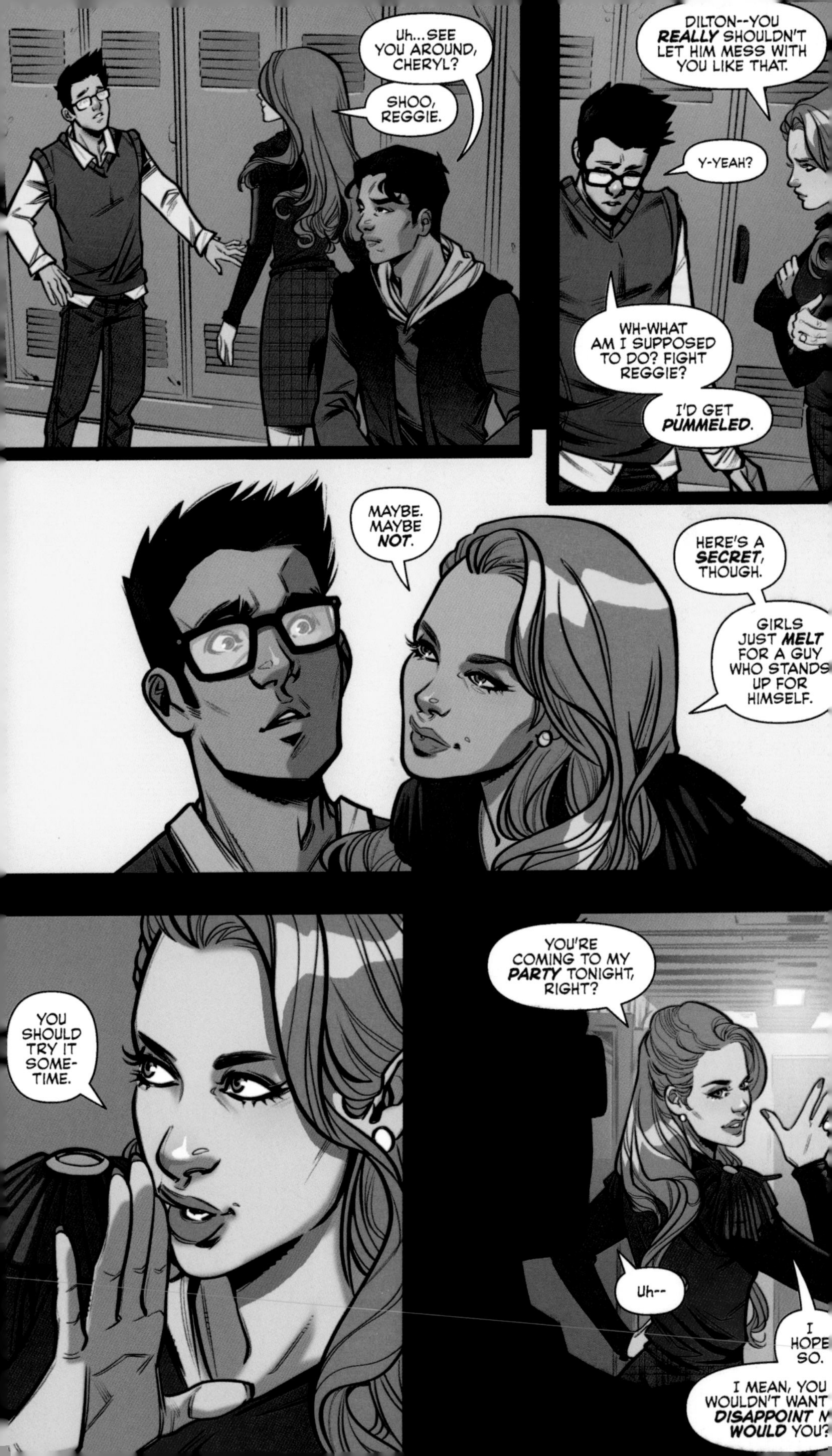

Uh...SEE YOU AROUND, CHERYL?
SHOO, REGGIE.
DILTON--YOU REALLY SHOULDN'T LET HIM MESS WITH YOU LIKE THAT.
Y-YEAH?
WH-WHAT AM I SUPPOSED TO DO? FIGHT REGGIE?
I'D GET PUMMELED.
MAYBE. MAYBE NOT.
HERE'S A SECRET, THOUGH.
GIRLS JUST MELT FOR A GUY WHO STANDS UP FOR HIMSELF.
YOU SHOULD TRY IT SOME-TIME.
YOU'RE COMING TO MY PARTY TONIGHT, RIGHT?
Uh--
I HOPE SO.
I MEAN, YOU WOULDN'T WANT DISAPPOINT WOULD YOU?

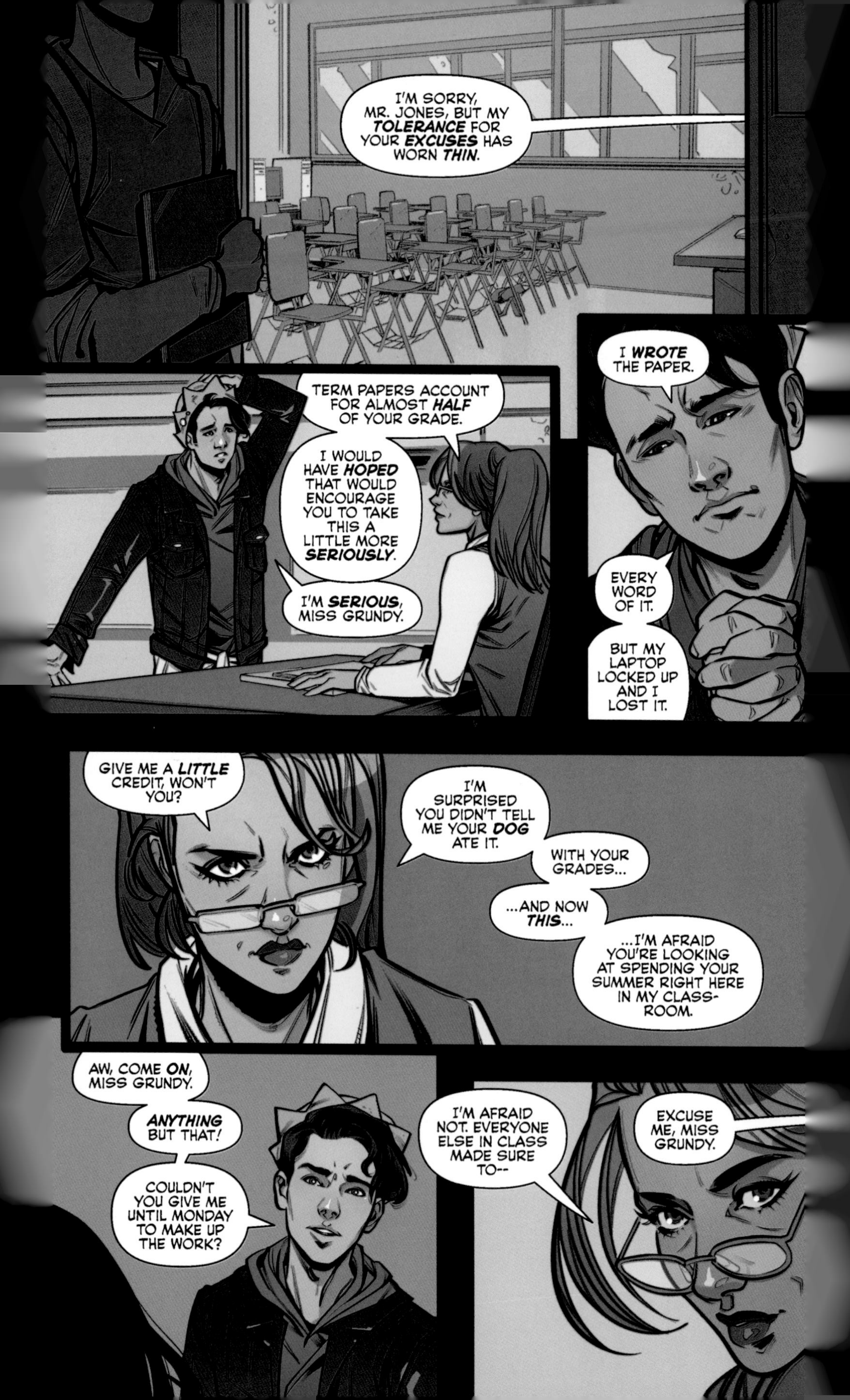
I'M SORRY, MR. JONES, BUT MY TOLERANCE FOR YOUR EXCUSES HAS WORN THIN.
TERM PAPERS ACCOUNT FOR ALMOST HALF OF YOUR GRADE.
I WOULD HAVE HOPED THAT WOULD ENCOURAGE YOU TO TAKE THIS A LITTLE MORE SERIOUSLY.
I'M SERIOUS, MISS GRUNDY.
I WROTE THE PAPER.
EVERY WORD OF IT.
BUT MY LAPTOP LOCKED UP AND I LOST IT.
GIVE ME A LITTLE CREDIT, WON'T YOU?
I'M SURPRISED YOU DIDN'T TELL ME YOUR DOG ATE IT.
WITH YOUR GRADES...
...AND NOW THIS...
...I'M AFRAID YOU'RE LOOKING AT SPENDING YOUR SUMMER RIGHT HERE IN MY CLASS-ROOM.
AW, COME ON, MISS GRUNDY.
ANYTHING BUT THAT!
COULDN'T YOU GIVE ME UNTIL MONDAY TO MAKE UP THE WORK?
I'M AFRAID NOT. EVERYONE ELSE IN CLASS MADE SURE TO--
EXCUSE ME, MISS GRUNDY.

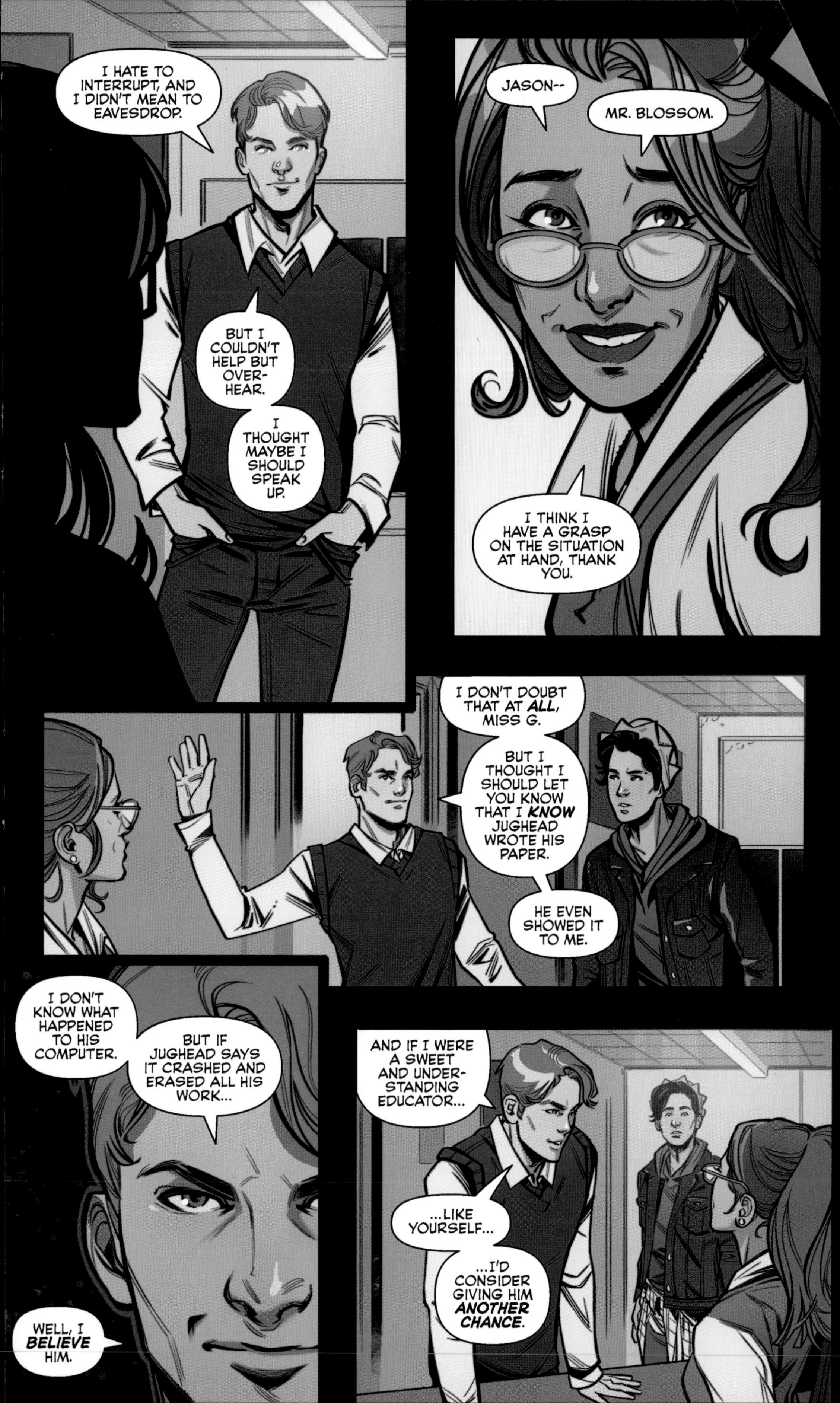
I HATE TO INTERRUPT, AND I DIDN'T MEAN TO EAVESDROP.
BUT I COULDN'T HELP BUT OVER-HEAR.
I THOUGHT MAYBE I SHOULD SPEAK UP.
JASON--
MR. BLOSSOM.
I THINK I HAVE A GRASP ON THE SITUATION AT HAND, THANK YOU.
I DON'T DOUBT THAT AT ALL, MISS G.
BUT I THOUGHT I SHOULD LET YOU KNOW THAT I KNOW JUGHEAD WROTE HIS PAPER.
HE EVEN SHOWED IT TO ME.
I DON'T KNOW WHAT HAPPENED TO HIS COMPUTER.
BUT IF JUGHEAD SAYS IT CRASHED AND ERASED ALL HIS WORK...
WELL, I BELIEVE HIM.
AND IF I WERE A SWEET AND UNDER-STANDING EDUCATOR...
...LIKE YOURSELF...
...I'D CONSIDER GIVING HIM ANOTHER CHANCE.

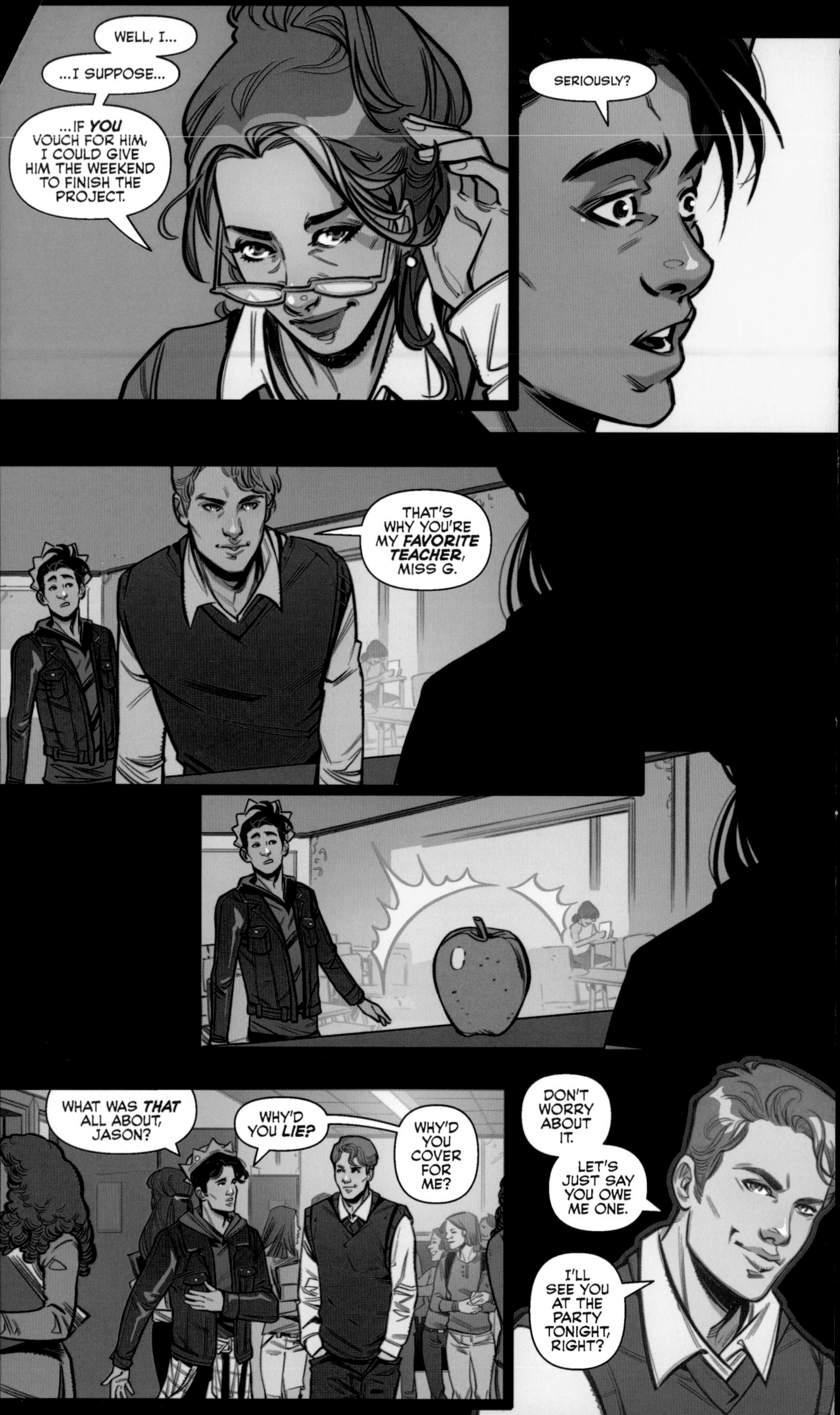
WELL, I...
...I SUPPOSE...
...IF YOU VOUCH FOR HIM, I COULD GIVE HIM THE WEEKEND TO FINISH THE PROJECT.
SERIOUSLY?
THAT'S WHY YOU'RE MY FAVORITE TEACHER, MISS G.
WHAT WAS THAT ALL ABOUT, JASON?
WHY'D YOU LIE?
WHY'D YOU COVER FOR ME?
DON'T WORRY ABOUT IT.
LET'S JUST SAY YOU OWE ME ONE.
I'LL SEE YOU AT THE PARTY TONIGHT, RIGHT?

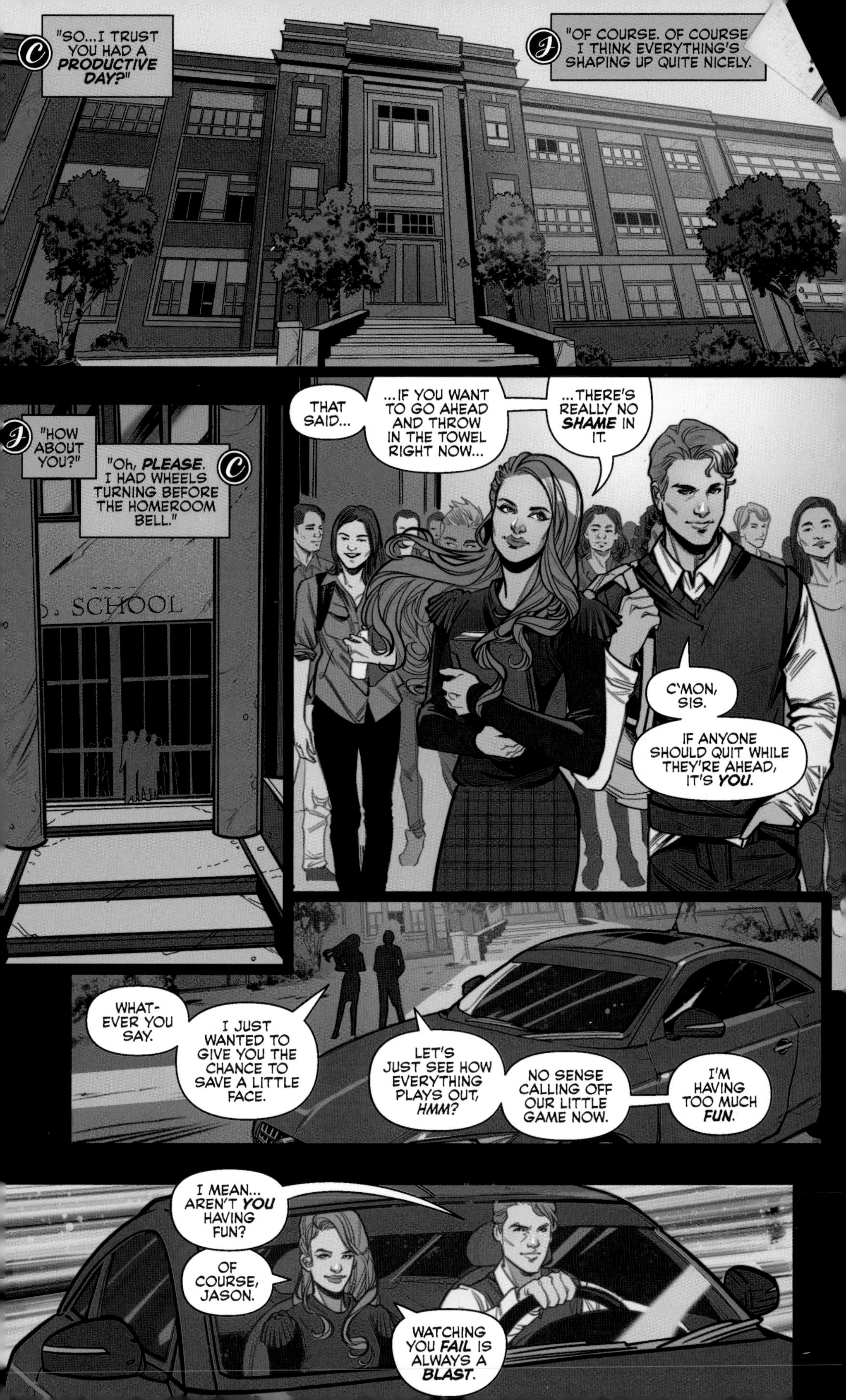
"SO...I TRUST YOU HAD A PRODUCTIVE DAY?"
"OF COURSE. OF COURSE I THINK EVERYTHING'S SHAPING UP QUITE NICELY.
"HOW ABOUT YOU?"
"Oh, PLEASE. I HAD WHEELS TURNING BEFORE THE HOMEROOM BELL."
SCHOOL
THAT SAID...
...IF YOU WANT TO GO AHEAD AND THROW IN THE TOWEL RIGHT NOW...
...THERE'S REALLY NO SHAME IN IT.
C'MON, SIS.
IF ANYONE SHOULD QUIT WHILE THEY'RE AHEAD, IT'S YOU.
WHAT-EVER YOU SAY.
I JUST WANTED TO GIVE YOU THE CHANCE TO SAVE A LITTLE FACE.
LET'S JUST SEE HOW EVERYTHING PLAYS OUT, HMM?
NO SENSE CALLING OFF OUR LITTLE GAME NOW.
I'M HAVING TOO MUCH FUN.
I MEAN... AREN'T YOU HAVING FUN?
OF COURSE, JASON.
WATCHING YOU FAIL IS ALWAYS A BLAST.

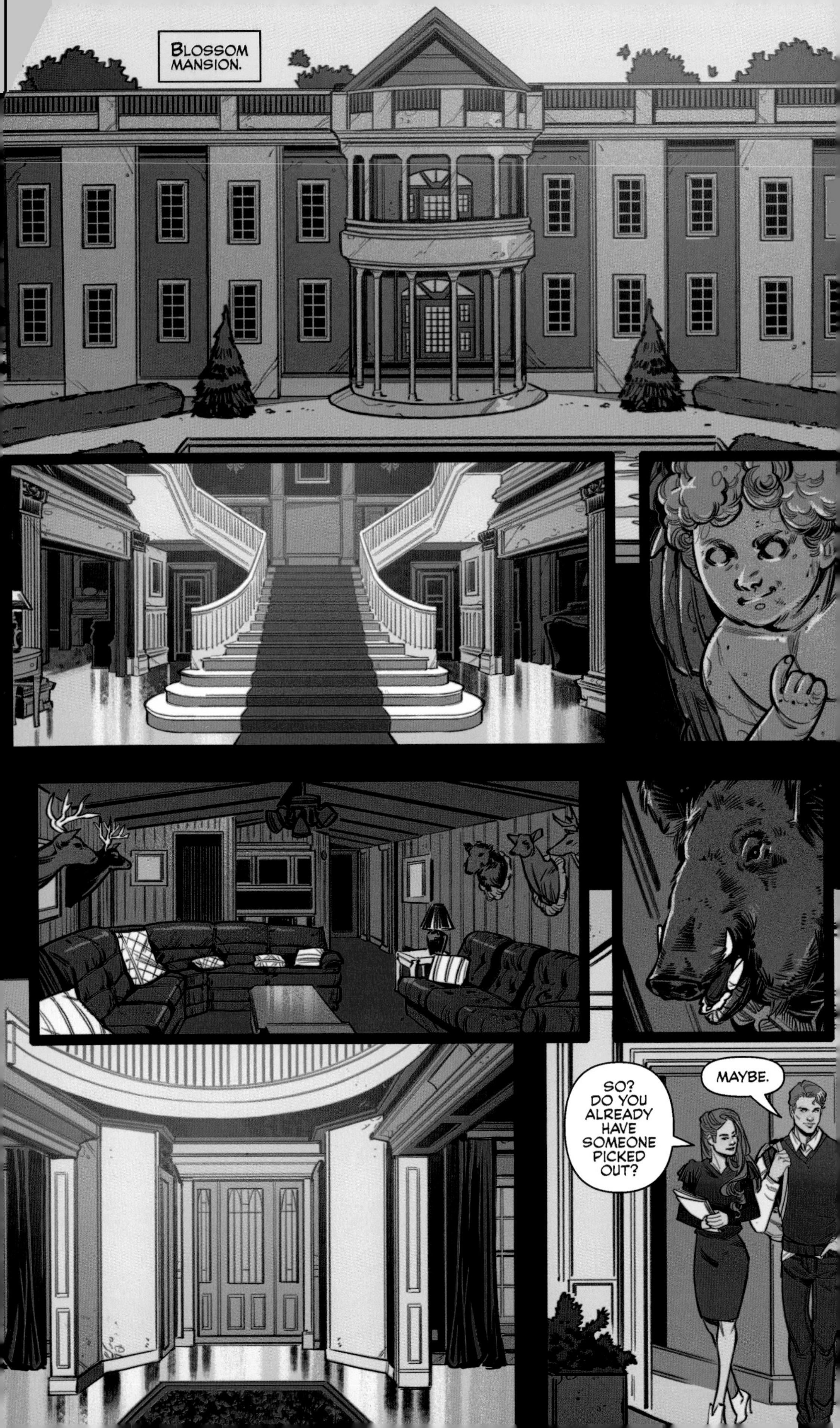

BLOSSOM MANSION.
SO? DO YOU ALREADY HAVE SOMEONE PICKED OUT?
MAYBE.

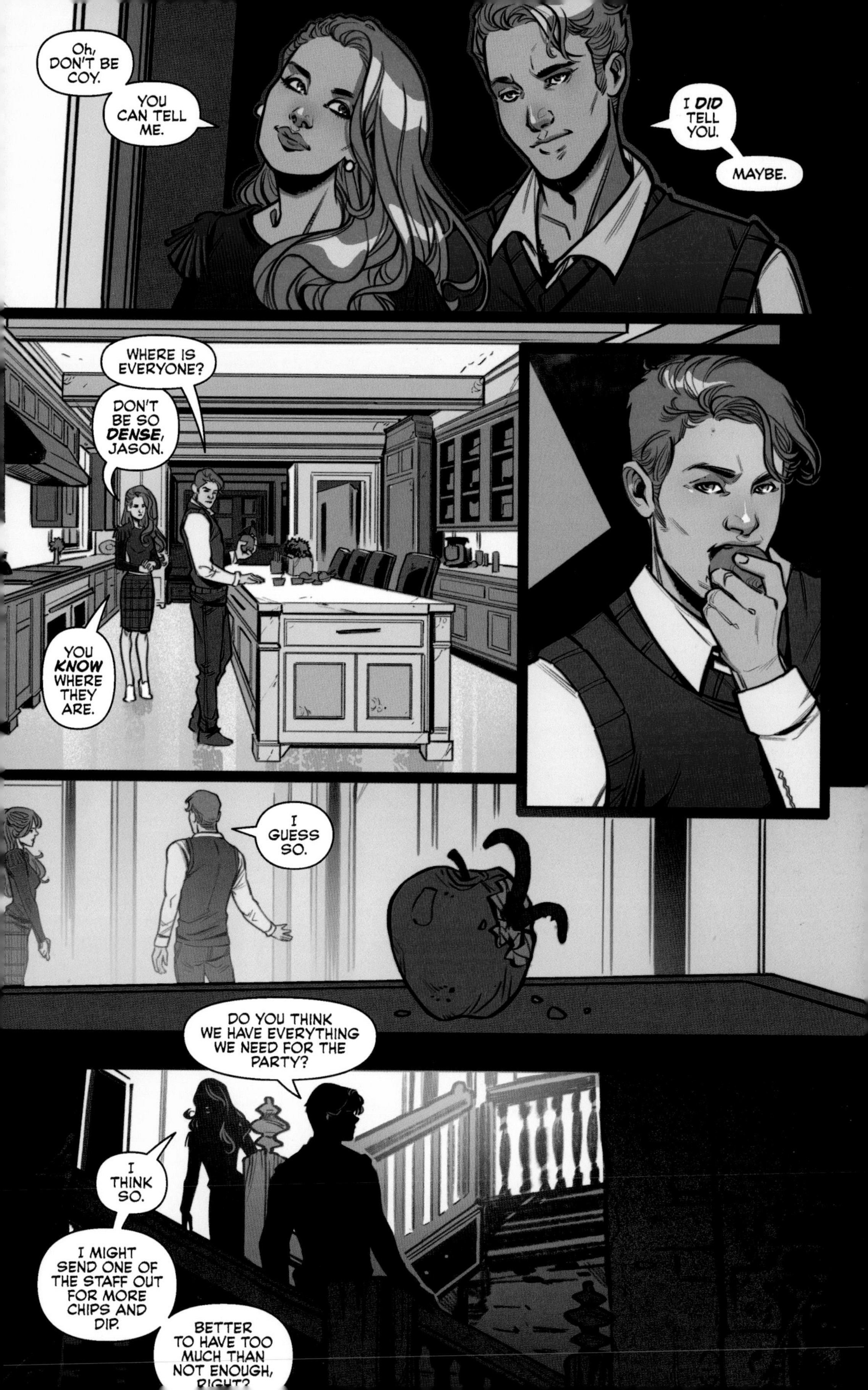
Oh, DON'T BE COY.
YOU CAN TELL ME.
I *DID* TELL YOU.
MAYBE.
WHERE IS EVERYONE?
DON'T BE SO *DENSE*, JASON.
YOU *KNOW* WHERE THEY ARE.
I GUESS SO.
DO YOU THINK WE HAVE EVERYTHING WE NEED FOR THE PARTY?
I THINK SO.
I MIGHT SEND ONE OF THE STAFF OUT FOR MORE CHIPS AND DIP.
BETTER TO HAVE TOO MUCH THAN NOT ENOUGH, RIGHT?

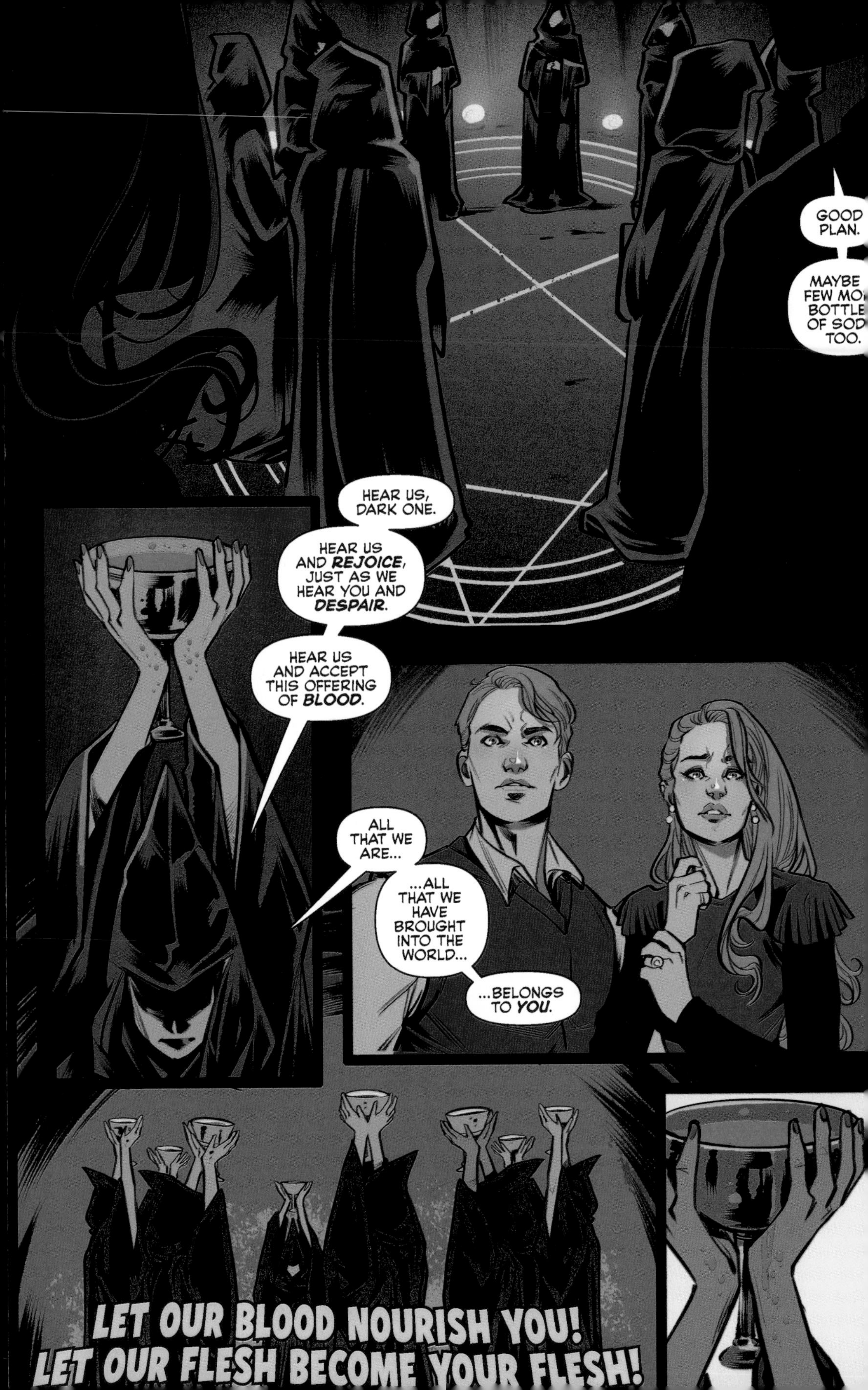

GOOD PLAN.
MAYBE FEW MO BOTTLE OF SOD TOO.
HEAR US, DARK ONE.
HEAR US AND REJOICE, JUST AS WE HEAR YOU AND DESPAIR.
HEAR US AND ACCEPT THIS OFFERING OF BLOOD.
ALL THAT WE ARE...
...ALL THAT WE HAVE BROUGHT INTO THE WORLD...
...BELONGS TO YOU.
LET OUR BLOOD NOURISH YOU!
LET OUR FLESH BECOME YOUR FLESH!

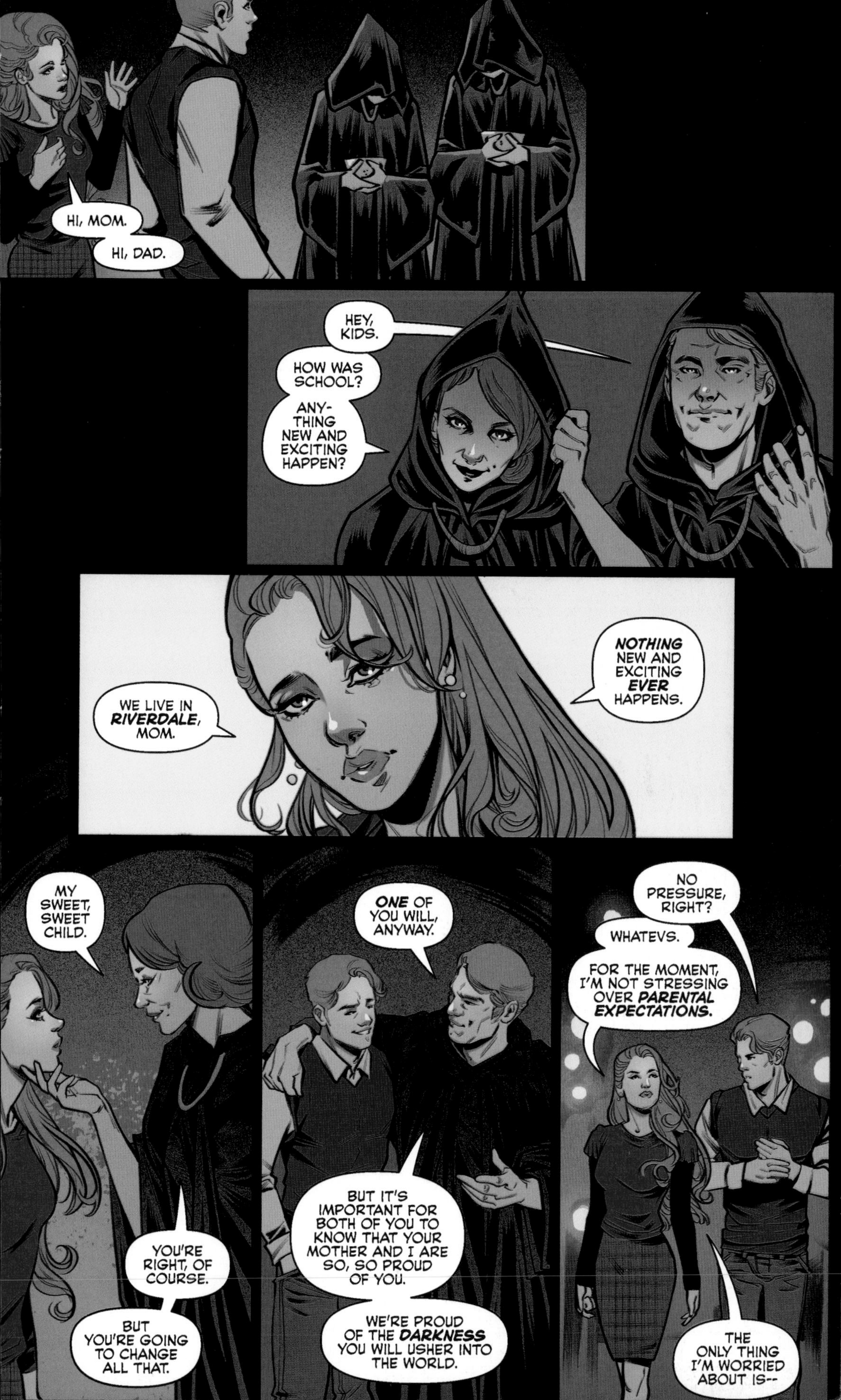

HI, MOM.
HI, DAD.
HEY, KIDS.
HOW WAS SCHOOL?
ANY-THING NEW AND EXCITING HAPPEN?
WE LIVE IN ***RIVERDALE***, MOM.
NOTHING NEW AND EXCITING ***EVER*** HAPPENS.
MY SWEET, SWEET CHILD.
YOU'RE RIGHT, OF COURSE.
BUT YOU'RE GOING TO CHANGE ALL THAT.
ONE OF YOU WILL, ANYWAY.
BUT IT'S IMPORTANT FOR BOTH OF YOU TO KNOW THAT YOUR MOTHER AND I ARE SO, SO PROUD OF YOU.
WE'RE PROUD OF THE ***DARKNESS*** YOU WILL USHER INTO THE WORLD.
NO PRESSURE, RIGHT?
WHATEVS.
FOR THE MOMENT, I'M NOT STRESSING OVER ***PARENTAL EXPECTATIONS.***
THE ONLY THING I'M WORRIED ABOUT IS--

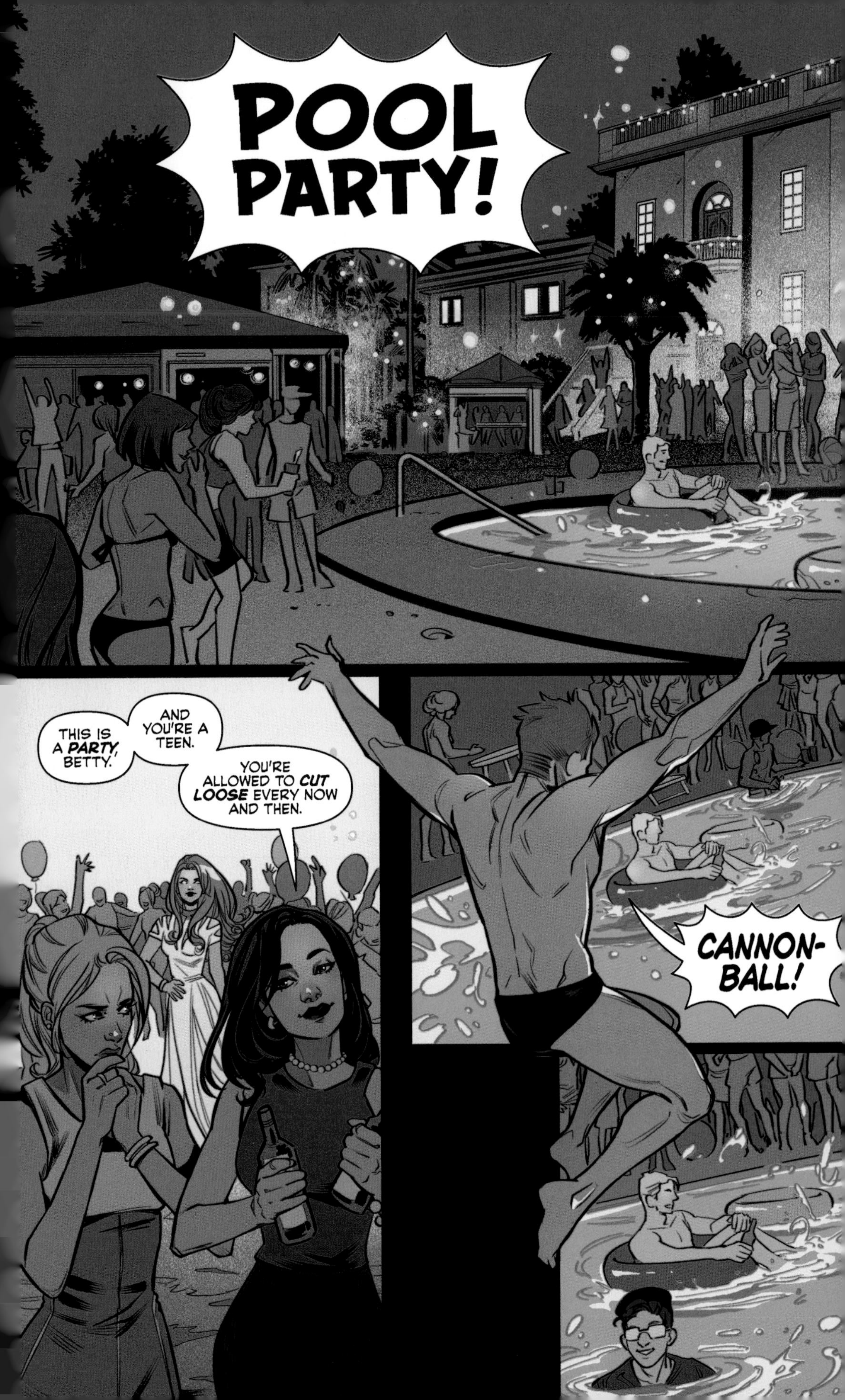
POOL PARTY!
THIS IS A **PARTY**, BETTY.
AND YOU'RE A TEEN.
YOU'RE ALLOWED TO **CUT LOOSE** EVERY NOW AND THEN.
CANNON-BALL!

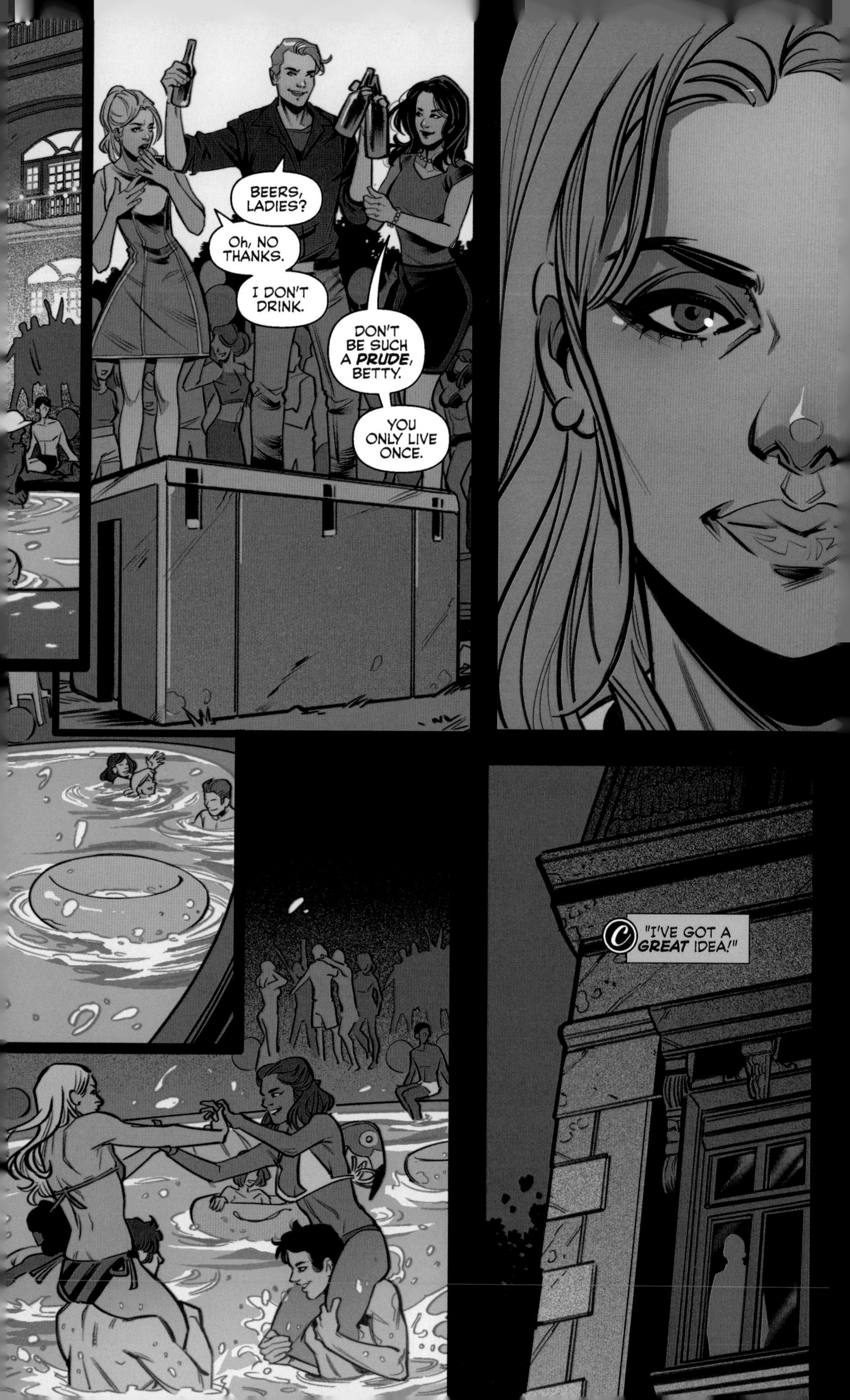
BEERS, LADIES?
Oh, NO THANKS.
I DON'T DRINK.
DON'T BE SUCH A **PRUDE**, BETTY.
YOU ONLY LIVE ONCE.
"I'VE GOT A **GREAT** IDEA!"

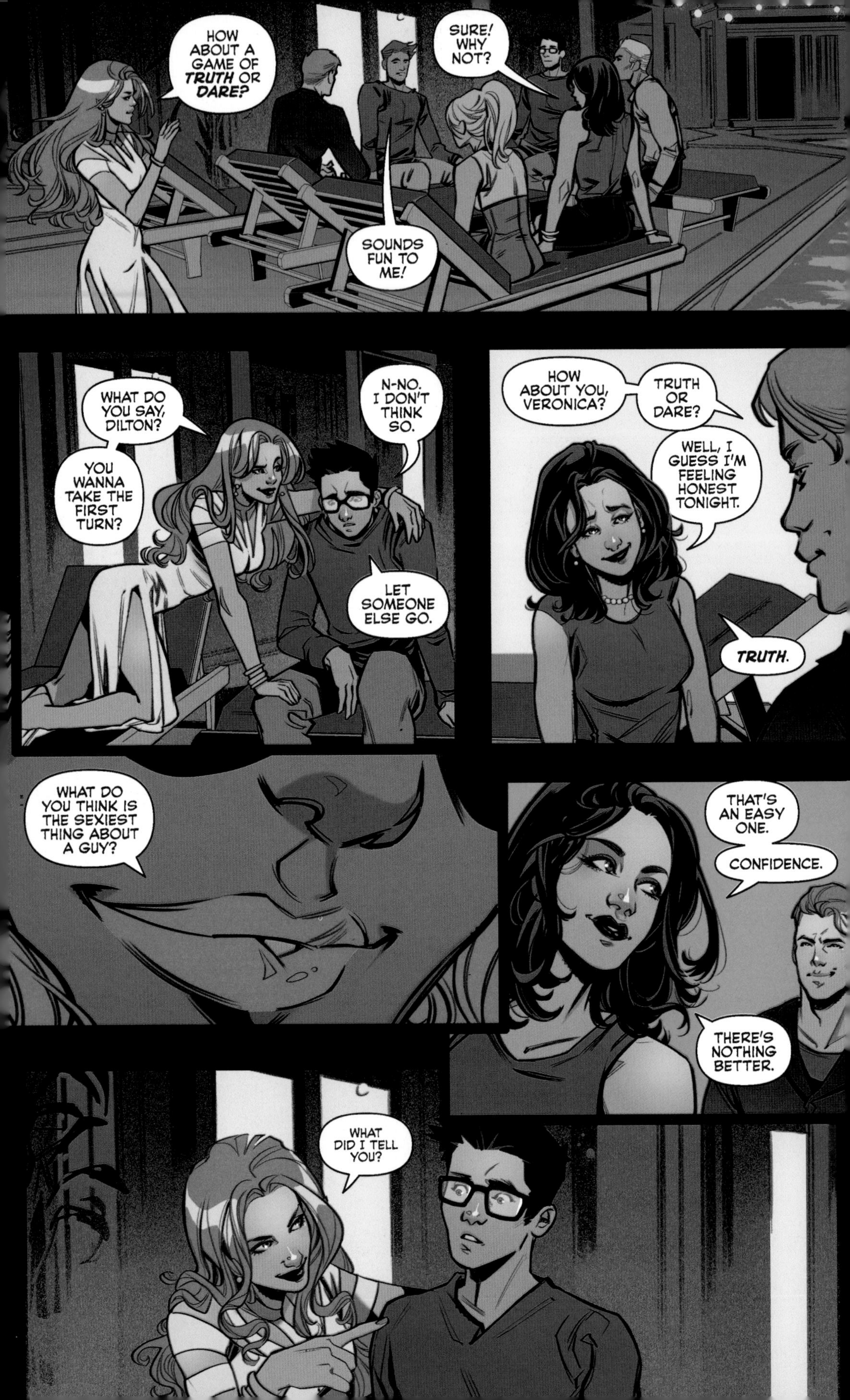
HOW ABOUT A GAME OF *TRUTH* OR *DARE?*
SURE! WHY NOT?
SOUNDS FUN TO ME!
WHAT DO YOU SAY, DILTON?
YOU WANNA TAKE THE FIRST TURN?
N-NO. I DON'T THINK SO.
LET SOMEONE ELSE GO.
HOW ABOUT YOU, VERONICA?
TRUTH OR DARE?
WELL, I GUESS I'M FEELING HONEST TONIGHT.
TRUTH.
WHAT DO YOU THINK IS THE SEXIEST THING ABOUT A GUY?
THAT'S AN EASY ONE.
CONFIDENCE.
THERE'S NOTHING BETTER.
WHAT DID I TELL YOU?

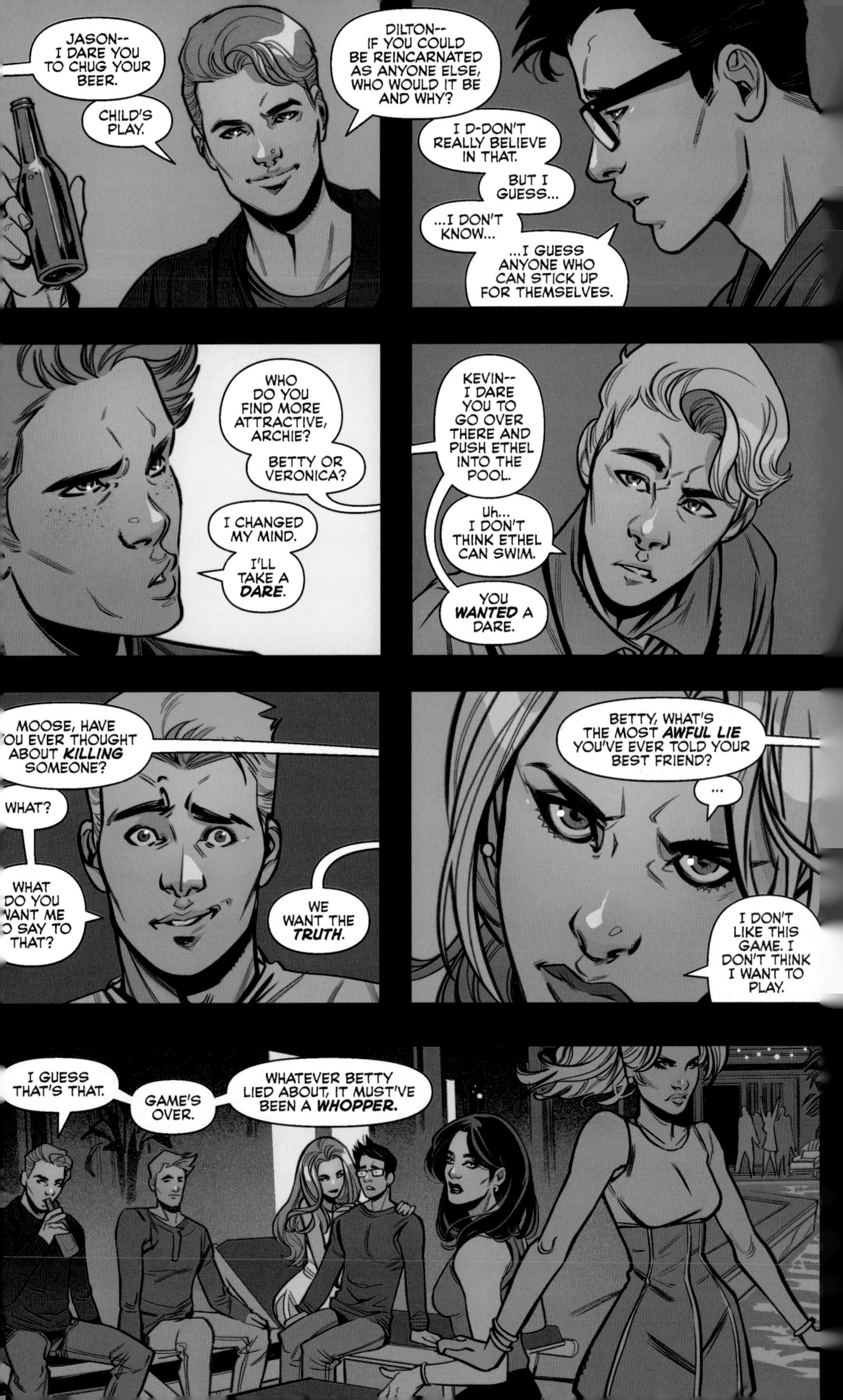
JASON-- I DARE YOU TO CHUG YOUR BEER.
CHILD'S PLAY.
DILTON-- IF YOU COULD BE REINCARNATED AS ANYONE ELSE, WHO WOULD IT BE AND WHY?
I D-DON'T REALLY BELIEVE IN THAT.
BUT I GUESS...
...I DON'T KNOW...
...I GUESS ANYONE WHO CAN STICK UP FOR THEMSELVES.
WHO DO YOU FIND MORE ATTRACTIVE, ARCHIE?
BETTY OR VERONICA?
I CHANGED MY MIND.
I'LL TAKE A ***DARE***.
KEVIN-- I DARE YOU TO GO OVER THERE AND PUSH ETHEL INTO THE POOL.
Uh... I DON'T THINK ETHEL CAN SWIM.
YOU ***WANTED*** A DARE.
MOOSE, HAVE OU EVER THOUGHT ABOUT ***KILLING*** SOMEONE?
WHAT?
WHAT DO YOU ANT ME SAY TO THAT?
WE WANT THE ***TRUTH***.
BETTY, WHAT'S THE MOST ***AWFUL LIE*** YOU'VE EVER TOLD YOUR BEST FRIEND?
...
I DON'T LIKE THIS GAME. I DON'T THINK I WANT TO PLAY.
I GUESS THAT'S THAT.
GAME'S OVER.
WHATEVER BETTY LIED ABOUT, IT MUST'VE BEEN A ***WHOPPER***.

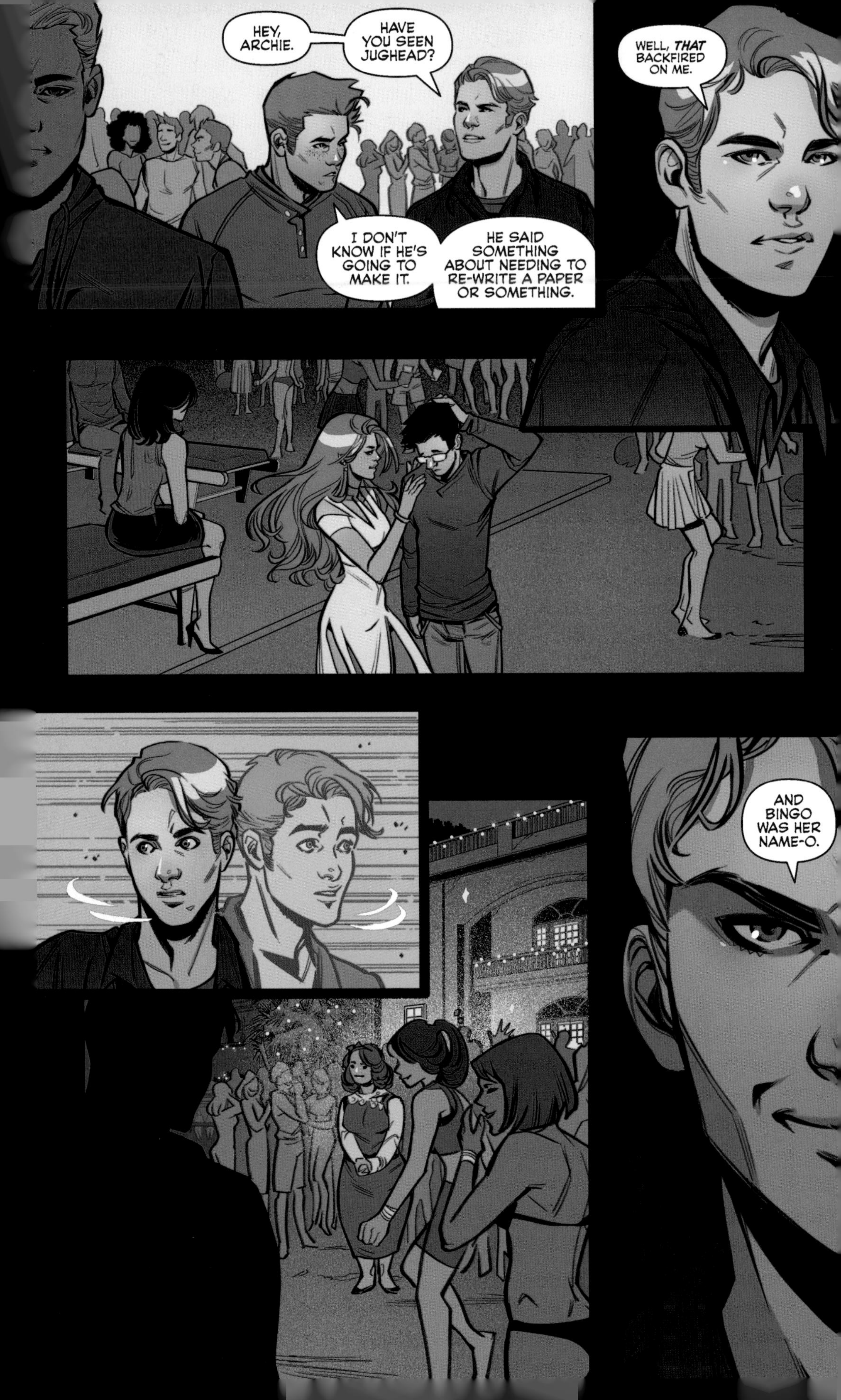
HEY, ARCHIE.
HAVE YOU SEEN JUGHEAD?
I DON'T KNOW IF HE'S GOING TO MAKE IT.
HE SAID SOMETHING ABOUT NEEDING TO RE-WRITE A PAPER OR SOMETHING.
WELL, *THAT* BACKFIRED ON ME.
AND BINGO WAS HER NAME-O.

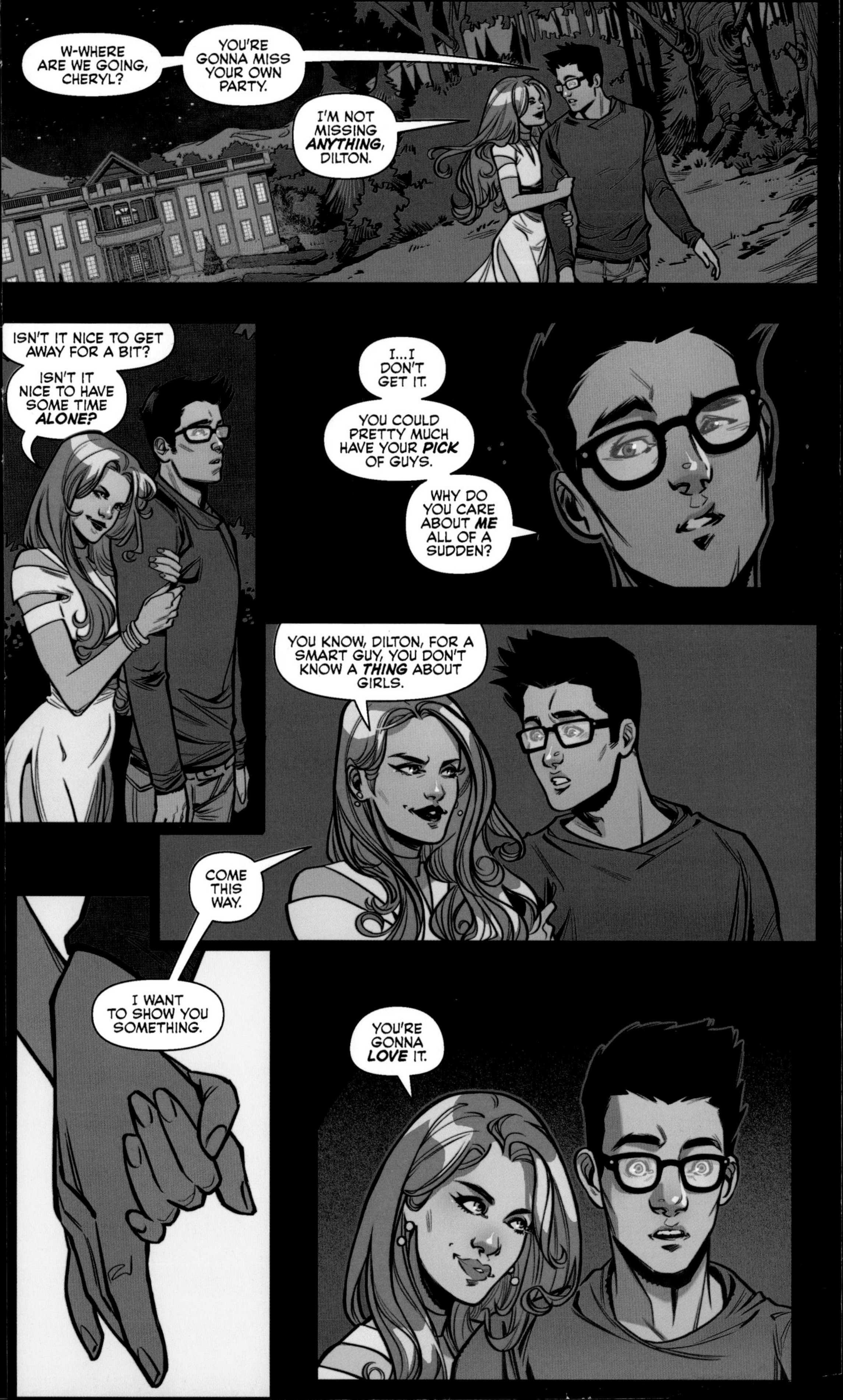
W-WHERE ARE WE GOING, CHERYL?
YOU'RE GONNA MISS YOUR OWN PARTY.
I'M NOT MISSING ***ANYTHING***, DILTON.
ISN'T IT NICE TO GET AWAY FOR A BIT?
ISN'T IT NICE TO HAVE SOME TIME ***ALONE?***
I...I DON'T GET IT.
YOU COULD PRETTY MUCH HAVE YOUR ***PICK*** OF GUYS.
WHY DO YOU CARE ABOUT ***ME*** ALL OF A SUDDEN?
YOU KNOW, DILTON, FOR A SMART GUY, YOU DON'T KNOW A ***THING*** ABOUT GIRLS.
COME THIS WAY.
I WANT TO SHOW YOU SOMETHING.
YOU'RE GONNA ***LOVE*** IT.

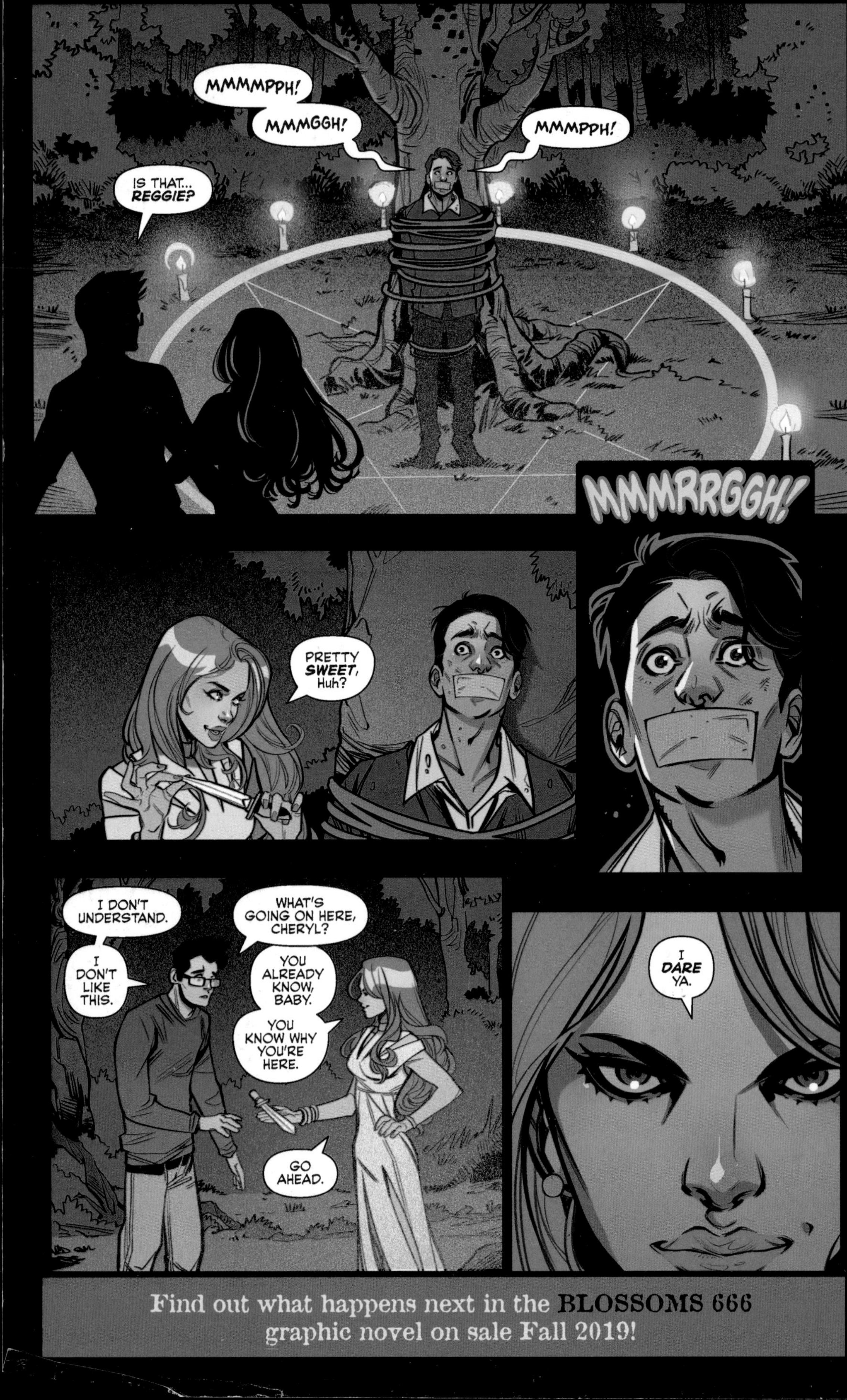
MMMMPPH!
MMMGGH!
MMMPPH!
IS THAT... REGGIE?
MMMRRGGH!
PRETTY SWEET, Huh?
I DON'T UNDERSTAND.
I DON'T LIKE THIS.
WHAT'S GOING ON HERE, CHERYL?
YOU ALREADY KNOW, BABY.
YOU KNOW WHY YOU'RE HERE.
GO AHEAD.
I DARE YA.

Find out what happens next in the BLOSSOMS 666 graphic novel on sale Fall 2019!